Foreword

The British Crime Survey (BCS) has now been carried out four times in England and Wales—in 1982, 1984, 1988 and 1992—and has established itself as one of the major regular household surveys in this country. Its main purpose is to provide an index of the extent of crime and of crime trends. The need for such an index has been convincingly demonstrated by the survey's findings that police statistics often fail to reflect the underlying trends in crime. However, the BCS yields a great deal of additional information about people's experience of crime and criminal justice, and the survey has increased our stock of knowledge appreciably.

This report does not present all the findings of the 1992 survey. Other reports will appear in due course on topics taken up in the last sweep including, attitudes to and contacts with the police, ethnic minorities' experience of crime, teenagers and crime, drug use, fear of crime and obscene telephone calls.

ROGER TARLING

Head of the Research and Planning Unit

September 1993

HOME OFFICE RESEARCH STUDY NO. 132

The 1992 British Crime Survey

by Pat Mayhew, Natalie Aye Maung and
Catriona Mirrlees-Black

A HOME OFFICE
RESEARCH AND PLANNING UNIT
REPORT

LONDON: HMSO

ISBN 0 11 341094 8

HOME OFFICE RESEARCH STUDIES

'Home Office Research Studies' comprise reports on research undertaken in the Home Office to assist in the exercise of its administrative functions, and for the information of the judicature, the services for which the Home Secretary has responsibility (direct or indirect) and the general public.

On the last pages of this report are listed titles already published in this series, in the preceding series *Studies in the Causes of Delinquency and the Treatment of Offenders*, and in the series of *Research and Planning Unit Papers*.

HMSO

Standing order service

Placing a standing order with HMSO BOOKS enables a customer to receive other titles in this series automatically as published.

This saves time, trouble and expense of placing individual orders and avoids the problem of knowing when to do so.

For details please write to HMSO BOOKS (PC11B.2), Publications Centre, P.O. Box 276, London SW8 5DT and quoting reference 25.08.011.

The standing order service also enables customers to receive automatically as published all material of their choice which additionally saves extensive catalogue research. The scope and selectivity of the service has been extended by new techniques, and there are more than 3,500 classifications to choose from. A special leaflet describing the service in detail may be obtained on request.

Acknowledgements

So many people contributed in some way to the 1992 BCS, they are too numerous to mention individually. However, particular thanks go to the teams of SCPR (Jon Hales, Peter Lynn and Jo Periam) and BMRB (Jenny Turtle and Bruce Hayward) whose skills and dedication made the 1992 BCS run so smoothly. Thanks are also due to the interviewers who coped so well with a long and complex questionnaire.

We are indebted to a number of academics for their suggestions and comments on the questionnaire including in particular: Wesley Skogan (police); Paul Wiles (police); Ken Pease (obscene telephone calls; multiple victimisation); Richard Kinsey (teenagers).

Within the Research and Statistics Department, thanks are due to Joy Mott and Malcolm Ramsay for their help with the self-completion questionnaire, and to David Heppenstall, a university student, who made a significant contribution to the data analysis. Many other colleagues also helped at various stages of the survey. But we are particularly grateful to Mike Hough for his invaluable contribution to the questionnaire, for his perceptive comments on this report and for his unstinting commitment to the BCS. Chris Nuttall, Director of the Research and Statistics Department, gave us considerable support and encouragement too.

NATALIE AYE MAUNG

PAT MAYHEW

CATRIONA MIRRLEES-BLACK

Contents

Summary

The British Crime Survey (BCS) provides an index of crime in England and Wales to set beside the crime statistics compiled by the police. Many crimes are not reported to the police, and some that are reported go unrecorded. Police statistics are thus an unreliable guide to the extent of crime. They can also be misleading about trends, as readiness to report crimes to the police varies over time. The BCS avoids this problem by asking people directly about their experience as victims.

The BCS has been carried out in England and Wales in 1982, 1984, 1988 and 1992, each survey measuring crime in the previous year. In each sweep a representative sample of over 10,000 people aged 16 and over were interviewed. BCS estimates cannot provide a complete count of crime. Many crimes cannot readily be covered in household surveys, such as fraud, shoplifting and commercial burglary. The survey will also pick up some incidents which are not notifiable offences. Crime surveys are also prone to various forms of error, mainly to do with the difficulty of ensuring that samples are representative, the frailty of respondents' memories, their reticence to talk about their experiences as victims, and their failure to realise an incident is relevant to the survey. In sum, the BCS does not claim to chart the 'true' level of crime; for some offence categories, however, it provides a better guide to the extent of crime and to trends than recorded crime figures.

Chapter 2 describes the extent of crime in 1991 and looks at trends in crime since the first survey, providing estimates of unreported and unrecorded crime. Chapter 3 examines the reasons why some crimes are reported to the police and others are not, together with the views of victims about the service they receive from the police. The rest of the report considers in turn burglary, theft of and from cars and violence, looking at who is at risk of these offences and what typically happens. The main findings are:

The extent of crime

*   For those crime categories which can be compared, recorded crime figures nearly doubled between 1981 and 1991, but the BCS suggests a lower rise of about 50%. Recorded crime shows a larger rise than the BCS mainly because of increased reporting to the police.

*   Since 1987, recorded crime figures for this comparable sub-set of offences

have risen particularly steeply—by 39%—whereas BCS figures indicate a rise of 14%.

* This pattern is not consistent across crime types. Since 1981, acquisitive crime has risen broadly as indicated by recorded crime figures. But violent crime has risen more slowly than recorded figures would suggest. Vandalism has increased hardly at all, though the police statistics show a large rise.

* Reporting to the police has increased for most BCS offence categories. For all BCS offences combined, 31% were reported in 1981, but 43% in 1991. For BCS crime categories which can be compared with police statistics, reporting rose from 36% in 1981 to 50% in 1991. Incomplete reporting and recording mean that only 30% end up in police records. The gap between BCS and police figures has narrowed, particularly for vandalism, wounding and robbery.

* Higher levels of reporting may be due to wider insurance cover and changing public tolerance to crime may also be a contributory factor. Changing attitudes to the police seem unlikely to be implicated. It cannot be ruled out that the increase in reporting is in part an artefact; that is, as crime rises there may be an increasing tendency for respondents to recall only the more serious or salient incidents at interview—the ones most likely to be reported.

* There were an estimated 15 million incidents in 1991 falling within BCS categories of crimes against individuals and their private property. The vast majority were against property, as is the case in police figures. Vehicles are a very common target of crime: 36% of all BCS offences involved theft of and from vehicles and damage to them. Five per cent of BCS incidents were crimes of violence (wounding and robbery) and a further 12% were common assaults (involving little or no injury).

Reasons for not reporting

* Crimes go unreported mainly because in the eyes of the victim they are too trivial or not amenable to police action. Nonetheless, many incidents regarded by their victims as serious go unreported, while many less serious incidents are reported.

* Factors that influence reporting other than seriousness are insurance considerations, the practical help the police might give in helping to retrieve cars and bicycles, assessments made by victims of the likely police response, and the intricacies of victim-offender relationships. Assaults are among the most seriously regarded offences which go unreported, especially those where victims know the offender.

* The feeling that the police could not or would not want to deal with the offences is cited by a minority of those not reporting incidents, though it has increased since the two previous sweeps of the BCS.

The police response to victims of crime

* Most victims who *do* report are satisfied with the service they receive from the police: 65% were very or fairly satisfied in 1992. This figure was an improvement on 1988 (60%), but lower than in 1984 (68%).

* Victims who notified the police were, for the most part, satisfied with the politeness of the police. The vast majority of victims were also happy with the time the police took to attend to their call. The biggest source of dissatisfaction was feedback of information from the police. There seems little improvement since 1988. The next biggest criticism was inadequate effort by the police, although six out of ten were satisfied on this score.

* The young, those from ethnic minorities, manual workers, victims who knew the offender, and victims of more serious offences tended to be less satisfied with the service they received from the police.

* When victims see the police personally after reporting they are more likely to be favourably impressed about all aspects of police response.

Burglary

* Set against General Household Survey (GHS) and BCS survey figures, police statistics have overstated the increase in burglary since 1971. The surveys indicate that burglaries with loss have risen since the early 1970s by only a third as much as police figures show. Increased reporting explains this in part, but so does increased recording of offences. The sharp increase in recorded burglaries since 1987 is supported by BCS estimates.

* Inner city residents and those in certain ACORN neighbourhoods have higher burglary risks. So too do residents of flats, maisonettes or rooms, single-adult households, and those with lower levels of occupancy.

* There are higher risks of burglary for households with poorer security protection. But while preventive devices do help keep burglars out, a sizeable number of burglaries still occur against householders with security in place.

* Levels of security protection have increased since 1988.

* In a fifth of incidents with entry, doors or windows had been left open or unlocked, but this had decreased since 1981. Thus, while burglary has increased there is no suggestion that greater carelessness is to blame.

* In successful break-ins, entry through doors and from the back of the property was most likely, although the *single* most likely point of entry was a back window.

* Most burglaries are 'anonymous' crimes, with the house empty or victims unaware of the incident. Violent or threatening confrontation between burglar and victim occurred in 3% of cases in 1991: about half the confrontations involved strangers.

* Slightly more than half of burglaries happened in the evening or at night. In a quarter of incidents, the respondent was asleep when the incident took place. One out of ten incidents happened when the respondent was on holiday or away for the weekend.

* Damage occurred in most incidents, although usually when the burglar was trying to get in. Cases involving gratuitous damage (such as 'soiling' or graffiti) were extremely rare.

* The most common items taken in burglaries were cash, jewellery, videos, stereos/hi-fi equipment and televisions.

* Stolen property was seldom recovered, although in about half of incidents householders were insured, fully or partly, against the loss or damage. When burglars got in and the household was insured, four out of five made a claim, but only one in three victims of attempted burglary bothered to.

* Most burglaries involved relatively minor *net* losses of less than £50, but in some, losses were extensive: the average net loss was £370, and for incidents with entry, £560.

Thefts involving cars

* In 1991 thefts of and from cars, including attempts, comprised a quarter of the offences mentioned in the BCS, and a similar proportion of recorded offences. If vandalism to cars is included, cars are the target in over one in three BCS crimes.

* The BCS estimate of thefts *of* cars is similar to that from police statistics as most offences are reported by victims. But the number of thefts *from* cars is about three times higher than that recorded by the police as by no means all are reported to or recorded by the police. The number of *attempts* is a full seven times higher. Thefts *from* cars are the major problem: for every car successfully driven away, there were nearly five thefts from a car.

* Since 1981, attempts have risen by a factor of about four according to both the BCS and police figures. One can infer that offenders are being thwarted either by owners' heightened security-consciousness, or by better car

design. Police figures have shown a sharper rise in thefts from vehicles since 1981 than the BCS.

*   Three-quarters of stolen cars were recovered in 1991 according to BCS figures, and these are generally assumed to have been taken for 'joyriding'. The proportion of stolen cars recovered has declined since 1981, indicating that theft of cars for other purposes (stripping, resale, export etc) is increasing more steeply than those used for 'joyriding'.

*   A third of all thefts took place in the street near home at night, and a fifth in other locations at or near the home.

*   In one in twenty thefts in 1991 where method of entry was known, thieves gained access through an unlocked door or window. This figure is lower than in previous surveys, perhaps indicating more driver care or more central locking. Over half of thefts *from* cars involved thieves breaking windows; a quarter forced the lock—the method of entry in half of thefts *of* cars.

*   The main factors that increase risks of theft for owners are: living in an inner city or an area in which the level of car ownership is relatively low; being in a higher-income group; and parking at night on the street or in housing estate car parks. Those who live in flats and terraced houses (which are less likely to have garages) are also more at risk.

*   Financial loss, even after any insurance payment, was significant for thefts of cars, whether or not the vehicle was recovered. Victims said their net loss was £500 or more in two-thirds of incidents in which cars were not recovered and in a quarter of those in which they were.

Violence

*   The BCS count of violence is unlikely to be a full one; for a number of reasons, many incidents will go unmentioned in the interview. Offences between non-strangers are particularly likely to be undercounted.

*   Of an estimated 2.64 million incidents, some 20% were domestic assaults, involving partners, ex-partners and other relatives and household members. Nearly half of assaults mentioned by women in the survey were of this nature.

*   Street assaults were nearly as common as domestic assaults, amounting to 19% of violent incidents. Male victims were involved in over eight out of ten of them. Sixteen per cent of incidents of violence were in pubs and clubs, again with over eight out of ten victims men.

* A tenth of violent incidents were 'muggings' (robberies and snatch thefts) fairly evenly split between men and women. The number of robberies against men was higher than against women, but 'snatch thefts' were more often against women.

* Age is strongly related to violence, with younger people facing higher risks. Areas with higher levels of social disorder produced more victims. Men who went out frequently, especially to the pub, ran higher risks. Insofar as the BCS data are representative, individuals who were single, or separated or divorced, ran higher risks of violence, but for offences involving known offenders, having children was associated with increased risk. The elderly were infrequent victims, though 10% of muggings involved those 60 or over. Women were considerably less at risk than men of all types of violence except domestic assaults and mugging. Slightly less than 1% of women overall reported at least one incident of domestic assault in the 1992 survey; among 16-29 year old women, the proportion was just over 2%.

* About a third of all violent incidents against Afro-Caribbeans and Asians were felt to be racially motivated. More than a half of street assaults were said to be. Asians also said race was involved in two-thirds of incidents around the home, usually citing white offenders.

* Victims of violent crime are more likely to be repeatedly victimised than is the case with most property crimes. Half of female victims of domestic assault had experienced more than one incident in 1991. For violent crime as a whole, some 17% of the sample accounted for 45% of the incidents counted.

* About five out of ten pub brawls involved people known to the victim to some degree; and this was even more often the case with violence at work. Mugging was most likely to involve strangers, followed by street assaults.

* The vast majority of pub assaults involved offenders said to be drunk. But many other incidents of violence were also committed by drunken offenders.

* Most violence is perpetrated by men, whether directed against men or women. However, one in five incidents of violence against women were committed by other women, and a further 6% by men and women acting together. The highest proportion of women-on-women violence took place in pubs. But women offenders caused less injury.

* Muggings and offences around the home were most likely to be reported to the police: about half were. About a third of work-related, street and pub assaults were reported. Reporting of domestic assaults was low: only one in five women brought in the police. Violent offences involving strangers were more frequently reported.

*   Domestic assaults and other home-based assaults against women were regarded most seriously by their victims, despite low reporting. But many pub assaults were considered serious by men.

*   On the definition of violent crime used here, the number of offences measured in the survey has risen by 24% between 1981 and 1991, and by 15% since 1987. The number of domestic assaults has risen by 79% since 1981, though greater willingness to talk about these cannot be ruled out. The number of assaults at work has more than doubled since 1981, but as more are now being reported to the police, changing perceptions about their criminality may be implicated. There was no statistically significant change in the number of muggings, street assaults, and pub assaults.

1. Introduction

This report presents results from the fourth sweep of the British Crime Survey (BCS) which was conducted in England and Wales in 1992. Earlier surveys were carried out in 1982, 1984 and 1988.[1] The survey questions a large, random sample of those aged 16 and over about offences they have experienced in the last year. Its main purposes are:

*   **To provide an alternative measure of crime to statistics of offences recorded by the police.** Recorded crime is a good measure of police workload, but is deficient as an *index* of crime because many offences go unreported by victims and some which are reported go unrecorded. The BCS now provides a measure of trends in crime between 1981 and 1991.

*   **To provide a picture of the nature of crime.** The BCS collects detailed information on the crimes reported at interview, showing for instance how victims are financially and emotionally affected. Some of this information is also collected in police records, but by no means all is, and much is not made routinely available.

*   **To provide information on crime risks.** The survey helps show how risks of crime vary for different groups: where, for instance is burglary most common; and, what are the risks of crime for the elderly? Police statistics show risks across different police force areas, but are not easily analysed to show risks against different *victims*.[2] The BCS offers more flexibility in constructing measures of risk.

*   **To take up other crime-related issues.** The large sample needed to estimate victimisation risks can be asked about a variety of other crime-related issues.

The BCS is one of a growing number of crime (or victimisation) surveys whose origins can be traced to the United States President's Commission on Crime (eg, Ennis, 1967; Biderman *et al*, 1967). The US National Crime Survey followed

---

[1]The first survey was carried out in England and Wales and in Scotland (see Hough and Mayhew (1983) and Chambers and Tombs (1984), respectively). The second was carried out in England and Wales alone (see Hough and Mayhew, 1985), but the third in both countries (Mayhew *et al*, 1989; Payne, 1992).

[2]Police forces are now tending to carry out fuller analysis of their statistics, and much work has been done recently by the Home Office Research and Statistics Department (see, eg, Davidoff and Dowds, 1989).

from this, beginning in 1972 and repeated annually since. Other countries have mounted national or large-scale surveys—though not as frequently as in the US.[3] A recent development has been standardised, albeit small surveys in a number of countries, to provide more comparable results than independently organised surveys allow; these have all differed in coverage, questionnaire content and methods, making comparisons difficult (see Van Dijk and Mayhew, 1993).

In Britain, the first full-scale survey was in London in the early 1970s (Sparks *et al*, 1977), and two other local surveys predated the BCS (Bottoms *et al*, 1987; Tuck and Southgate, 1981).[4] Over the 1980s, there has been a growth in local surveys, mounted either to measure crime alongside other issues (eg, fear of crime and attitudes to the police), or to assess the effect of crime prevention initiatives, which themselves can change levels of reporting to the police.[5] Many of these surveys have adopted BCS methods and questions.

All crime surveys have shown that a great many crimes go unreported to the police, mainly because they are not seen as sufficiently serious, or because calling the police is not thought to provide any remedy. But few have tried, as the BCS does, to relate the *number of reported* offences to the *number recorded* by the police in order to estimate the extent of unrecorded crime. Offences which are not reported or recorded make up the so-called 'dark figure' of crime, and the BCS has been able to show the size of this for different offences.

One of the main strengths of the BCS is that, as a regular survey, it yields trends in crime. Recorded crime statistics are still extensively used for this purpose but there is now far greater awareness of their shortcomings. The large 'dark figure' for many offences means that any change in the public's propensity to report can alter the number of recorded offences independent of any change in the underlying volume of crime. Changes in police recording practice can have the same effect.

The BCS has shown trends in different crimes that differ from those based on police statistics (Mayhew and Aye Maung, 1992). The US National Crime Survey has shown a flatter increase in crime than police Uniform Crime Reports (eg, Blumstein *et al*, 1991), and the Dutch surveys have also indicated generally shallower trends than police figures, as well as explaining reductions in some categories of police statistics in terms of falling reporting rates (Van Dijk, 1982).

---

[3]There have been surveys, for example, in Canada, Australia, the Netherlands, Israel, Scandinavia, Switzerland, and the Republic of Ireland. Most 'crime counting' surveys are free-standing, but in some countries questions about victimisation have been added to other surveys.

[4]An earlier use of crime survey techniques was in a 1966 OPCS survey which asked questions about victimisation (Durant *et al*, 1972). Since 1972, the General Household Survey has intermittently carried questions on residential burglary (see, eg, OPCS, 1992).

[5]See, for example, Farrington and Dowds (1985); Anderson *et al* (1990); Crawford *et al* (1990); Lea *et al* (1988); and Painter *et al* (1989).

Crime surveys have also shown that police statistics can mislead when used to make comparisons across different areas. Farrington and Dowds (1985), for instance, demonstrated that levels of crime in Nottinghamshire were actually only slightly higher than in adjacent counties, and that its very high recorded crime rate could be largely attributed to distinctive recording practices on the part of the Nottinghamshire police. The 1982 BCS showed that the extent of crime in Scotland was much on a par with England and Wales, though police statistics indicated Scotland was more crime-ridden (see Mayhew and Smith, 1985). The 1988 BCS indicated that in both Scotland and England and Wales crime, as measured by the survey, increased less than police figures indicated between 1981 and 1987, though the survey increase in Scotland was lower than in England and Wales (Payne, 1992; Kinsey and Anderson, 1992).

The British Crime Survey count of crime

Differences in coverage from police statistics

The count of crime in the BCS differs from that of the police as follows:

* The survey *includes* unreported as well as reported offences. There will be the largest discrepancy in the two sets of figures for poorly reported crimes such as vandalism (Chapter 2). The BCS count of *unreported* crime however is not simply a count of incidents 'not worth worrying about'. Chapter 3 shows that a good number of unreported incidents are judged to be serious (cf Pease, 1988).

* The BCS also *includes* some categories of crime—eg, common assaults — which are excluded from the 'notifiable offences' series collated by the police. (Other offences are covered by both series, but cannot always be matched. Household thefts are an example, being subsumed in police statistics in the very broad category of 'other thefts'.)

* The BCS *excludes* crimes against organisations (eg, fraud, shoplifting, fare evasion, commercial burglary and robbery).[6]

* It *excludes* so-called 'victimless' crimes (eg, drug and alcohol misuse), consensual sexual offences, or crimes where people may not be aware of having been victimised, as in an assortment of frauds.

---

[6] The early NCS Commercial Crime Survey covered burglary and robbery against businesses and some non-governmental organisations. Commercial targets were much more at risk than private ones: about six times more for robbery, and about three times more for burglary, although private targets generated greater *numbers* of offences—about four times more (US Dept of Justice, 1976). More crimes against commercial targets were reported to the police which was one reason why the Commercial Surveys were discontinued.

3

* Crime against children are also *excluded* (the lower age limit in the BCS 'core' sample being 16), and, for obvious reasons, homicide.

Differences in definitions of crime

Both the BCS and police statistics apply legal definitions in classifying and counting crimes; they do not simply accept respondents' definitions of what is crime.[7] But there will be some differences:

* The BCS applies no threshold of severity; any incident that is technically a crime is counted.[8] Thus, it applies what might be called a *nominal* definition of crime: a count of incidents which according to the letter of the law could be punished, regardless perhaps of the value of doing so, and regardless always of whether a layman would really see the incident as 'crime' as such.

* The police use an *operational* definition of crime. They count incidents reported by victims which: (i) could be punished by a court; (ii) are felt to merit the attention of the criminal justice system; and (iii) meet organisational demands for reasonable evidence.

For many offences, public and police definitions will coincide. Burglaries and car thefts, for example, will clearly be regarded by respondents as a breach of law, even if they do not always think it worth bringing in the police; and the police themselves would be unlikely to leave such incidents unrecorded. Other offences, while criminal, may be left unreported—fights in clubs, minor criminal damage, some types of domestic trouble. Or, when the police *are* called, they might be left unrecorded because formal action is seen as inappropriate, or weak evidence leads the police not to record, or to 'no-crime' the incident subsequently. The count of recorded crime reflects the successive judgements of victims and the police. The process of attrition at the various stages is difficult to pinpoint precisely, and it will vary for different offences. The definitional agreement between the public and the police will certainly be weakest for less serious incidents, those about which moral consensus is weak, and those where the legal criteria for taking action are most fluid. On balance, the BCS will count a broader and more value-free set of incidents than police statistics—as indeed it has to if the survey is to be able to detect shifts in reporting and recording practices over time.

---

[7] Other surveys (eg, the Australian one, the International Crime Survey, and many local ones) *do* leave the task of defining crime to respondents. They use legal or quasi-legal terms in asking screening questions about whether respondents have been 'burgled' for instance, and apply no checks on respondents' definitions. They yield a count of crime, therefore, as defined by the sampled population.

[8] Or more or less: some 7% of incidents in the 1992 BCS were excluded because no apparent valid crime had been committed.

The accuracy of the survey count

While the BCS may take a more inclusive count of incidents than the police, the survey process itself means there is undoubtedly much *undercounting* in the survey, as well as possible bias in response. There are several reasons why the BCS count will be imprecise.[9]

* Like any sample survey, the BCS faces problems of adequately representing the total population. In the 1992 sweep, the Postcode Address File was used to overcome problems associated with the Electoral Register (see below). Even so, some selected respondents were impossible for interviewers to locate at home, and others refused to be interviewed. Though the 1992 BCS achieved a good response rate of 77%, non-respondents may have included a disproportionately high number of victims.

* Those in institutions are not covered in the survey, and again their experience of crime could differ.

* Crime surveys question only a sample of the population and sampling error may arise because of this. The BCS sample is large by the standards of most surveys, but its estimates are imprecise, in particular for rare crime such as robbery and serious assault. Bearing in mind sampling error, a few crime types which are exceptionally well-reported to the police (eg, theft of vehicles) are probably counted more accurately by police statistics. (Estimates of sampling errors are provided in Appendix E.)

* The BCS tends to undercount crimes where victim and offender know each other; respondents may not think of these as 'real crimes' and may in any case be reticent with interviewers. This will affect counts of domestic and non-stranger violence. Sexual offences, too, are very likely to be underestimated. In view of this and the fact that risk estimates are sensitive to question wording, which has been changed in the BCS to try to prompt better response, this report does not cover sexual offences.

* There may be differential undercounting between social groups. For example, some types of offence such as assault are more often reported by better-educated respondents, though it is unlikely they are really more at risk. The most likely explanation is that they are able to complete survey questionnaires better, and may be more prepared to define incidents as falling within the scope of the survey. While this so-called 'education effect' has been found in several surveys (Skogan, 1990), it has never been quantified precisely—nor could it, in the absence of a more accurate measure. In a review of the evidence, Gottfredson (1986) optimistically

---

[9]See Sparks (1981), Block and Block (1984), and Skogan (1986) for discussions of how well surveys count crimes.

concludes that the 'education effect' does not seriously jeopardise the relationship between risks and other demographic factors.

* Other things, too, prevent respondents giving accurate answers to questions about their experience of crime over a 14-month period (the 'recall' period in the BCS). They may:

    * simply forget a relevant incident (or be ignorant of it);

    * remember the incident, but think it happened before the reference period;

    * remember an earlier incident as happening within the reference period.

    Methodological work shows that response biasses of various sorts work, on balance, to *undercount* survey-defined offences, but there will be differential losses across crime categories. In checks where respondents have been asked about offences *known* to have been reported to the police, more trivial crimes (eg, minor thefts, vandalism and some assaults) are the ones less likely to be recalled in interview. More serious incidents are disproportionately likely to be captured, and indeed may even be overcounted because more salient events tend to be pulled forward in time ('forward telescoping'). Overall, memory loss seems to exclude more incidents than 'forward telescoping' includes.

* It is a moot point how far in a regular survey like the BCS rising crime affects the accuracy of the survey count. It may be that frequent victims will be more likely to forget trivial incidents, leading to a relatively greater undercount of crime. Chapter 2 takes up this issue and, in brief, suggests that an effect of this kind *may* have occurred.

In summary, the BCS and police figures are complementary measures. The BCS will give a higher tally because it counts any incident that is technically criminal, and because it is concerned with unreported as well as reported crime. As against this, it omits certain classes of offences and victims, and may well undercount certain types of crimes. Its estimates are also subject to sampling error, and in conditions of increasing crime the survey may lead to a change in the number of incidents respondents recall in the interview. As some of these sources of error are linked to the distribution of victimisation itself, this causes problems for the crime counting function of the survey, and it may be even more important for analysing patterns of risk. (For instance, young men register the highest risks of assaults in crime surveys (see Chapter 6), but as they are particularly hard for interviewers to contact, and may 'define out' some assaults, their level of risk may still be understated.) But to say these limitations vitiate survey-based indices of crime is to overstate the case. For a wide range of offences against individuals and their property, the BCS provides the best available national yardstick.

Organisation and design

Fieldwork was carried out in early 1992 by a consortium of Social and Community Planning Research (SCPR) and British Market Research Bureau (BMRB) who were heavily involved in the design of the survey.[10] The 1992 'core' sample was similar in size to that of earlier surveys, covering a nationally representative sample of 10,059 households in England and Wales. The response rate in 1992 was 77%, the same as in 1988 and 1984, but slightly lower than in 1982 (81%). (Further details of the survey are in Appendix D and in SCPR (1993).) As in 1988, the 1992 survey carried an additional 'booster' sample of Afro-Caribbeans (mainly West Indians and Africans) and Asians (Indians, Pakistanis and Bangladeshis); 1,654 were interviewed. The response rate was 64%. A new feature for the survey was an additional sample of children aged 12-15 years who lived in households selected for either the 'core' or ethnic minority booster sample. Results in this report exclude these teenagers.

The Electoral Register served as the sampling frame in the first three surveys, but because of doubts whether this still provided adequate coverage of all households, the Postcode Address File (PAF) was used in 1992 as it represents the fullest register of household addresses. (The PAF is a listing of all postal delivery points in the country, almost all households having one delivery point, or letter box.) Methodological work was carried out to assess whether the change to PAF had any effect on victimisation levels—which would occur to the extent that the PAF sample picks up households with different experiences of crime to those on the Electoral Register. The results showed, as expected, a slightly higher rate of victimisation for those on PAF but not traceable on the Electoral Register, but the overall difference was not large enough to merit any adjustment to results to take account of the change in sampling frame.

One adult in each household was interviewed. All of them answered a **Main Questionnaire**. This included some attitudinal questions and then 'screened' people to see if they had been the victim of crime.[11] Anyone giving a positive answer completed a supplementary questionnaire about the incident, on the basis of which an offence classification was made. Respondents were asked about their own experience and that of others in the household for **household crimes**: burglary, thefts of and from vehicles, vandalism, and theft from the home. They were asked only about their own experience with respect to **personal crimes**: assaults, robberies, thefts from the person, and other personal thefts. This distinction reflects the fact that for some crimes, such as burglary, the household

---

[10]SCPR did the fieldwork in the first survey; NOP Market Research in the second, and a consortium of both companies in the third.

[11]The large number of 'screening' questions are couched in everyday language rather than using legal terms: eg, "in the last . . . months, has anyone got into your home without permission, in order to steal or try to steal anything?".

is a natural unit of analysis, whereas for others the individual is a better choice.

Details of each incident revealed by the screen questions were collected in **Victim Forms**, which provide the basis for classifying incidents. (Close attention is paid to legal criteria in classification, and procedures deliberately mirror those followed by the police.) Most victim forms corresponded to one incident. However, some victims may experience a number of very similar offences which are difficult to separate into discrete events. In this case, one Victim Form was completed for the whole series, with full information collected only about the most recent incident (see Appendix D for fuller details). There was a limit of five Victim Forms.[12] All respondents completed one or other of two versions of a **Follow-Up** questionnaire. The first covered questions principally about attitudes to sentencing and crime prevention. (All those in the ethnic minority booster sample completed this Follow-Up questionnaire.) The second covered the public's contacts with, and attitudes to the police. Personal details were collected from all respondents. Teenagers and those aged 16-19 were given a self-completion questionnaire relating to self-reported offending and drug misuse. Those aged 20-59 were also given a self-completion questionnaire, covering drug misuse only.

To maintain consistency, questions about victimisation have remained largely the same in each BCS sweep, but other areas of questioning have varied. The main topics dealt with in 1992 are shown in Table 1.1.

---

[12]In previous surveys, the maximum number of Victim Forms was four. The change to five was made in 1992 to reflect a possible increase in multiple victimisation. Information from the fifth Victim Form is included in rate estimates for 1992, though the effect is extremely small. Only 3% of victims filled out five Victim Forms.

Table 1.1
Coverage of the questionnaire in the 1992 British Crime Survey

	Core sample	Ethnic boost	Teenage boost (1)
FULL SAMPLE			
Victimisation screeners	✓	✓	✓
Socio-demographic information	✓	✓	✓
Attitudes to crime in the neighbourhood	✓	✓	
Experience of household fires	✓	✓	
VICTIMS			
Questions on victimisation	✓	✓	✓
Victim support	✓	✓	
HALF SAMPLES			
Security behaviour	✓	✓	
Membership of Neighbourhood Watch	✓	✓	
Experience of obscene telephone calls	✓	✓	
Awareness of Police Complaints Authority	✓	✓	
Attitudes to crime and sentencing	✓	✓	✓
Experience of and attitudes to drugs	✓(2)	✓(2)	✓
Self-reported offending	✓(3)	✓(3)	✓
Contacts and attitudes to the police	✓		✓

Notes:
1. The coverage of topics for teenagers was not always exactly the same as for the other samples.
2. Drugs questions were asked only of those aged 16-59 years.
3. Self-reported offending questions were asked of those aged 16-19.

The structure of this report

This report does not cover all the topics mentioned above, and further reports will follow. **Chapter 2** deals with levels of risk in 1991, provides estimates of unreported and unrecorded crime, and examines changes in risks since previous surveys. The picture for the BCS is contrasted with that from offences recorded by the police. The results in this chapter have been summarised in Mayhew and Aye Maung (1992). **Chapter 3** looks in more detail at reporting to the police, examining reasons why victims do *not* report, and then at how people who *did* report felt they had been handled by the police; some attention is paid to contact with, and attitudes to Victim Support. The next three chapters deal with specific offences: burglary (**Chapter 4**), theft of and from cars (**Chapter 5**), and violent crime (**Chapter 6**). These document what happened and how risks are distributed across different social groups, and in different areas. The concluding chapter (**Chapter 7**) draws out the most important new findings from the survey and discusses their implications. Additional results are provided in **Appendices A, B and C**. Details of the survey design are presented in **Appendix D**. A technical note on sampling error is included in **Appendix E**. **Appendix F** describes the comparison made between BCS figures and offences recorded by the police. **Appendix G** gives details about the comparisons of findings on burglary from the General Household Survey and the BCS. **Appendix H** describes the ACORN system of neighbourhood classification. A bibliography of BCS reports is included in **Appendix I**.

2 The extent of crime

The British Crime Survey yields estimates of the extent of various crimes including those unreported to the police. It covers some forms of violence and most theft of and damage to private property.[1] Respondents describe the offences they have experienced in the preceding year, so the results of the four surveys cover crime occurring in 1981, 1983, 1987 and 1991. Many of the findings in this chapter have been reported in Mayhew and Aye Maung (1992).

This chapter discusses first the extent of crime in 1991; it then describes the extent of reporting and recording of crime and BCS estimates of the 'dark figure' of unrecorded crime. There is then some attention paid to how the 'dark figure' of unrecorded offences has changed over the 1980s. One reason is an increase in the reporting of crime, for which some explanations are put forward. We turn finally to the picture of trends in crime according to the BCS. Here, we begin by comparing BCS trends to those from recorded offences for the sub-set of offences for which this can be done, and then take up trends in other BCS offences.

The survey estimated a total of 15 million crimes in 1991. Figure 2.1 shows numbers and relative frequencies of offences. (As do statistics of recorded offences, some offences include attempts.) Estimates have been derived by applying rates from the 'core' sample to the household and adult populations in England and Wales. As the estimates are derived from a sample they are subject to sampling error: another survey with a different sample might have resulted in different estimates. For instance, the survey's best estimate of the number of incidents of burglary in 1991 is 1,365,000; with 95% certainty the number that would have been estimated from another equivalent survey would fall between 1,184,000 and 1,546,000.[2] (Table A2.1 in Appendix A shows the detailed figures on which Figure 2.1 is based. Table A2.2 gives details of the victimisation rates

---

[1]The BCS questionnaire also deals with sexual offences, doorstep thefts of milk bottles, and threats. Sexual offences are not included in analyses in the present report as changes in question wording make trends unreliable, and many women will be reluctant to report sexual offences anyway. Milk bottle thefts are also excluded, though 7% of households said they had milk stolen at least once over about 14 months. Threats are also not covered as few meet the criteria of criminal offences. Only a minority can be prosecuted *qua* threats as indictable offences (threats to murder, blackmail and threats to commit criminal damage). A threat is a possible route to an offence of robbery. And a threat may be involved in some summary Public Order offences. Many of the 'frightening threats' uncovered by the BCS are reported to the police and are viewed seriously. They comprised 11% of crimes and threats counted in the 1992 BCS.

[2]Strictly, we should say that if the BCS was repeated many times under the same conditions, in the long run 95% of the intervals derived would contain the number of burglaries in the population. The interval above will either contain the 'true' number or not: we do not know for certain, but are 95% sure that it does.

**Figure 2.1
British Crime Survey estimates of certain offences in England and Wales, 1991**

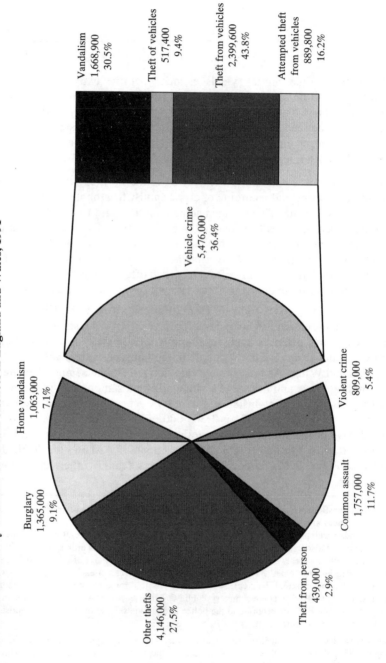

Vandalism
1,668,900
30.5%

Theft of vehicles
517,400
9.4%

Theft from vehicles
2,399,600
43.8%

Attempted theft
from vehicles
889,800
16.2%

Vehicle crime
5,476,000
36.4%

Home vandalism
1,063,000
7.1%

Burglary
1,365,000
9.1%

Violent crime
809,000
5.4%

Common assault
1,757,000
11.7%

Theft from person
439,000
2.9%

Other thefts
4,146,000
27.5%

on which the *numbers* of offences are based. Table A2.3 shows rates of vehicle offences for vehicle owners.)

The vast majority of offences were against property. Motor vehicles (cars, vans and motorcycles) emerged as a strikingly common target: over a third of all incidents uncovered by the BCS involved theft of, theft from, or damage to vehicles (Figure 2.1). In contrast, burglaries formed a smaller proportion of survey crimes, at around 9%. Wounding and robbery accounted for only 5% of BCS crime, although less serious common assaults made up another 12%.

Throughout the rest of this chapter, we distinguish three broad groups of BCS offences: acquisitive crime, vandalism, and violence. Within these groups there is a further division between offences which can be compared with offences recorded by the police (some 65% of all BCS offences) and those which cannot. The former are called the 'comparable sub-set' hereafter. They *exclude* common assaults, which are not notifiable offences, and 'other household theft' and 'other personal theft', which cannot be readily matched to any police category. Various adjustments are made to recorded crime categories to maximise comparability with the BCS. (For instance, crimes against those under 16 are excluded as they are not covered by the BCS. Recorded vehicle thefts are adjusted to exclude incidents involving commercial vehicles. And the large amount of vandalism against public and corporate property is also excluded.) The table below shows which offences fall into which category. Appendix F gives details of the adjustments to recorded crime figures.

	Comparable with police figures (comparable sub-set)	Not comparable with police figures
ACQUISITIVE CRIME	Burglary[1] Bicycle theft Theft from the person[1] Theft of/from motor vehicles[1]	Other household theft[1,2] Other personal theft[1]
VANDALISM	Incidents against household property and vehicles	
VIOLENCE	Wounding Robbery[1]	Common assault[1]

Notes:
1. Including attempts.
2. Including theft in a dwelling. In previous publications on the BCS these thefts have been in the comparable sub-set. However, numbers are small thus trends are unreliable.

Figure 2.2
Levels of recorded and unrecorded crime, 1991. British Crime Survey estimates

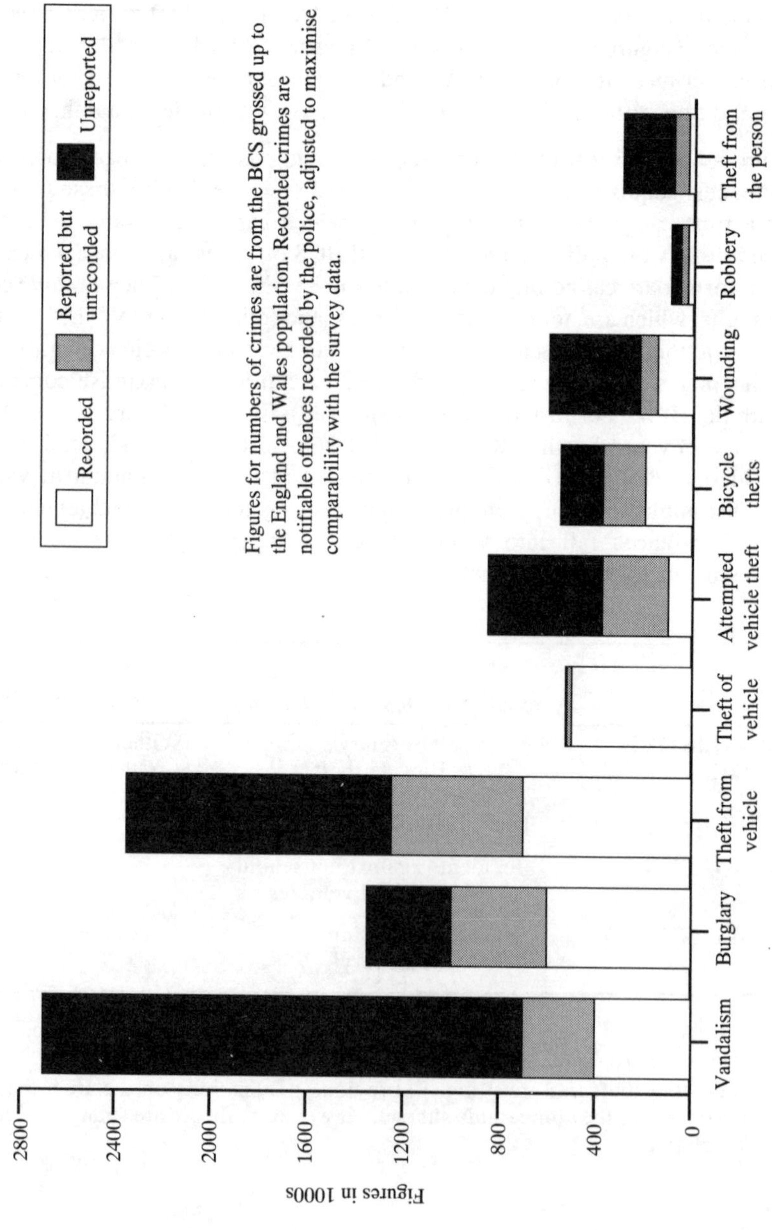

Figures for numbers of crimes are from the BCS grossed up to the England and Wales population. Recorded crimes are notifiable offences recorded by the police, adjusted to maximise comparability with the survey data.

14

Reporting and recording of crimes

By combining information from the BCS with police statistics, estimates can be derived of the proportion of crimes reported to, and recorded by the police. Figure 2.2 shows unreported incidents, those which were reported but not recorded, and those which found their way into police records (see also Table A2.4, Appendix A).

A large proportion of incidents goes unreported for all categories of crime except vehicle theft and burglary with loss (Figure 2.3). The overall reporting rate for the comparable sub-set of crimes shown in Figure 2.2 was 50%. Particularly low reporting rates emerged for vandalism, common assault and other household theft: roughly a quarter were brought to police attention. Trends in reporting are looked at later and victims' contacts with the police after reporting are taken up in Chapter 3.

Figure 2.3
Percentage of incidents reported to the police (1992 BCS)

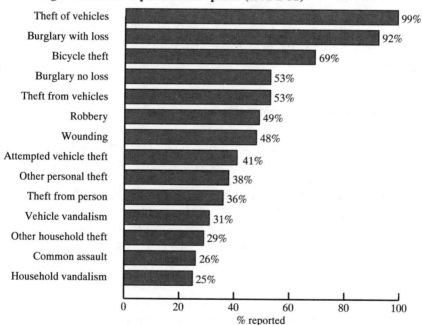

Many offences reported to the police do not get recorded as crimes—or at least not in the crime categories shown in the BCS. There is a great deal of variation by offence type (see Table A2.4) but, for instance, the police would appear to record about six out of ten incidents of acquisitive crime and vandalism reported to them, and about half of violent incidents. For the comparable sub-set overall, around 60% of reported offences in 1991 were recorded by the police. Taking account of both incomplete recording *and* reporting, only 30% of the sub-set ended up in police records.

The four surveys have shown a consistent recording shortfall, and there can be little doubt that many reported incidents are not recorded, or at least not in the crime categories suggested by victims' descriptions. However, BCS estimates of the 'recording shortfall' are not precise. This is both because of sampling error on the survey estimates and because of the difficulties in comparing like with like when matching BCS offence classifications with those used by the police (though in principle the same rules are adhered to). Some incidents will have been recorded but in different crime categories—where, for example, it is indisputable that criminal damage has been committed, but less clear that a *burglary* has been attempted.

One reason for the shortfall is that the police do not always accept victims' accounts of incidents; they may think that a report is mistaken or disingenuous, or may feel that there is simply insufficient evidence to say that a crime has been committed. Some incidents may have been regarded as too trivial to warrant formal police action—particularly if complainants indicated they wanted the matter dropped or were unlikely to give evidence, or if the incident had already been satisfactorily resolved.

Changes in reporting and recording

Over the last ten years, the proportion of BCS offences reported to the police has increased. For the comparable sub-set, 36% of offences were reported in 1981, but 50% in 1991. For all BCS offences, reporting has increased from 31% in 1981 to 43% in 1991 (Table A2.5 in Appendix A shows details.) The proportion of reported offences which are recorded has remained the same over the 1980s for the comparable sub-set *overall*, but the stability of the recording ratio masks differing trends for acquisitive crime—for which recording has *decreased*—and for vandalism and violence—for which recording has *increased* (Table A2.6 in Appendix A shows details).

The overall result of changes in reporting and recording has been a decrease in the ratio of BCS crime to recorded offences, or a contracting of the 'dark figure' of crimes unrecorded by the police. In 1981, the BCS estimated that for the comparable sub-set, there were 4.5 BCS incidents for every one incident recorded by the police—due to non-reporting and non-recording. This had dropped to 4.4 in 1983, to 4.1 in 1988 and to 3.4 in 1992 (Figure 2.4).

The contraction in the 'dark figure' has been especially marked for incidents of vandalism, and this is explained much more by increased recording by the police

16

Figure 2.4
The ratio of BCS offences to recorded offences (the 'dark figure')

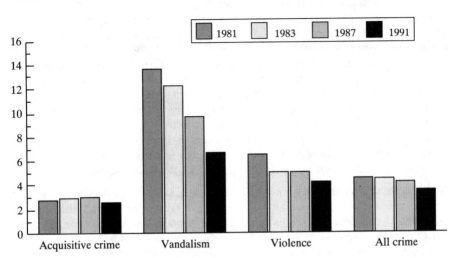

than by an increase in reporting. The 'dark figure' for woundings and robberies has also declined since 1981; increased reporting plays some part in this, but changes in police recording again appear more important. For acquisitive crimes, the proportion now recorded is the same as in 1981, the effect of higher reporting rates being largely cancelled out by lower recording levels.

Explaining the increase in reporting

The BCS shows that the decision of victims to report to the police turns largely—although not entirely—on the seriousness of what happened. Overlaying judgements about seriousness is a calculation of the personal costs and benefits of reporting, and of the chances that notifying the police will achieve something. Thus, the reasons given by 1984 victims who *did* report (the question has not been asked in other sweeps) stressed mainly: (i) the personal advantages of doing so (eg, getting property recovered, reducing the risks of further victimisation, getting police help, and insurance requirements); and (ii) the feeling that there is a social obligation on victims to notify the police (see Hough and Mayhew, 1985: pp 20-21).

Reasons for *not* reporting given by respondents in the 1992 survey are taken up in Chapter 3, but in brief they reflect judgements that the incident was too minor, or that there was little chance of any satisfactory outcome in terms, for instance, of getting property back, or offenders caught. Victim-offender relationships also play an important part (see Skogan, forthcoming).

There is no way of saying for certain why reporting to the police has generally gone up over the decade. Other analysis of BCS data (Skogan, forthcoming) highlights the importance of being insured in deciding victims whether or not to report—so certainly one factor may be that more victims are insured against property loss or damage.[3] (For instance, 50% of theft and damage incidents were covered by insurance in 1991 as against 37% in 1987.) Between 1987 and 1991 it can be roughly estimated that wider cover and the fact that insured victims are more likely to report may have accounted for about a fifth of the extra incidents of theft and damage (in the comparable sub-set) which the police had available to them to record. Higher owner-occupation may be implicated in this since owners are much more inclined to take out insurance. (According to the GHS, some 54% of households were owner-occupiers in 1981 (GB), as against 67% in 1991.) Skogan also finds that older people report more often and, reflecting national trends, they are a growing proportion of the BCS sample.

Another possibility is that it may have become easier to report as more people have a telephone at home than a decade ago. This is plausible, although in analysing the effects of various factors in relation to reporting crime, Skogan does not find telephone ownership to be associated with higher reporting rates when other factors, which are themselves associated with telephone ownership, are taken into account.

That more people now report because of increased confidence in the police seems unlikely. The BCS provides no evidence that attitudes to police performance have improved either among reporters or non-reporters. While most people still feel that the police are performing well, levels of general satisfaction with the local police are slightly below those observed in previous years.[4] Moreover, according to 1992 results more victims did not report because they felt that the police could not or would not want to deal with what happened, which is inconsistent with any improvement in attitudes (see Chapter 3).

Is there any reason to think that reporting has increased because the nature of offences has changed, and in particular because offences have become more serious? The 1984 and 1992 BCS asked victims to assess what happened to them using a 'seriousness scale' where zero represented a very minor crime like theft of milk bottles, and twenty murder.[5] The results show first that increases in

---

[3] Skogan looks at the independent effect on reporting of a range of variables (eg value of loss, victim-offender relationships, degree of injury and social class). Accounting in multivariate analysis for overlaps between these factors, the single fact of a loss being covered by insurance made it 7% more likely that an incident would be reported to the police, holding other factors constant.

[4] In 1992, 69% of respondents said the police did a good or fair job in their local area, compared to 75% in 1982 and 1988. Among reporters, favourable opinion dropped from 74% in 1982 to 70% in 1992. (Those with no opinion are included in the base.)

[5] Obviously, no meaning can be attached to an isolated score, but the scale allows one to distinguish groups of crimes according to seriousness. There is considerable variation within crime categories in ratings of seriousness, in that most means had large standard deviations. This variation will reflect in part differences between respondents in the use of the scale, albeit that previous work has shown a fair degree of consensus between people in judgements about seriousness. The variations, then, may be due more to the fact that offences *within* crime categories will vary considerably in nature.

reporting to the police between 1983 and 1991 were sharper for offences regarded as *less serious*. This indicates that the additional offences reported to the police are those which were previously thought less worth bothering the police with. This may be because increased public sensitivity to crime is contributing to higher reporting, or even that attitudes towards anti-social behaviour are becoming less tolerant. Secondly, in the 1992 BCS, particular sub-categories of crime (eg, attempted burglary, personal thefts) were on average rated more seriously by victims than in 1984. This again may signify increased public sensitivity to crime, or less tolerance of it. But it also raises the possibility that the findings on reporting are an artefact of the survey method. Thus, it may be the greater seriousness of incidents reported to interviewers in the 1992 BCS reflects the fact that victims who have been often victimised tend to forget more trivial incidents. Also, the interview process may result in either interviewers or respondents rationing themselves to a limited number of incidents. When crime is rising, the effect of these processes would be to reduce the rate of increase in crime indicated by the BCS, and to increase the proportion of more serious or more salient incidents recalled in the survey—which are more likely to have been reported to the police. Detailed methodological work will be needed to investigate whether this is actually occurring.

Changes in crime between 1981 and 1991: BCS and recorded offences

This section looks first at trends in crime over the last ten years as measured by the BCS for those offences which can be compared with police statistics. Trends in other BCS crimes (eg common assault) are dealt with next. Table A2.4 in Appendix A shows trends in BCS and police recorded offences since 1981.

The comparable sub-set

In comparing trends in recorded offences and the BCS comparable sub-set, there are three relevant measures:

* the number of offences recorded by the police,

* BCS offences, *whether or not* reported to the police, and

* BCS offences which *were* reported to the police.

Generally, there has been a flatter rise in BCS estimates of crime over the last ten years than in recorded offences. Figure 2.5 shows this with figures for 1981 indexed at 100. The number of *recorded* offences rose by 96% between 1981 and 1991; BCS offences, whether reported or not, rose by 49% —a difference which is well outside the range of sampling error. The number of *reported* offences rose by just over 100%, reflecting partly the underlying growth in crime and partly an increase in reporting. The result is that the dotted line in Figure 2.5, which covers reported offences, shows a similar trend to police statistics.

Figure 2.5
Indexed trends in crime 1981-1991—comparable sub-set (all 1981 numbers = 100)

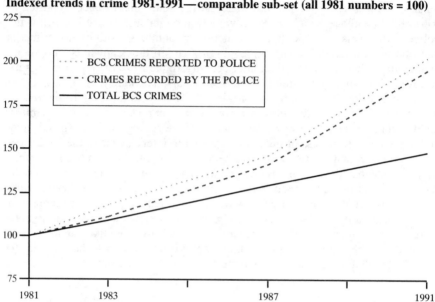

Between 1987 and 1991, the rise in BCS crime was 14% compared to 39% for police figures—again a statistically significant divergence.

Within sub-groups of offences the pattern is by no means consistent, however. Figure 2.6 shows the results for acquisitive crime, vandalism and violence. Where trends diverge, this may be explained by reporting changes, or changes in the extent and manner of recording by the police of offences reported to them. Estimates of the proportion of reported offences which are *recorded* should be treated cautiously, but possible changes in the proportion seem important for some offences (Table A2.6 in Appendix A shows details).

Acquisitive crime

Around two-thirds of the comparable sub-set is made up of property thefts. These have nearly doubled since 1981, and have increased by a quarter since 1987. Police figures show the same increase over the last ten years, although a statistically significantly greater increase since 1987. Despite the parallel trends, the BCS shows that more property thefts are now being reported. This implies that fewer reported crimes are being recorded, or that they are being recorded under other types of crime (eg vandalism or other types of household theft).

There is some variation in the picture for individual offence categories within the acquisitive crime group. (Chapter 4 gives fuller details for burglary, Chapter 5 for thefts of and from cars and Appendix B for other individual offences.) In brief, thefts from motor vehicles have risen more in police figures than in the BCS since 1981, while bicycle thefts have risen less (mainly because of a steeper increase in BCS figures before 1987). Since 1987, recorded offences have risen more than BCS estimates for attempted burglary, thefts from vehicles and vandalism. (Divergences appear for other offences but are not statistically reliable.)

Vandalism

Overall, vandalism of private property has shown no significant change in the BCS since 1981, and has decreased since 1987 (Figure 2.6). Police figures indicate a doubling since 1981, and an increase of a third since 1987. Separate police-recorded estimates are not available for incidents against vehicles and against other household property, but the BCS indicates that *vehicle vandalism* (comprising 62% of vandalism offences) has been most stable. *Household vandalism*, however, increased slightly between 1981 and 1987, but has shown a more marked decline in the last four years.

For vandalism in general, reporting has increased significantly since 1981,

Figure 2.6
Indexed trends in different offence groups, 1981-1991 (all 1981 numbers = 100)

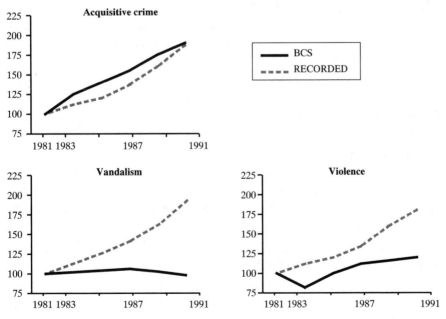

though this masks an increase in reporting of vehicle vandalism and a decline for household vandalism. Given the low level of reporting of vandalism generally, any rise in reporting translates into a much larger increase in recorded crime. The increase in reporting of vehicle vandalism, then, seems to play some part in the higher rise in police figures, but does not account fully for the divergence in trends. It may be that the police are now recording a larger proportion of incidents reported to them, or are classifying incidents as vandalism that the BCS classifies elsewhere (eg as attempted vehicle theft).

Wounding and robbery

Wounding and robbery have together risen less than police statistics indicate, and this is statistically reliable. BCS figures have increased by a fifth since 1981, while recorded offences have almost doubled (Figure 2.6). The BCS suggests that reporting has increased somewhat, but again not enough to account fully for the divergence. This may suggest increased recording by the police. Another possibility is that the police are now giving higher priority to some types of violent crime, such as domestic crime and street robbery; and where there are two options for classification (for instance, between wounding and common assault, or between robbery and theft from the person), they may now choose the more serious.

Interpretation of the divergence between BCS and police figures is made more complex by the fact that the dividing line between 'wounding' and 'common assault' is often difficult to draw, both for the BCS and, no doubt, the police. Common assaults as measured by the BCS have increased by a quarter since 1981, and this—if accompanied by a tendency by the police to classify more of these as 'wounding'—may have contributed towards the observed rise in recorded woundings.

Other crimes not comparable with police statistics

Common assault

Common assault has risen by a quarter since 1981, although sampling error is such that this is not a statistically significant increase. Levels of reporting to the police have changed little.

Other household theft and other personal theft

The BCS covers a miscellany of 'other household thefts' (eg, from gardens and sheds) and 'other thefts of personal property' (eg, from work, cloakrooms, etc).

They each comprised 12% of BCS offences. These thefts did not show any statistically significant increase over 1981 or 1987 figures according to BCS estimates. However, levels of reporting have increased for both categories of offence.

Summary

*   There were an estimated 15 million incidents in 1991 falling within BCS categories of crimes against individuals and their private property. The vast majority were against property, as is the case in police figures.

*   Some undercounting of violence in the survey is likely, but present figures show that wounding, robbery and common assault—the most comprehensive coverage of violent crime—comprised 17% of survey offences, or 5% with common assaults excluded.

*   Vehicles are a very common target of crime: 36% of all BCS offences involved theft of or from vehicles or damage to them.

*   Under half of offences in the BCS were reported to the police in 1991 — though reporting rates vary according to the offence involved. There is low reporting of vandalism, common assault and other household theft (about three-quarters go unreported). But most thefts of vehicles and burglaries with loss were drawn to police attention.

*   Reporting has increased for most BCS offence categories. For all BCS offences, reporting rose from 31% in 1981 to 43% in 1991. For BCS crime types which can be compared with police statistics, reporting rose from 36% in 1981 to 50% in 1991.

*   Changing attitudes to the police seem unlikely to be implicated in explaining the higher levels of reporting, but wider insurance may be. Changes in public sensitivity to crime may also be a contributory factor, but it cannot be ruled out that as crime rises, respondents may be forgetting to tell interviewers about less serious incidents—the ones least likely to be reported.

*   Incomplete reporting and recording mean that only 30% end up in police records. But this proportion is higher than in earlier years, due mainly to a shrinking of the 'dark figure' of unrecorded crimes of vandalism, wounding and robbery.

*   BCS crime *as a whole* increased by 36% between 1981 and 1991, and by 13% between 1987 and 1991.

* For those crime categories which can be compared, recorded crime figures nearly doubled between 1981 and 1991, but the BCS suggests a lower rise of about 50%. Since 1987, recorded crime figures for the comparable sub-set of offences have risen particularly steeply—by 39% —whereas BCS crimes have risen by 14%. Recorded crime shows a larger rise than the BCS mainly because of increased reporting to the police.

* Behind the overall picture of trends, there are differences for different offences. Since 1981, 'acquisitive crime' (burglary, motor vehicle crime and other thefts) have risen broadly in line with recorded crime figures. But violent crime has risen more slowly than recorded figures would suggest. Vandalism has increased hardly at all, compared to a large increase in the police statistics.

3 Reporting to the police

This chapter looks first at the reasons why many victims do *not* bring their offence to the attention of the police. It then focuses on people who *did* report to look at how satisfied they were with the response they got. Finally, the chapter covers contact with Victim Support schemes, to which the police now often refer victims after an offence is reported.

Reasons for not reporting

Victims of incidents which went unreported were asked why the police had not been involved.[1] Their most common explanation (55%) was that the incident was too trivial or involved no loss—as, for example, in cases of low-value criminal damage or attempted offences. Other common reasons were that the police could do nothing (25% of cases), that they would not be interested (13%), or that the incident was not a matter for the police or better dealt with privately (12%); 6% of incidents had been reported to another authority.[2] Rarely cited overall, was the inconvenience of reporting, dislike of the police, and fear of reprisals. These results are consistent with previous BCS findings, and are closely in line with results from other surveys (see, eg, Skogan, 1984; Gottfredson and Gottfredson, 1988; van Dijk and Mayhew, 1993).

The reasons for not reporting varied by offence. A higher than average proportion of personal thefts—often taking place at work—were not reported to the police because they were reported to someone else (20%). In a higher proportion of assaults, respondents said that it was inappropriate to report the incident, or that they had dealt with the matter themselves (40% of unreported assaults). Table A3.1 in Appendix A shows details.

Table 3.1 shows that over the last three surveys (a comparison is difficult with the 1982 survey because of questionnaire changes) there has been some increase

---

[1] Surveys less often ask why people *do* report crimes. Results from the 1984 BCS showed that, overall, slightly more than a third of victims offered motives stressing the advantages of reporting: recovery of property; reducing the risk of further victimisation; getting help from the police; and notifying the police to satisfy insurance requirements. Another third referred to the obligation to notify the police. Retributive motives—the hope that the offender would be caught and punished—weighed with 16% of victims.

[2] These incidents are treated as unreported to the police in this chapter, although some victims might have thought that they would become known to police in due course.

in the proportion of incidents going unreported because of 'police-related' factors: principally, because it was felt the police could do nothing, or that they would not be interested.[3] The view that the police's hands were tied was cited more in 1992 than in earlier surveys by victims of burglaries and thefts; lack of interest on the part of the police was mentioned more often for most types of offence (see Table A3.2 in Appendix A). The increase in 'police-related' reasons for not reporting does not suggest any improvement in attitudes among victims as to the ability, or commitment of the police to deal with the relatively less serious incidents which typically go unreported.[4]

Table 3.1
Reasons for not reporting crime: 1984, 1988 and 1992 British Crime Surveys

	84	88	92
Reasons for not reporting:	%	%	%
Too trivial/no loss	58	50	55
Police could do nothing	17	24	25
Police would not be interested	7	10	13
We dealt with matter ourselves/ inappropriate for police	11	11	12
Reported to other authorities	4	6	6
Inconvenient to report	2	2	3
Fear reprisals	1	1	2
Fear/dislike police	1	1	1
Other	7	13	4
All 'police-related' reasons(1)	24	32	35
Unweighted N	2705	2803	2905

Notes:
1. 'Police-related' reasons comprise any of the following reasons: police could do nothing, police would not be interested, fear/dislike police. Multiple responses were allowed, so these three categories may sum to more than the combined category.
2. Based on all incidents not reported to the police. 'Vague/not stated' responses are excluded from the base.
3. Source: incident-based analyses 1984, 1988 and 1992 BCS (weighted data).

[3]These reasons are not without ambiguity. "Nothing could be done" can mean both that the harm, loss or damage cannot be rectified; that there is insufficient proof of what happened; or that it seems impossible that an offender could be apprehended. "The police would not be interested" may signify that the victim feels uneasy about bothering the police in a relatively minor matter; or that he/she feels that the police would not want, or be able to give the matter due attention.

[4]One possibility seemed to be that as reporting has increased, respondents with more favourable attitudes to the police have been 'siphoned off' as reporters, leaving as *non*-reporters those more disposed to judge the likely police response unfavourably. If this were the case, then the proportion of incidents not reported because of police reasons based on *all* incidents (whether reported or not) would remain more stable. However, analysis shows that this does not explain the pattern of results; police-related reasons have increased on an all-incident basis.

Factors related to reporting

How much is reporting determined by victims' perceptions of the seriousness of their crime, and how significant a part do other factors play? In both the 1992 and 1984 surveys, victims were asked to assess the seriousness of their offence, using a 'seriousness scale' where zero represented a very minor crime like theft of milk bottles, and twenty, murder.[5] Seriousness ratings are clearly influenced by objective factors such as financial loss, degree of injury, etc, and it is not surprising that seriousness ratings are higher for well-reported offences.

Nonetheless, the decision to report is not wholly a function of the seriousness of what happened. Table 3.2 divides offences into three levels of seriousness, showing the percentage of each reported to the police. Nearly two-thirds of the most serious incidents were reported, as against only a quarter of the least serious. Table 3.2 also estimates the *number* of offences in the most serious category which went unreported in 1991. (The estimates are derived by applying the percentage of incidents not reported in the top seriousness band to the number of offences at this seriousness level in England and Wales in 1991 as estimated by the BCS.)

Table 3.2
Offence seriousness[1] and reporting to the police, 1991

| | % reported | | | Estimated no. of 'most serious' offences, not reported, 1991 |
	Least serious	More serious	Most serious	
Vehicle thefts[2]	33	60	75	343,000
Bicycle theft	60	84	68	53,000
Burglary	51	71	82	150,000
Other household thefts	21	39	44	170,000
Other personal thefts	25	49	56	176,000
Robbery/theft from person	11	41	62	107,000
Assaults[3]	20	27	40	647,000
Vandalism	15	31	53	262,000
All offences	25	48	62	1,891,000

Notes:
1. The 'least serious' offences (39% of all offences) were those with seriousness scores of 0-3; the 'more serious' (29%) those with scores of 4-6; and the 'most serious' (33%) those with scores of 7-20.
2. Thefts of and from vehicles; all attempts.
3. Assaults comprise woundings and common assaults.
4. Numbers do not sum to total due to rounding.
5. Source: 1992 BCS (weighted data).

[5] See footnote 5, page 18.

Table 3.2 shows that even for serious crimes, a great many incidents do not become known to the police. The figure of 1.9m compares with an estimated 3m *reported* offences considered similarly serious, and with 6.5m reported offences in total. Thus, even though the majority of incidents judged to be not particularly serious went unreported, so too did a good number of those which had most impact on victims. Conversely, many incidents which *were* reported were thought to be relatively trivial, and these will comprise a good proportion of recorded offences (cf. Pease, 1988). Broadly, three factors appear relevant to the decision whether to report, as well as seriousness. Firstly, there are practical considerations of self-interest. At all levels of seriousness, a higher than average proportion of burglaries, vehicle thefts and bicycle thefts are reported. One reason will be because claiming on insurance is seen to demand a police report. And for those whose car or bicycle has gone missing, police assistance will be needed in retrieving them. Secondly, victims' expectations of the police will play a part. 'Police-related' reasons for not reporting were more often cited for more seriously rated crimes than ones of lesser seriousness: ie, deciding not to report turned more on views of the effectiveness and interest of the police (Table A3.3 in Appendix A shows details).

Thirdly, victim-offender relationships are important. When victims know the offender(s), they will often fight shy of the consequences of bringing in the police, even when what has happened is seriously regarded and upsetting. Thus, of the most serious assaults, some 43% of which were related-party incidents, only four in ten were reported. For those which were not, over a third were considered to fall outside the remit of the police, or better dealt with privately. Fear of reprisals is another element, with one in five of the most serious assaults not being brought to the attention of the police because of what might happen as a consequence. (Fear of reprisals was also relevant for some more serious unreported incidents of vandalism.)

This analysis is consistent with that of Skogan (forthcoming), who has also looked at how much reporting is determined by the nature of what happened and by characteristics of victims themselves. In multivariate analysis, he too shows that indicators measuring intrusiveness, harm, level of loss and insurance coverage are most influential, but that in addition to this, related-party incidents go unreported more often. Skogan finds that while some victim characteristics are important, others, such as income and gender, do not have much to do with reporting differences once offence-related factors are taken into account.[6]

---

[6]Skogan does not examine attitudes to the police as a *determinant* of reporting on the grounds that attitudes reported in the BCS may have been a *result* of the police contact.

The police response when victims report

Previous BCS sweeps have asked a few questions of victims about how they were treated by the police after reporting. More detailed questions were asked in the 1992 survey in the light of renewed commitment by police forces to respond to victims more effectively.[7]

One question has been included in the last three surveys: "Overall, were you satisfied or dissatisfied with the way the police handled the matter?"[8] There was a drop in satisfaction between the second (1984) and third (1988) surveys—from 31% of victims who felt *very* satisfied in 1984 to 22% in 1988 (see Table 3.3). The percentage who were *very* or *fairly* satisfied also dropped from 68% to 60%. The fall in satisfaction between these two sweeps was consistent across all offence categories, with the exception of robbery/theft from the person, for which the numbers involved are too small to be reliable. It was also evident across sex, age and class (Mayhew *et al*, 1989).

Between the third (1988) and fourth (1992) surveys, overall satisfaction with police performance improved, in particular among victims of burglary, vandalism, robberies and thefts from the person. Levels of satisfaction, nonetheless, remained lower in 1992 than in 1984, with the exception of burglary and robbery/theft from the person.

---

[7]In previous sweeps of the survey, victims expressing dissatisfaction with the service they received were asked what aspects had disappointed them. In 1992, all victims who had reported incidents to the police, whether satisfied or dissatisfied, were asked to evaluate the service they had received on those aspects that had previously been identified as potential problems. Dimensions of performance were also covered in the 1992 BCS questions on other types of contact with the police, in order to facilitate comparisons across different types of contacts between police and public. Results are reported in Skogan (forthcoming).

[8]A similar question was asked in the 1982 survey, but it lacks strict comparability as it was only asked of those who had face-to-face contact with the police.

Table 3.3
Satisfaction with police response 1984 to 1992, by offence

	% very satisfied		
	1984	1988	1992
Theft of motor vehicle	48	30	39
Theft from motor vehicle[1]	21	17	21
Bicycle theft	33	21	24
Burglary	30	23	32
Other household theft	37	25	35
Other personal theft	24	21	20
Robbery/theft from the person	19	30	45
Assault	37	22	29
Vandalism	34	20	32
All offences	31	22	29
	% very and fairly satisfied		
All offences	68	60	65
Unweighted N	1755	2008	2469

Notes:
1. Including attempted thefts of and from vehicles.
2. Only incidents that the police came to know about through someone reporting them are included to maintain comparability between survey years.
3. 'Don't know' and 'too soon to tell' responses are included in the analysis.
4. Source: 1984, 1988 and 1992 BCS (weighted data).

Initiatives within police forces to improve service to victims began to take hold towards the end of the 1980s. It gained momentum with the police Quality of Service initiative, the Citizen's Charter, and the Victim's Charter (published in 1990 by the Home Office), which set out how victims should be treated and what they are entitled to expect from the criminal justice system. These initiatives may explain the improvement in victim satisfaction in 1992 over 1988, when opinion among victims about their response from the police seemed at a particularly low ebb.

Another BCS question on how good a job the local police do—asked of victims and non-victims—shows the percentage of respondents who rated the police as 'very' or 'fairly' good dropping from 89% in 1984, to 86% in 1988, and to 81% in 1992.[9] This suggests that improvements in dealing with victims have not necessarily been reflected in more general improvements—or perceived improvements—in police work in general.

---

[9]The percentage who gave the police the highest rating ('very good') dropped from 34% in 1984 to 25% in 1988, stabilising somewhat in 1992 at 24%. Skogan (forthcoming) discusses these results and those of other public attitude surveys.

Of course, how victims feel they have been handled by the police when they report crime may be coloured by what they think about policing generally. But there is some evidence that the reverse is more true. Thus, while the majority of those who were 'very satisfied' with the police after reporting a crime claimed this had no effect on their opinion of the police, a quarter said they now felt more positively about them. But 15% of those who were 'fairly dissatisfied' and half of those who were 'very dissatisfied' said their opinion had gone down. Overall, 11% of reporting victims said they now had a more favourable opinion and 10% said they had a less favourable one. Given that reporting a crime is the single most frequent way in which contact is made with the police (16% of BCS respondents came into contact with the police through reporting in 1991), dealing effectively with victims is clearly important in maintaining overall public confidence in the police.

Aspects of the police response

Victims in the 1992 survey were asked a series of questions about the service they had received: whether they had **waited** a reasonable time for the police to attend; whether the police had shown enough **interest** in what they had to say;

Figure 3.1
Victims' assessments of police performance

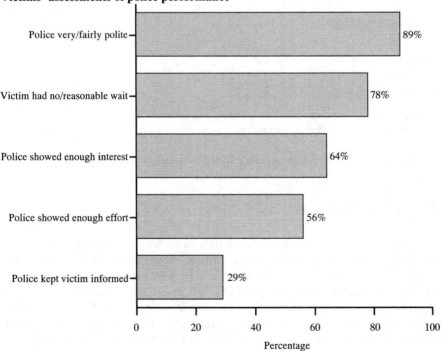

whether the police had put enough **effort** into dealing with their report; whether they had been **polite**; and how well they had kept the victim **informed** of the progress of the investigation (if there had been one). Figure 3.1 shows results.

The politeness of the police was highly rated: nine out of ten considered them to have been very or fairly polite. There was also relatively little criticism of the length of time victims had to wait to have their matter dealt with: three-quarters considered it to have been reasonable. Two-thirds felt the police had shown enough interest, and over half felt enough effort had been made. The lowest ratings were for how well victims felt they had been kept informed.

All five measures were related to **overall satisfaction** (Table 3.4). In particular, those who felt they had been treated impolitely were much more likely to express dissatisfaction. And victims who felt they had been kept well informed during the investigation were very much more likely to be very satisfied.

Table 3.4
Overall satisfaction on reporting to the police, by various aspects of police performance

| | Overall satisfaction on reporting | |
	% very satisfied	% very dissatisfied
Showed enough interest		
Yes	44	2
No	2	38
Had no, or reasonable wait		
Yes	35	8
No	7	41
Showed enough effort		
Yes	49	2
No	2	35
Kept victim informed		
Yes	61	2
No	11	20
Were very/fairly polite		
Yes	32	10
No	4	61

Note:
1. Source 1992 BCS (weighted data). Base: incidents reported to the police.

Feedback of information

The police service's duty to keep victims informed is a central tenet of the Victim's Charter. This specifies that victims should be given the names and telephone numbers of contacts at the police station whenever possible, and be told of developments in their case, notably the arrest of a suspect, prosecution decisions, and outcome of any trial. However, according to 1992 BCS results, only 14% of victims felt they had been kept 'very well' informed, and only 29% felt 'very' or 'fairly well' informed—a figure just 3% higher than in 1988.

These figures need some qualification however, as 'less well-informed' victims did not always feel the police *should* have done more.[10] Of this group, about half said either that the police would have had no information to pass on, or that they did not feel the need to be given more information. In total, some six out of ten victims were happy with the amount of information they were given by the police, or *else* (and more usually) were realistic enough to see that probably not much more information could have been provided. But four out of ten victims still remained dissatisfied with the level of information feedback.

Those more and less satisfied

How the police were rated in relation to different aspects of performance varied by the nature of the offence involved (see Table A3.4, Appendix A). Those who had cars or bicycles stolen gave higher than average ratings. Burglary victims were also comparatively favourable in their views, though not especially about being kept well informed. Those experiencing robbery and thefts from the person were also more likely to feel the police had taken the matter seriously and had reacted quickly. In contrast, victims of thefts from a vehicle, other personal thefts and assault—least satisfied overall—felt the police were uninterested, showed insufficient effort, and did not keep them informed.

Offence type apart, how does satisfaction vary in terms of age and gender of the victim, for instance, their relationship to the offender, or offence seriousness? Multivariate analysis is needed to answer this since the various factors can be interrelated. For example, victims from ethnic minorities (who are generally less satisfied) are also younger (who are also less satisfied); and those lower down the social class scale (less satisfied) are also more likely to know who was involved (less satisfied). We used logistic regression analysis to unravel what most affects judgements about the five elements of police performance.

The results show that those over the age of 30 were consistently more positive, as were those whose offenders were strangers. White respondents were more satisfied than those from ethnic minorities, and those in households in which the head was in a non-manual profession were more satisfied than those in which he/she was in manual work. Those who had made a claim on insurance were also more satisfied. This is perhaps because the police are seen to act as facilitators of a claim, or it may be that victims themselves provoke a better police response in the way they interact with the police when they expect to make a claim. If the police caught an offender or recovered property, this increased satisfaction, as one might expect. There was little evidence of any gender difference

---

[10]The question on whether the police should have provided more information was not asked of victims who said they had been kept 'very well' informed.

in satisfaction once other factors had been taken into account. Table C.12 in Appendix C illustrates these results by showing what factors were related to how victims felt about the *interest* the police had shown. Table 3.5 shows the differences in satisfaction on the dimensions identified as important in multivariate analysis, using a summary 'police performance score' based on the five separate questions about what happened. It also shows differences in scores

Table 3.5
Judgements about police performance on reporting crime

	Police performance score		Police performance score
Race		Type of police contact	
White	3.5	At home	4.4
Non-white	2.6	At police station	3.8
		Elsewhere	3.4
Social class (head of household)		No face-to-face contact	1.1
Non-manual	3.9		
Manual	2.9	Age	
		61+	5.2
Perpetrator identified		31-60	3.4
Yes	4.6	16-30	2.9
No	3.1		
		Offence	
Property recovered		Theft of vehicle	4.9
Yes	5.3	Bicycle theft	4.2
No	3.2	Robbery/theft person	4.2
		Burglary	3.9
Insurance claim		Other household theft	3.8
Yes	4.0	Vandalism	3.1
No	3.1	Other personal theft	2.9
		Theft from vehicle[2]	2.8
Relationship to offender		Assault	2.7
Stranger	3.5		
Known casually/well	2.7		
Seriousness of offence			
Low/medium	3.7		
High	3.1	All offences	3.4

Notes:
1. The police performance score was computed from the responses to the five questions on the various aspects of police service victims had received. 'Don't know' and missing responses were set to zero before the scores were computed; each item was recoded so that the total score could range from -10 to +10. The higher the positive score the more satisfied victims were with the service they received from the police after reporting a crime.
2. Including attempted thefts of and from vehicles.
3. Source: 1992 BCS (weighted data; core and ethnic boost samples).

for different types of offence.[11] The higher the scores, the more satisfied victims were with the service they received.

Face-to-face contact

Table 3.5 shows that when victims had face-to-face contact with the police they were consistently more satisfied with their response. It may not, of course, be that face-to-face contact *per se* improves victims' assessment of policing, but what the police convey (or are able to convey) when a more personal contact is made.

In total, 82% of victims had face-to-face contact with the police, and in 43% of cases this was at home. Home contacts were more common for burglary (four out of five cases), and for incidents of vandalism and household theft (about half the incidents). Of those who were not seen by an officer, a quarter felt they should have been—in particular victims of vandalism, theft of motor vehicles and burglary.[12]

Although only an 18% minority had no face-to-face contact with the police, these victims were consistently less satisfied with their response on all dimensions (Table 3.6). The most satisfied were victims visited at home—clearly indicating that the show of interest this represents is an important factor in meeting victim's expectations.

---

[11]Skogan (forthcoming) takes a slightly different approach in his multivariate analysis. He looks at which factors were related to *overall satisfaction* with the police, including, as independent variables, what victims felt about the five elements of police performance. These proved overridingly important, indicating that the way the police actually behave towards victims (or are perceived to behave) is paramount in affecting their general judgement. Possibly, of course, the police behave differently towards different types of victims.

[12]A quarter of victims met the police by going to the police station themselves. Those most likely to go had had their cars or bikes stolen, or were victims of robbery or theft from the person. Fifteen per cent of victims came into contact with the police by stopping them in the street, or encountering them at the scene of the offence. But face-to-face contact most often occurs at home, usually after a telephone call from the victim, or because a follow-up visit is made by the police after a previous encounter. Face-to-face contact of any kind was least likely for victims of thefts from motor vehicles, vandalism and other personal and household thefts.

Table 3.6
Satisfaction with police response, by type of contact

Percentage of incidents in which police:

	Showed enough interest	*Victim had no/reasonable wait*	*Showed enough effort*	*Kept victim informed*	*Were very/ fairly polite*
No face-to-face contact (18%)	43	48	43	13	70
All face-to-face contact (82%)	69	85	59	33	93
Personal contact at home (43%)	73	86	62	36	95
All incidents police came to know about	64	78	56	29	89

Notes:
1. 'Don't knows' on method of contact excluded.
2. Source: 1992 BCS (weighted data).

Case outcome

In few of the crimes uncovered by the BCS were the offenders identified, and where they were, the victim rarely knew what subsequently happened to them. In reported property incidents, some 12% of victims knew that the police had identified a perpetrator, but in only half of these cases was the victim told what subsequently happened (6% of all cases). Even when victims knew that some action had been taken against the offender (for instance, that an arrest had been made), only about half knew that someone had been taken to court (3% of all reported incidents). When the victim knew the offender had been taken to court, a third were told the date of the case (1% of all incidents). Table 3.7 summarises these findings.

As one might expect, the picture is different for cases involving assaults. An offender was identified in seven out of ten reported cases, and (again) about half the victims were told something about what happened subsequently (43% of incidents). For this group, half knew the offender went to court, often because they were required as witnesses. In total, 18% of reported assaults resulted in a court case—or at least one which the victim knew about.

Whether or not victims would want to be informed of the date of a court appearance if this arose has been the subject of some debate recently. One view is that victims are entitled to know as many of the facts about case outcome as possible; another is that they may dislike being reminded of their victimisation. The BCS suggests that more victims than not *would* want to be told about court appearances. Among those who knew a court visit was due but had not been told its date, six out of ten had expected to be told, and the figure was higher for victims of assault (70%). Moreover, among victims who had not been told whether an offender had been identified, or who were unaware of any court case, over three-quarters said they would have expected to be told where and when any case was being heard.

Table 3.7
Victim's knowledge about progress of investigation (incidents reported to the police)

	Assaults	Property offences	All offences
	%	%	%
Knew offender was identified	70	12	19
Told what happened to offender	43	6	10
Aware offender went to court	21	3	5
Told date of court case	18	1	3

Note:
1. Source: 1992 BCS (weighted data). Base = all incidents police came to know about.

Victim Support

Victim Support schemes are voluntary organisations which aim to provide support and advice for all victims of crime and to increase awareness of the effects of crime.[13] Nearly two-thirds of respondents in the BCS had heard of Victim Support, in contrast to a third in 1984. Women and those aged 30 to 60 are the most aware of the schemes.

The usual means of referral to Victim Support is by the police, who for certain types of crime, in particular burglary, pass on the victim's name and address unless the victim asks them not to. A few victims may make contact themselves. Victims are then visited, telephoned, or written to with an offer of support. Among victims who had reported to the police, 6% recalled being contacted by Victim Support, half of them burglary victims.[14] The percentage of BCS victims who had contact with Victim Support has increased from less than 1% in 1983, to 3% in 1987, to 6% in 1991. Numerically, the sample with experience of Victim Support in 1991 was small—just 148—and the results presented below are thus tentative.

[13]There are some 385 local Victim Support schemes covering 97% of the country. There is some central government funding for schemes, but the vast bulk of work is done by volunteers. The number of referrals to Victim Support was over 600,000 in 1991/92, involving over 7,500 volunteers.

[14]On the basis of all victims, whether or not they reported to the police, the contact rate is of course much lower (3%).

Effort seems to be fairly well targeted. Contact was made in 7% of offences judged to be in the top third of seriousness, compared with 2% of incidents of lesser seriousness; as a corollary of this, the majority of contacted victims said that they had been "very" or "quite" upset by their crime. Higher contact rates were also evident for victims who knew their offender well, female victims, and older victims—groups that the BCS shows to be particularly keen to have contact with Victim Support.

Half of contacted victims had received a letter telling them how to obtain further help, just over a third a home visit, and 13% a telephone call. This broadly mirrors the pattern of known contacts (Victim Support, 1992). Most approaches were considered to have been useful: 32% judged it very helpful and another 42% fairly helpful; 14% said it had not been very helpful and 8% felt it to have been not at all helpful. There was little apparent difference between those who had received a visit as opposed to a telephone call. (This question was not asked of those who had received a letter.)

All victims, regardless of whether they notified the police, were asked whether contact with Victim Support *would* have been helpful. When incidents were not reported, victims usually did not think so, but some 4% did. Interest was higher, as would be expected, among victims who notified the police: 10% said they would have liked contact. This is small proportionately, but would translate into a sizeable *number* of victims receptive to help. Victims of burglary, assault (including domestic violence) and robbery/theft from the person were most likely to have appreciated contact.

The best way of contacting victims is obviously a major issue for Victim Support, albeit one which needs to take into account both the helpfulness of different approaches, as well as resource considerations. There is concern that victims who need help will not always respond to a letter, or admit it in a telephone call, so that 'cold calling' is usually felt the best way of making contact (see, eg, Reynolds *et al*, 1993; Maguire and Wilkinson, 1993).

Victims who would have liked to have been contacted (a sample of 230) were asked whether they would have preferred a home visit, a telephone call, or a letter. They were also asked whether they would have minded an *unannounced* visit at home. A letter was the most popular option (half favoured it), followed by a home visit, particularly among more elderly victims. A telephone call was least popular (16%). Overall, two-thirds would not have minded an unannounced visit. This is rather higher than suggested by Maguire and Wilkinson (1993), and may reflect the fact that Victim Support is now becoming better known.

Summary

* Crimes go unreported mainly because in the eyes of the victim they are too trivial or not amenable to police action. But a large number of incidents regarded as serious are kept from the police, while many incidents at the less serious end of the range are reported.

* Other than seriousness, factors that influence reporting are insurance considerations, the practical help the police might give in finding stolen cars and bicycles, assessments of the likely police response, and victim-offender relationships. Assaults are among the most serious offences which remain unreported, especially those where offenders are known.

* The feeling that the police could not or would not want to deal with the offences is cited by a minority of those not reporting incidents, though it has increased since the two previous sweeps of the BCS.

* Most victims who *do* report are satisfied with the service they receive from the police: 65% were very or fairly satisfied in 1992. This figure was an improvement on 1988 (60%), but lower than in 1984 (68%).

* Victims who notified the police were, for the most part, satisfied with the politeness of the police. The vast majority of victims were also happy with the time the police took to attend to their call. Victims were most disappointed with feedback of information from the police. There seems little improvement since 1988. The next biggest criticism was inadequate effort by the police, although six out of ten were satisfied on this score.

* The young, those from ethnic minorities, manual workers, victims who knew the offender, and those experiencing more serious offences tended to be less satisfied with the service they received from the police.

* When victims see the police personally after reporting they are more likely to be favourable about all aspects of their response.

* Victims of burglary were among the more satisfied with the police. So too were those who had cars and bikes stolen. Part of the basis for their greater satisfaction may be that the police are seen to act as facilitators of an insurance claim.

* Very few victims end up knowing whether any sanction has been brought to bear on their offender. Only 3% of property offences were known to have resulted in a court case.

* Awareness of Victim Support has increased. Two-thirds of respondents in the 1992 survey had heard of Victim Support as against one-third in 1984.

39

* Of incidents reported to the police in 1991, 6% resulted in contact with Victim Support, most often by letter. Three-quarters of those contacted found it fairly or very helpful.

* Overall, Victim Support appears to be contacting the types of victims who are most likely to want help.

* In 10% of reported incidents, the victim would have appreciated being contacted by Victim Support—a small proportion but one that would translate into a sizeable *number*. Victims of burglary, assaults (including domestic violence), robbery and theft from the person were most likely to say they would have liked contact—albeit these are groups already seen most by Victim Support.

4 Residential burglary

This chapter looks first at trends in residential burglary since 1972, combining data from the BCS and the General Household Survey. It then considers the risks of burglary and how these vary across area and for different types of household. We then look into the circumstances of burglaries—how burglars get into houses, for instance, and the impact of security.

Where numbers of cases are sufficient, 1992 data are used; but to increase the reliability of some analyses, we have combined the data-sets from different sweeps of the BCS. This chapter uses two definitions of attempted and substantive burglary. Where survey data are compared with police statistics in the section on trends, attempts *include* cases where the house was entered but nothing was taken. Elsewhere in the chapter, attempts are defined as cases where the burglar failed to secure entry at all.

In common parlance, burglary involves entering a home and stealing household property. In law, however, burglary involves any incident in which an offender enters or tries to enter the home as a trespasser with the intention of committing theft, rape, grievous bodily harm, or unlawful damage. The BCS uses this legal definition to classify burglary, but in nine out of ten BCS break-ins, the motivation was theft.[1]

Trends in burglary

Since 1972, the General Household Survey (GHS) has intermittently included a question on household burglary. By combining its results with those from the BCS, a survey trend in burglary over the last two decades can be compared with that of police statistics. The most reliable comparisons can only be made for *burglaries with loss* (ie, where a burglar entered the home and stole something). Technical details about the comparability of GHS and BCS figures are given in Appendix G. The BCS can also say a little about the trends in attempted burglary since 1981.

---

[1]There are some offences whereby when trespass occurs, an offence other than burglary is committed (eg, when trespass results in very serious wounding). Reflecting these, a number of BCS incidents which involved actual or attempted trespass are classified as something other than burglary, and they are omitted in this chapter.

THE 1992 BRITISH CRIME SURVEY

Burglary with loss

Figure 4.1 shows burglary trends as measured by survey and police figures. In the 20 years from 1972-1991, combined GHS/BCS results indicate that burglaries with loss have risen by 61%; police figures over the same period have increased much more steeply, by 189%. The police statistics have thus very considerably overstated the rate of increase. Despite this divergence in the volume of change, the survey and police figures show the same picture in terms of direction of change: a peak around 1984/85; a slight dip, and then an upswing from the late 1980s.

Why have police statistics exaggerated the rate of increase in burglary? Changes in levels of reporting to the police, and in police recording practices are both probably implicated. The GHS and BCS can yield estimates of *reporting* rates; levels of police *recording* have to be inferred from the shortfall between survey estimates of reported crime and the police statistics themselves (see Chapter 2).

There has been a steady increase in the proportion of burglaries involving loss reported to the police—from 78% in 1972 (GHS figures) to 94% in 1991 (BCS figures adjusted for comparability to the GHS). Some of the factors behind this were discussed in Chapter 2; changing patterns of insurance may be particularly important for burglaries with loss. According to the GHS, 19% of incidents were covered by insurance in 1972, whereas the BCS figure was 58% in 1991.

The steeper increase in police statistics also implies a rise in the proportion of offences reported to the police which are recorded (although 1991 figures indicated a fall since 1987). Our best estimate is that just over half of reported burglaries were recorded in 1972, whereas about 8 out of 10 were in 1991. Increasing police numbers, standardisation of recording procedures, and computerisation may underlie the increase in recording particularly until 1987.

The BCS and GHS estimates of burglaries with loss have generally seemed consistent, but there has previously been no way of confirming this. For 1991, however, a direct comparison was possible since, for the first time, the reference period in the two surveys overlapped.[2]

---

[2]The reference periods for incidents used in the comparison for the two surveys are not identical. BCS figures refer to incidents in the calendar year 1991. The GHS question asks about incidents "in the last 12 months"; the questionnaire was administered over the 12 months April 1991-March 1992, so the bulk, but not all of incidents answered about will have occured in the calendar year 1991.

Figure 4.1
Residential burglaries involving loss, 1972-1991

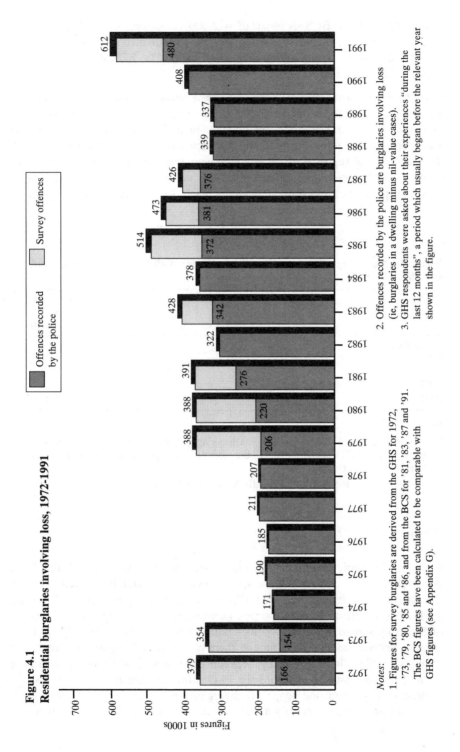

Legend: Offences recorded by the police | Survey offences

Notes:

1. Figures for survey burglaries are derived from the GHS for 1972, '73, '79, '80, '85 and '86, and from the BCS for '81, '83, '87 and '91. The BCS figures have been calculated to be comparable with GHS figures (see Appendix G).

2. Offences recorded by the police are burglaries involving loss (ie, burglaries in a dwelling minus nil-value cases).

3. GHS respondents were asked about their experiences "during the last 12 months", a period which usually began before the relevant year shown in the figure.

43

Compared with the BCS estimate of 612,000 residential burglaries with loss committed in England and Wales, the 1991 GHS indicated a figure of 606,000. This 1% difference is not statistically significant. (The BCS figure for 1991 is used in Figure 4.1.)

Over the last decade (1981-91), the number of burglaries with loss estimated by the BCS rose rather more (88%) than recorded offences (74%). This was accounted for mainly by a steeper increase in BCS figures after 1987 (Figure 4.2). Reporting of burglaries with loss has increased steadily since 1981, though the proportion of reported offences which were recorded has recently decreased (Table 4.1). One possible explanation for this is that with increased reporting, a higher proportion of less serious incidents reach the attention of the police, who are less likely to record them.

Table 4.1

Trends in reporting and recording of burglaries with loss: 1982, 1984, 1988 and 1992 BCS

	% reported	% recorded of reported incidents	% recorded of all incidents
Incidents in:			
1981	85	87	74
1983	87	87	75
1987	86	84	73
1991	92	74	68

Notes:
1. Recording rates are derived by expressing police figures as a proportion of grossed-up BCS estimates of (i) the number of reported offences, and (ii) the number of all offences.
2. Source: 1982, 1984, 1988, 1992 BCS (weighted data).

Attempted burglaries

Attempted burglaries can be charted only since 1981, and the picture differs from that for burglary with loss (Figure 4.2). Between 1981 and 1991, attempts rose *less* sharply according to the BCS (76%) than police figures (96%). Between 1981-1983 specifically, the two series showed parallel trends; between 1983-87 BCS attempts rose more (45%) than police figures (19%); since 1987, BCS offences showed no change, although there was a sizeable increase in recorded attempts (35%). The discrepancy between the two sets of figures is due to a particularly low rate of reporting in 1987, although the reasons for this are unclear. In any event, the scope for divergence between the trends is wide as recorded figures represent only a minority of incidents recalled in the BCS.

Figure 4.2
Indexed trends in burglary, 1981-1991 (all 1981 numbers = 100)

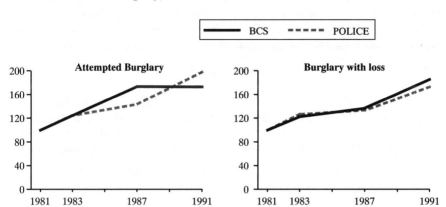

Risks

In this section we show first how relative risks differ according to area of residence and a number of other household factors. After this, a multivariate analysis is reported which takes into account the overlap between the different factors which influence the likelihood of burglary.[3]

Table 4.2 shows the relative risks of burglary for different types of household. The overall average incidence risk is indexed at 100. Inner city households run risks of burglary around twice the national average. The pattern is similar for both burglaries with entry and attempts.

Another way of looking at the spread of risks across area is through the ACORN classification, which assigns each home in the country to one of 11 neighbourhood groups according to the demographic, employment and housing characteristics of its immediate area as measured in the 1981 Census (see Appendix H).[4] The characteristics of neighbourhoods that feed into the ACORN

---

[3]Broadly speaking, risks may be expressed either in the form of *prevalance* rates or *incidence* rates. Prevelence rates are based on the number of victims per head of population, discounting the number of times they have been victimised; incidence rates use the number of crimes per head, counting all incidents for those victimised more than once. Both types of rates are used in this report. In this chapter, incidence rates have been used to look at relative risks. The multivariate analysis, however, was based on prevalence risks (ie, simply whether a household was a victim or not).

[4]ACORN was developed by CACI on the basis of cluster analysis of some 40 variables from the 1981 Census including age, class, tenure, dwelling type and car ownership. On the basis of this, each Enumeration District in the country (comprising 150 households on average) has been assigned an ACORN code. BCS respondents' census enumeration districts are identified via their postcode. It is important to remember that ACORN categories are not actual areas; rather, they refer to the *type* of area in which groups of individual respondents live.

classification are likely to encompass a number of factors associated with risk—for instance, inner city residence. In Table 4.2, the ACORN classification has been collapsed into three broader groups reflecting risks of crime in general.[5] Of households in the three highest-risk ACORN neighbourhoods, 50% live in inner city locations on the BCS inner city definition as against 17% overall.

Households in areas with the highest *overall* crime risks run over twice the national average burglary risk. (Table A4.1 in Appendix A gives indexed rates for the eleven ACORN groups.) Households in ACORN area F (containing the most tenants in 'less well-off' council estates) also run higher than average risks, particularly for attempted burglary. These patterns underline the greater vulnerability of household in more urban and poorer areas—those where offenders are more likely to be active. However, they may also reflect differences in target vulnerability. Properties in better-off areas may be better secured for instance—even though they may contain richer pickings.

Aside from area differences, other factors which seem to influence burglary risks are the number of adults in the household, the type of accommodation, occupancy patterns, tenure and socio-economic status of household head. There is a 'U'-shaped relationship between risk of burglary and household income, with those in the lowest and highest income bands experiencing the highest risks. Security also seems important.

These risk factors, however, will overlap with each other. For instance, houses are less vulnerable than flats, but as houses are more common in less urban areas, their lower risks could simply reflect an 'area' rather than a 'dwelling type' effect. Similarly, although there are higher risks for renters, this could reflect area, dwelling type, or the likelihood of renters having made poorer provision for security. Multivariate analysis is needed to disentangle the importance of any one particular factor. The multivariate approach used here was a series of logistic regression models which looked at whether households had been a victim or not of burglary (ie, a prevalence measure). This was done separately for all burglaries, burglary with entry, and attempted burglary in relation to a number of variables which bivariate analysis (ie, simple two-way tables) suggested were implicated in risks. The models were applied to half samples of combined 1988 and 1992 BCS data, since data on occupancy and security at the time of the burglary, felt to be important factors in risk, were not collected for the full samples.

---

[5]This is irrespective of the location of crime. The three areas with highest overall crime risks are:

ACORN H: Mixed inner metropolitan, or multi-racial areas with a mixture of poor, private rental housing and owner occupation.

ACORN I: High-status non-family areas, with a mix of affluent houses and privately rented buildings in multiple occupation.

ACORN G: The poorest council (or local authority) estates. These are located either in inner cities, or in the outer ring of conurbations.

Table 4.2
Relative risks of burglary[1]

Inner city	190[2]	Renters etc	155
Non-inner city	80[2]	Owner-occupiers	75
ACORN risk group:		SEG of household head	
High	225[2]	Manual	110
Medium	120[2]	Non-manual	90
Low	65[2]		
		Household income[5]	
Number of adults		Lower	110
One	130	Medium	90
Two or more	90	Higher	105
Flats/maisonettes	150	Number of evenings out in last week	
Houses	90	Two or more	110[3]
		None or one	90[3]
Security devices:[4]			
None	130[3]		
One or more	65[3]		

Notes:

1. Unless otherwise stated, rates are indexed at the pooled rate for the full 1988 and 1992 BCS samples.
2. Indexed at the pooled rates for the 1984, 1988 and 1992 samples.
3. Indexed at the pooled rate for half-samples of the 1988 and 1992 BCS.
4. A measure of security currently or at the time of the burglary was constructed, based on three types of device: alarms, double/dead locks on doors, and window locks.
5. Higher income households, £20,000 per annum household income or more; medium, £10,000 to under £20,000; lower, under £10,000.
6. Source: various BCS sweeps (weighted data).

Fuller details of the models are given in Appendix C.[6] Here we discuss the factors that emerged as important in their own right in the model for *all* burglary.[7]

a) **Where you live.** The strongest correlates of burglary, after all other factors have been taken into account, were measures of the type of area people lived in: namely, ACORN neighbourhood and inner city residence. We interpret this as indicating that the main determinant of risk is— unsurprisingly—proximity to offenders.

---

[6]Because it is better to make sure that what is being measured about the household relates to their circumstances at the time of a burglary, final models were based on those who had lived in their current address since the 1st January of the preceding year. However, models including movers and non-movers showed similar effects.

[7]See note 3 to Table C.1, Appendix C for all factors considered.

b) **Dwelling type.** Houses are less at risk of being burgled than other types of accommodation, regardless of the sort of area where they are located and any other factors. Houses differ from other types of dwellings (flats, maisonettes, rooms and bedsits) in that they are, by definition, self-contained, with separate (rather than communal, and possibly open) entrances. Their greater privacy may help keep burglars out.

c) **Security.** The presence of security devices was associated with a lower risk of burglary. This 'security effect' would seem to explain the simple association that is observed between tenure and burglary risk: owner-occupiers are less at risk of being burgled, but on the whole have better security than private renters and council tenants. The security issue is returned to later.

d) **Household composition.** Single-adult households run greater risks of burglary than households with two or more adults, net of other effects. This is not simply explained by the fact that single-adult households will provide a lower level of 'guardianship', since they still ran higher risks of burglary even after levels of occupancy had been taken into account (see below). Other factors may also be at work. For example, there is a higher than average proportion of single-adult households in rooms and bedsitters specifically, and these may be particularly insecure forms of accommodation. Also, there was a noticeably higher risk of burglary for 'single parent' households; the relatively high proportion of incidents committed by ex-partners may be a factor in this since illegal entry even by a known offender is still technically burglary.

e) **Occupancy.** Occupancy was measured by the number of evenings the respondent had spent outside the home in the previous week. Lower levels of occupancy were associated with a higher risk of burglary.

Multiple victimisation

One finding not discussed so far is that households were more likely to be burgled in 1991 if they had been burgled in the four years previously: their risks in 1991 were over double those who had avoided a burglary over the longer period. There is an obvious circularity in saying that houses which have been burgled in the past are 'at risk' of burglary. But previous victimisation nonetheless may encapsulate the factors that determine current levels of risk—factors which survey data cannot cover in their entirety, nor usually measure with sufficient accuracy. Previous victimisation will not explain *why* a household is at higher risk, and since in the modelling procedures the aim was less to identify *which households* are at higher risk than to assess *what factors* rendered them at risk, previous victimisation was excluded as a variable. But it deserves some attention even so.[8]

Table 4.3 shows that repeated burglary victimisation is commonplace. Eighteen per cent of victims had been burgled more than once over the recall period, accounting for just over a third of the incidents related to interviewers. If victims were selected at random, the proportion of households burgled more than once in the space of a year would be very small.[9] The non-random nature of victimisation has been observed for most types of crime (eg, Sparks, 1981; Gottfredson, 1986; Farrell and Pease, 1993). And for some it is even more pronounced than is the case with burglary (see Chapter 6, and Farrell and Pease, 1993).

Table 4.3
Multiple burglary victimisation: 1982, 1984, 1988 and 1992 BCS

	% respondents	% victims	% incidents
Number of burglaries:			
None	95	—	—
One	4	83	65
Two	1	12	18
Three or more	<1	6	17
TOTAL	100	100	100
Unweighted N	42,386	2,296	2,912

Notes:
1. Columns do not necessarily add to 100% because of rounding.
2. Source: 1982, 1984, 1988, 1992 BCS (weighted data).

The pattern of multiple victimisation should be understood in part as an inevitable consequence of the geographical 'pocketing' of risks coupled with the fact that burglars' choices of target within any area are purposive and not random

---

[8]When previous victimisation was included in other models, it was still associated with a greater risk of burglary even after other factors were accounted for. It *weakened* the impact of the other factors on risk, with one exception: security devices had a greater reductive effect on burglary risk. This may reflect the fact that some households will have installed security devices in response to a previous victimisation, but this is still not sufficient to overcome other factors which make them prone to being burgled.

[9]A Poisson distribution is most appropriate to calculate probabilities of rare, discrete events. It also assumes that events are independent of each other. If victimisation followed a Poisson distribution (with the same overall risk of burglary), 3% of victims would be burgled more than once in the course of a year, whereas the actual figure was 18%.

(Maguire, 1980; Bennett and Wright, 1984). If burglars are active in a defined area, with marked preferences for particular types of property, homes which fit their requirements on one occasion are likely to do so on another.

However, a victimisation might also lead directly to further victimisation. For instance, once having succeeded in gaining entry to a house, burglars may return for a 'second bite at the cherry'—or else tip their friends off as to how to get in. A repeat burglary also appears likely to occur fairly soon after the first. Farrell and Pease's (1993) review concludes that "the risk of revictimisation is greatest in the period immediately after victimisation". The BCS is far from ideally suited to assessing the *timing* of repeated victimisations.[10] However, analysis of the small number of BCS victims who were burgled in the first six months of the recall period suggest that the bulk of re-victimisation occurred within three months of the first. This is consistent with Forrester *et al* (1988) and Canadian research by Polvi *et al* (1990). The phenomenon of multiple victimisation has clear preventive implications, which are taken up in Chapter 7.

Burglars' modus operandi

When burglaries occurred

Slightly more than half of burglaries happened in the evening or at night—evenly split between the periods 6pm-12pm and 12pm-6am (Figure 4.3). Daytime incidents were most often in the afternoon. In a substantial proportion of incidents, particularly attempts, respondents did not know when the incident had happened.[11] Around 30% of incidents took place at the weekend (from early evening on Friday), indicating that risks were no higher than during the week.

In 1988 and 1992, respondents were asked what they themselves had been doing at the time of the incident—though this may, or may not, tie up with the activities of other household members. Looking at all incidents, 11% of burglaries occurred when the respondent was away on holiday or for the weekend.[12] This compares to 23% of incidents when the respondent was sleeping at home, 16%

---

[10]There are also problems with dating incidents accurately. In the BCS, single incidents are dated to the nearest month. For series incidents, only the last incident in the series is so dated—other incidents are dated to the nearest quarter.

[11]In 12% of burglaries, respondents could not estimate when the incident had happened; the figure for attempts was 18% and for incidents with entry 8%.

[12]Whether or not this indicates that risks of burglary are higher for people on holiday depends on the assumptions made about how often people go on holiday. For instance, assume that on average a household spends 26 days, or 7% of the year on holiday or away for the weekend (2 weeks holiday and 6 weekends away from home). In this case, if burglars paid no heed to what victims were doing, about 7% of burglaries would occur when individuals were away. This is slightly lower than the 11% actually observed, so if these assumptions were correct, the risk of a home being burgled when the occupants are on holiday would seem slightly higher than otherwise.

Figure 4.3
Time of day of burglaries (1992 BCS)

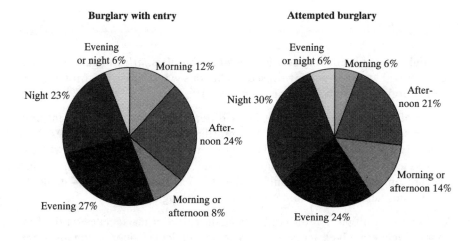

Figure 4.4
Method of entry in burglaries (1992 BCS)

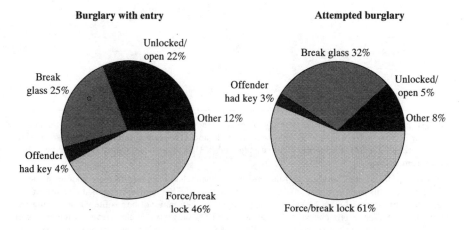

when they were engaged in leisure activities, 16% when they were at work and 15% when they were otherwise at home.[13]

Mode of entry

As might be expected, very few homes where burglars *failed* to gain entry had been left with doors or windows insecure; but this was the case in a fifth of cases where burglars got into the home (Figure 4.4).[14]

Means of entry in *successful* break-ins differed for day-time and night-time incidents, although for attempts the profiles were similar (Table A4.2 in Appendix A). Nearly half of burglars got in at night by forcing locks, whereas this was less common during the day. During the day, nearly a third got in through insecure entry points, but this only applied to 17% of cases at night —no doubt because householders are more careful about locking up then.

A much lower proportion of burglaries against flats or maisonettes on the first floor or higher involved access through an open/unlocked door or window—8% compared to 15% of houses and 21% of lower flats/maisonettes (Table A4.3). Houses were more vulnerable to having locks forced or broken, whereas in a higher proportion of incidents against flats, the offender had a key. This might reflect the greater 'turn-over' of individuals living in flats, with keys being more easily obtained and retained.

Over the years, there has been an increase in the proportion of burglaries involving forced entry, while the proportion involving insecure dwellings decreased—suggesting increasing security consciousness (Table 4.4).

---

[13]Not surprisingly, the profile of respondent activity differs for day-time and night-time incidents. In day-time incidents, 34% of respondents were at work, and 21% were at home. By contrast, in 41% of night-time incidents, respondents were asleep, and in 19% they were engaged in leisure activities away from home.

[14]A higher proportion of burglary victims said that property had been left insecure than in incidents of car crime. This may be because windows and doors in the home may be opened because of the weather or to air rooms; and be easier to leave open as they may not be visible when leaving the home (cars are more easily checked). In addition, the BCS suggests that cars are at particular risk in 'public' places (e.g. on the street or in public car parks); places where owners are more likely to check that they are fully locked up.

Table 4.4
Trends in selected methods of entry for burglaries: 1982, 1988, 1992 BCS

	Burglary with entry			Attempted burglary		
	81	87	91	81	87	91
Method of entry:[1]	%	%	%	%	%	%
Force/break lock	30	44	46	64	63	61
Door/window unlocked/open	29	21	22	4	6	5
False pretences[2]	n/a	1	1	n/a	1	2
Unweighted N	303	329	378	188	225	211

Notes:

1. More than one response allowed. 'Don't know' and not answered responses excluded.
2. A similar form of question was used in the 1982 survey, but multiple responses were not allowed. False pretences were coded under 'other'.
3. Source: 1982, 1988, 1992 BCS (weighted data). Based on incidents in full recall period.

Point of entry

Table 4.5 shows where burglars got in, or tried to get in. Where there was a successful entry, a third of burglars got in through a back window; 30% got in through the front door and 21% through the back door. The back of the house was generally more vulnerable. The picture for attempts is broadly similar. Burglars were more likely to get into homes without having to force entry when they got in through a door rather than a window. One in four 'door entry' incidents involved the door being left open or unlocked; however a window had been left insecure in only 14% of 'window entry' incidents.[15]

---

[15]This conflicts with findings on housebreaking in Scotland where a higher proportion of 'window entry' incidents than 'door entry' incidents involved insecure entry points (McAllister *et al*, 1993)

Table 4.5
Point of entry for burglaries: 1992 BCS

	Burglary with entry	Attempted burglary	All
Point of entry:[1]	%	%	%
Back door	21	27	23
Back window	35	27	32
Back other	2	1	1
Front door	30	38	33
Front window	11	7	9
Front other	<1	—	<1
Side door	4	2	3
Side window	4	4	4
Side other	<1	—	<1
TOTAL	100	100	100
	%	%	%
All back	52	50	51
All front	38	44	40
All side	8	6	7
More than one approach	2	1	2
TOTAL	100	100	100

Notes:
1. The small percentage of incidents (4%) involving approach from more than one or an unknown direction are excluded. More than one response is allowed. 'Don't know' and not answered responses are excluded.
2. Source: 1992 BCS (weighted data).

The point of entry varied according to when the incident occurred (Table A4.4). In just under half of daytime incidents, the burglar entered through the front door; for burglaries committed at night, the most common point of entry was a back window. This may indicate that burglars feel more vulnerable at night when they are at the front of the house than in the day— though it is not obvious why. These strong differences were observed both for attempts and incidents with entry, although successful break-ins via the back door were less common at night than during the day, while back doors were a *more* common target at night for attempts.

Although the relative ease of access to a property will depend on many factors such as security, site layout and perhaps the extent to which it is overlooked by neighbours and passers-by, point of entry varies markedly by broad property type (Table A4.5). Thus houses and ground floor flats were more vulnerable to entry from the back, most often a back window. In contrast, in three-quarters of incidents against flats on the first floor or above, entry was gained or attempted through the front door.

Security

Ownership of security devices has increased between 1988 and 1992, according to the two last surveys.[16] Table 4.6 suggests that the use of burglar alarms has almost doubled, and that there has been a steep increase in the installation of window locks. There has also been a small increase in the use of double locks or deadlocks on doors. We cannot say whether the stimulus for this was Home Office and police security campaigns, or individuals' awareness of specific cases of burglary.

Table 4.6
Security precautions, 1988 and 1992 BCS (all respondents)

	1988	1992
Proportion of households with:	%	%
Burglar alarm	8	13
All/some windows with locks	35	52
All/some doors with double/dead locks	57	61

Note:
1. Source: 1988 and 1992 BCS (weighted data). 'Don't know' responses are included in the base.

Some victims felt that they had not been careful enough about security. This was mostly because someone had failed to lock or close a door or window. In 14% of incidents where a burglar had entered the home, it was felt that someone in the household was partly responsible.[17] However, this was down on previous years (being 23% in 1982 and 17% in 1988).

---

[16]The full list of measures asked about was a burglar alarm, double/dead door locks, door chains, window keys, window bars/grilles, a dog and sensor lights. Only 29 respondents in two surveys said that they had window bars/grilles at the time of the incident.

[17]In 1% of incidents with entry, respondents said that someone outside the household was partly responsible.

The effectiveness of security

The logistic regression analysis reported above showed security protection to be one element in reducing burglary risks, after taking other factors (eg, area of residence) into account. Two further assessments of the impact of security are taken up here.

Table 4.7 compares the current security level of non-victims with that of victims first at the time of their burglary, and then at the time they were interviewed. (The data are based on the 1988 and 1992 surveys, and victims are those who reported burglaries at their current address in the previous year.) The level of protection among those not victimised in the last year is higher than that for victims on the occasion of their break-ins—highly suggestive of a security effect. Analysis of data from the Labour Force Surveys in Scotland shows similar results (McAllister *et al*, 1993).

Many households install security devices in response to being burgled. Indeed, victims' *current* level of security was if anything higher than among non-victims. Households may also upgrade their security after being burgled (eg, installing a better window lock in place of an old one); this will not have been picked up by the survey.

Table 4.7
Victimisation and ownership of security precautions: 1988 and 1992 BCS

	Non-victims	*Victims*	
	currently	*At time of incident*	*currently*
Proportion of respondents with:	%	%	%
Burglar alarm	10	8	17
Doors with double/dead locks	58	39	67
Window locks (with keys)	43	30	49
Light timers/sensors[2]	22	9	24

Notes:
1. The table excludes victims of a burglary at a previous address during the recall period.
2. Based on 1992 data only.
3. Source: 1988 and 1992 BCS (weighted data); those answering Follow Up A only. 'Don't know' responses are included in the base.

A second slant on the security issue is how far, once burglars actually target a property, enhanced security confers protection. We have assessed this by examining in what proportion of incidents burglars *failed to gain entry* in homes with enhanced security and in those without. Table 4.8 shows that burglars did not gain access in half of the cases where the home was protected by at least three measures, but this was the case in only a third of houses with no measures. It suggests, then, that alarms and better locks offer some, but not absolute protection.

Table 4.8
Proportion of cases where burglars failed to gain entry, by level of security

	% of incidents where entry not gained	Unweighted N
No security measures	31	279
One measure	38	363
Two measures	36	280
Three or more measures	51	247
Door double/dead locks	42	493
Sensor lights	42	106
Window keys	42	387
Door chain	45	448
Dog	47	216
Burglar alarm	49	103

Notes:
1. The figures for those with window bars/grilles are not shown as the base is too small to give a reliable rate.
2. Source: 1988 and 1992 BCS (weighted data).

The BCS evidence on security is not absolutely conclusive.[18] For instance, while security devices might be installed they might not necessarily have been in use (the front door may not actually have been double locked, for example, or the window key used). Burglars themselves, moreover, usually claim not to be much put off by security.[19] Nonetheless, the general indication from the BCS is that householders benefit by installing and using security devices. The lower risks among those with more security may well suggest that some offenders pass onto easier targets. When other offenders do not, the chance of a successful entry is *reduced* by security protection—though not eliminated.

---

[18]The BCS gives a 'snapshot' of a situation at one point in time, and there are difficulties in teasing out the *sequence* of security installation and victimisation. Respondents may not remember very accurately what security devices were in place when they were burgled. There are also problems when respondents have moved house during the recall period, making it cumbersome to measure security levels and burglary risks at different properties—though for this reason movers are excluded in Table 4.7. Movers can also take over a house well-protected by the previous owner, whose experience (or not) of burglary remains unknown. The 1988 BCS used a complex series of questions to try and take account of victimisation and moving house, but failed to produce results any clearer than those presented here.

[19]See eg, Maguire and Bennett, 1982; Bennett and Wright, 1983; Wright and Logie, 1988; Nee and Taylor, 1988.

Contact with the offender

Victims had face-to-face contact with the offender in a small proportion of cases—around one in ten in 1991 (Table A4.6). Usually the householders were out when the incident occurred (about three-fifths of cases in 1991, and more often in incidents with entry). The proportion of incidents which happened when someone was at home is fairly high (38% of all incidents in 1991), but in most the incident was still 'anonymous' with either no-one aware of what was happening (a quarter of all cases) or unable to give any details about the offender (5%). The proportion of incidents where no-one was at home rose in 1992, due largely to a rise in this for attempts carried out during the day.

Violent or threatening confrontation between burglar and victim was rare: it occurred in 3% of cases in 1991 (6% of incidents with entry).[20] Looking at all such confrontations over the four survey years (as the number picked up in 1992 alone is too small for reliable examination), around half involved strangers—some 26 incidents out of more than 2,000 burglaries. The other cases involving confrontation were those in which an illegal entry was made into the home by someone known to the victims—most usually neighbours and ex-partners.

The pattern of contact differed according to the time of the offence and whether the offender gained entry (Table A4.7 in Appendix A). The following generally held true: daytime burglaries were most likely to take place when the home was unoccupied; night-time burglaries had the highest proportions of individuals at home but unaware of the incident taking place—because they were asleep. Higher proportions of attempted burglary victims were aware of the incident — probably because the burglar was disturbed before gaining entry. Violent or threatening confrontation was more likely to occur in incidents where the burglar gained entry.

Losses

The majority of burglaries involved theft. Table A4.8 in Appendix A gives a full list of the types of items stolen. Most commonly, cash and jewellery were taken (each in two-fifths of burglaries with loss). Other things commonly taken were videos, stereos/hi-fi equipment, televisions, clothes, purses, wallets or handbags and cameras.[21]

---

[20]Over the four sweeps of the BCS, seven trespass incidents which involved more serious levels of injury were coded as assaults or robberies—although even including these the percentage of violent burglaries remained 3%.

[21]The BCS also asks about what items offenders *tried* to steal: this is not presented as in many situations it will be difficult to guess the burglars' intentions.

Figure 4.5
Trends in items stolen

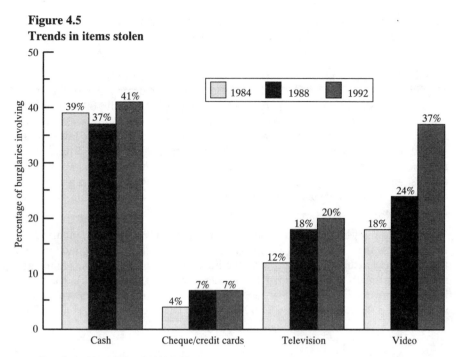

Based on 1984, 1988 and 1992 BCS

For some items, it is possible to see how the pattern of theft has changed since 1982 (Figure 4.5). The number of incidents involving loss of cash and cheque/credit cards has remained stable. However, since the early 1980s, the proportion of incidents involving theft of video equipment and televisions has increased. This will reflect, particularly for video equipment, increasing ownership of such items, though this does *not* mean that the presence of such goods in the home increases the risk of being burgled.[22] Rather, they are portable, easily sold and hard to identify as stolen goods; as such they are the obvious items for burglars to select.

The BCS asks about both initial losses (ie the value of property stolen and the cost of any damage caused in the incident) and net losses (ie how much the incident *cost* the victim after insurance payments and so on had been taken into account). There were pronounced variations in initial losses incurred by victims, which 'average' figures mask. In cases where something was stolen, the average value of goods taken was £1320, although in a fifth of cases less than £100 worth

---

[22]The General Household Survey shows that 74% of households had a colour television in 1981, 81% in 1983, 90% in 1987 and 95% in 1991. (The proportion owning either a colour or black and white set has been constant since 1981.) Ownership of a video recorder has increased from 18% in 1983, to 46% in 1987 and 68% in 1991. In 1989, 15% of households owned a compact disc player, in 1991 the proportion was 27%.

of property was stolen, while in 6% of cases the property taken was reckoned to be worth at least £5,000 (Table A4.9). Similarly, the average cost of damage was £190, although in 71% of cases the cost was under £50 (Table A4.10).

In only 9% of cases where something was stolen was any property returned. In roughly half of incidents in 1991, costs of stolen or damaged property were covered by insurance, fully or partly. Where burglars had got in, 80% of insured victims had made or planned to make a claim, while the figure was 31% for insured victims of attempted burglary (where costs were generally lower and a claim not always worth pursuing). A consistent finding of the BCS is that the risks of burglary for uninsured households are higher than for insured households (Lewis and Mo, 1986). Insurance is particularly common amongst owner-occupiers probably because contents insurance is often sold alongside, or as part of a mortgage.

Four out of ten of incidents with entry, and nine out of ten attempts, incurred *net* losses of less than £50 (Table 4.9). (A negligible percentage of respondents said that they were actually better off after the incident, presumably because they had received on insurance more than the goods were originally worth). But some households were involved in sizeable losses: in 16% of incidents with entry, victims rated their net losses as £1,000 or more. The average net loss was £370; for incidents with entry, the mean loss was £560.

Table 4.9
Net losses from burglary: 1992 BCS

	Burglary with entry	Attempted burglary	All
Net losses:	%	%	%
Less than £50	40	93	59
£50-£99	9	2	7
£100-£249	13	3	9
£250-£499	11	<1	7
£500-£999	12	1	8
£1,000-£4,999	13	1	8
£5,000 or more	3	—	2
Total	100	100	100
Mean net loss	£560	£30	£370
Unweighted N	382	220	602

Notes:
1. Victims were asked to assess the value of property stolen and damaged, and total costs after recovery and insurance payment. Net losses are the sum of property and damage losses, and loss of earnings, taking into account property recovered or compensated for. Mean loss figures are rounded.
2. Source: 1992 BCS (weighted data).

Grossing up BCS estimates to represent victims in the general population in 1991, net losses to victims of burglaries with entry were in the region of £480m, and to victims of attempts, £15m. These figures, however, are only an indication of losses to victims. Estimates will be least accurate for more minor incidents, such as attempted thefts, which the BCS is likely to undercount. They also take no account of the cost of insurance premiums, or any costs householders incur in home protection. Nor are criminal justice costs included, though if 5-10% of the costs of the criminal justice system are assumed to be spent because of burglary, the figure for 1991/92 would be around £440m-£890m. The financial cost of residential burglary to *society* compared to other types of crimes is also extremely difficult to judge. The costs of policing and insurance are widely borne and difficult to apportion; and stolen goods do not disappear from the economy (some people will benefit from the trade in VCRs).

Damage

In 60% of incidents in the 1992 BCS, the respondent said the burglar had caused some damage (a proportion similar to previous years). But in most cases this referred only to damage caused when the burglar was trying to get in or out. Cases involving gratuitous damage (such as 'soiling' or graffiti) were extremely rare: over all four sweeps of the survey, 'soiling' occurred in only 9 incidents out of more than 2,000 (under 1% of cases), and graffiti in six.

Summary

*   Set against GHS and BCS survey figures, police statistics have overstated the increase in burglary since 1971. The surveys indicate that burglaries with loss have risen since the early 1970s by only a third as much as police figures show. Increased reporting explains this in part, but so does increased recording of offences. The sharp increase in recorded burglaries since 1987 is supported by BCS estimates.

*   Inner city residents and those in certain ACORN groups have higher burglary risks. So too do residents of flats, maisonettes or rooms, single-adult households, and those with lower levels of occupancy.

*   There are higher risks of burglary for households with poorer security protection. But while preventive devices do help to keep burglars out generally, a sizeable number of burglaries still occur against householders with security in place.

*   Levels of security protection have increased since 1988.

* In a fifth of incidents with entry, doors or windows had been left open or unlocked, but the proportion has decreased since 1982. Thus, while burglary risks have increased, there is no suggestion that greater carelessness is to blame.

* In successful break-ins, entry through doors and from the back of the property was most likely, although the *single* most likely point of entry was a back window.

* Most burglaries are 'anonymous' crimes, with the house empty or victims unaware of the incident. Violent or threatening confrontation between burglar and victim occurred in 3% of cases in 1992: over all the four survey years, about half the confrontations involved strangers.

* Slightly more than half of burglaries happened in the evening or at night. In a quarter of incidents, the respondent was asleep when the incident took place. One out of ten incidents happened when the respondent was on holiday or away for the weekend, though it is hard to say whether going away is risky.

* Damage occurred in most incidents, although usually when the burglar was trying to get in. Cases involving gratuitous damage (such as 'soiling' or graffiti) were extremely rare.

* The most common items taken in burglaries were cash, jewellery, videos, stereos/hi-fi equipment and televisions. The proportion of incidents involving theft of video equipment and televisions has generally increased. This will reflect increasing ownership of such items. They are portable, easily sold and hard to identify as stolen goods; and as such are the obvious items for burglars to select once they have entered the home.

* Stolen property was seldom recovered, although in about half of incidents householders were insured, fully or partly, against the loss or damage. When burglars got in and the household was insured, four out of five made a claim, but only one in three victims of attempted burglary bothered to.

* Most burglaries involved relatively minor net losses of less than £50. Even so, the average net loss was £370, and for incidents with entry, £560. *Aggregate* net losses to victims of burglary may be in the region of £500m, excluding insurance and security costs.

5 Cars and theft

This chapter looks in detail at theft involving cars—ie, thefts of cars, thefts from and off cars, and attempts. It examines the scale of the problem, the risks that different car owners face, the main features of thefts, and their impact. On many of these questions, we have drawn on and sometimes combined data from several sweeps of the survey. Where findings are likely to have changed over time, we have used data from the 1992 survey relating to 1991 to present the most up-to-date picture.

Theft involving cars has become increasingly researched following a steep rise in offences over the 1980s (see eg, Clarke and Harris, 1992; Webb and Laycock, 1992). The work has included some BCS analysis (eg, Hope, 1987; Davidson, 1992), and this chapter expands on this. For the most part, it looks only at incidents in which cars and vans were stolen.[1] It excludes vandalism to cars.[2]

The analysis of *thefts of cars* includes the legal category of 'unauthorised taking', which on existing evidence is mainly committed by teenagers (cf Light *et al*, 1993). It also covers thefts for commercial gain (where cars are taken for stripping, resale, export, and insurance fraud), and thefts to provide offenders with temporary transport. *Thefts from cars* are incidents in which items were stolen off or from a vehicle, but the car was not driven away—though in half of thefts *of* cars which were recovered, items from the car were also stolen. Incidents categorised as *attempts* comprise both attempts to steal the car, and/or to steal from it; it is difficult for the victim to know what the thief's intention was.

Levels of theft involving cars

BCS estimates of the number of thefts involving vehicles in 1991 in England and

---

[1]Motorcycles are excluded. In 1991, they accounted for 11% of stolen vehicles and were the targets in 1% of all thefts from vehicles. The present analysis also excludes a small number of incidents in which cars were stolen, or items were taken from cars in the course of offences which were otherwise categorised in the BCS. Most of these cases were burglaries in which other things were also stolen (ie, the principal element was breaking into private property). A small number of cars which were stolen and then burnt out (coded as arson) are excluded, except for cost and damage findings.

[2]Vandalism to cars (scratches on paintwork, broken aerials etc) is a large component of 'car crime' but its pattern differs somewhat from car thefts. For instance, it involves more offenders who are known to the victim, and is particularly concentrated around the immediate vicinity of the home.

Wales are shown in Table 5.1.[3] These comprised 25% of all BCS offences, and if vandalism to cars is included the figures rises to 36%. Although the figures are not strictly comparable, thefts involving cars also comprise a quarter of all offences recorded by the police.

The number of *thefts from cars* is about three times higher than recorded by the police since only half are brought to police attention, and by no means all reported offences are recorded in the category of 'theft from vehicles'. The BCS estimate of *attempted thefts* is about seven times larger than police figures since even fewer incidents are reported, and some of those which are reported may not be recorded as attempts. (In the absence of evidence of intent to steal, the police may record some incidents as vandalism.) BCS figures indicate that for every car successfully driven away, there were nearly five thefts from cars, and nearly two attempts.

Table 5.1
Vehicle theft: numbers of offences, percent reported to the police, and trends

Figures in 000s	1991 BCS	1991 Police statistics	% reported	% change 1987-91 BCS	% change 1981-91 BCS
Theft of vehicles	517	481	99	34	81
Thefts from vehicles	2,400	769	53	14	86
Attempts	890	123	41	107	395
All thefts	3,805	1,373	56	31	117

Notes:
1. The total of all thefts may not sum to sub-totals because of rounding. Percentage changes are based on unrounded numbers.
2. 'Attempts' recorded by the police are cases of thefts of and from vehicles in which a 'nil value' was put on property loss.
3. Source: 1982, 1988, 1992 BCS (weighted data; based on cars, vans and motorcycles). 'Police statistics' refer to notifiable offences recorded by the police, with adjustments made to maximise comparability with the BCS (see Appendix F).

Trends in theft involving cars

Figure 5.1 shows the increase in all vehicle thefts between 1981 and 1991 according to BCS estimates and police statistics. Survey figures indicate a slightly steeper increase, although this does not reach statistical significance. The sharpest rise has been in attempted offences, which have risen by a factor of nearly four according to both sources. Since 1987, there has been a rather steeper

---

[3]To allow comparability with recorded offences, offences involving motorcycles are included here.

Figure 5.1
Indexed trends in vehicle thefts 1981-1991

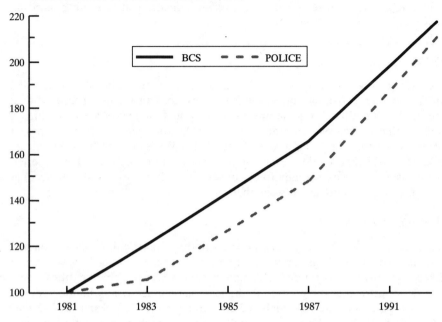

rise in thefts of vehicles than in thefts from them according to the BCS. Police figures have shown a statistically significant sharper rise in thefts from vehicles since 1981 than the BCS, and increased reporting to the police may explain this in part.

Recovery of stolen cars

Whether or not a stolen vehicle is recovered gives some guide to the motive of the crime. In the majority of cases where cars are taken for temporary use or for 'joyriding', they are recovered; in the majority of cases of thefts for commercial gain or resale, they are not. According to the 1992 BCS, some 76% of cars stolen in 1991 were recovered. This is higher than the recovery rate according to police statistics (64%).[4] The discrepancy could indicate sampling error on the BCS estimate, or the fact that some incidents in which the car was recovered quickly

---

[4]The BCS figure is not a very precise recovery rate since it will include some very recent thefts which may or may not end in recovery. The recovery rate in recorded offences is also somewhat crude, being based on vehicles which are recovered within a given time period. This is meant to be a month although according to the latest BCS in 9% of incidents where the car was recovered more than a month had elapsed before recovery.

were not reported to or recorded by the police. The recovery rate has declined since the 1982 survey, when 83% of stolen cars were recovered. This is in line with the picture from recorded offences, and indicates that 'joyriding' is rising less than other types of vehicle thefts.

Risks

According to BCS estimates, 3% of owners had a car stolen in 1991, 12% had a theft from their car at least once, and 5% experienced an attempt. These national figures are high, but for some groups of the population risks are much higher still. In this section, we consider first how risks vary across different types of areas (a common question asked of the BCS). We look next at other factors related to risks (household income for one). Multivariate analysis is then reported which assesses the causal importance of several such factors taking into account that there will be overlap between them.[5]

Area differences in risk

There are markedly higher risks for owners living in inner cities. One reason will undoubtedly be residents' proximity to offenders, though other factors are also likely to be involved—for instance, more limited private parking facilities. Table 5.2 shows differences in relation to the national average risk, which is indexed at 100. Figures are based on combined data from the 1984, 1988 and 1992 sweeps of the BCS. Risks of thefts *of* cars are particularly high in inner cities—double the average.

Table 5.2
Risks of theft involving cars in inner cities and elsewhere

	Inner cities	Elsewhere	National average
Thefts of cars	205	85	100
Recovered	220	80	100
Not recovered	185	85	100
Thefts from cars	155	90	100
Attempts	155	90	100
All 'home-based' thefts	130	60	100
All thefts	160	90	100

Notes:
1. Differentials are based on average incidence-based rates from the three surveys; risks based on car owners.
2. Source: 1984, 1988 and 1992 BCS (weighted data).

---

[5]The multivariate analysis used a prevalence rate base, while other risk analysis used incidence rates (see footnote 3 to page 45 in Chapter 4).

Another way of looking at the spread of risks across area is through the ACORN typology. This is best used for considering thefts committed around the home, since thefts that take place elsewhere may not necessarily occur where owners live.[6] ('Home-based' thefts are defined as those taking place in private or semi-private parking places by the home, or the streets by home.) Table 5.3 shows risks in different ACORN neighbourhoods in relation to the national average, again indexed at 100. The areas are grouped according to the level of *all* crimes measured by the BCS in the 1984, 1988 and 1992 sweeps.

Table 5.3
Relative theft rates for residents in different ACORN neighbourhood groups[1]

	Thefts involving cars around the home[2]	*% of all thefts involving cars which are home based*[3]
LOW RISK		
A. Agricultural areas	25	26%
K. Better-off retirement areas	75	52%
B. Modern family housing, higher income areas	70	40%
J. Affluent suburban housing	75	43%
C. Older housing of intermediate status	95	55%
MEDIUM RISK		
E. Better-off council estates	115	58%
D. Older terraced housing	155	59%
F. Less well-off council estates	150	63%
HIGH RISK		
H. Mixed inner metropolitan areas	210	70%
I. High status non-family areas	155	60%
G. Poorest council estates	245	71%
Indexed national average	100	

Notes:
1. Thefts involving cars comprise thefts of and from cars and attempts. Risks are based on car owners.
2. 'Around the home' comprises incidents taking place in private or semi-private parking places by the home, or the streets by home.
3. Source: 1984, 1988 and 1992 BCS (weighted data).

'Home-based' risks are ten times higher in poorest council estates than they are in agricultural areas. Where risks are highest, a greater proportion of thefts took place at home. For owners elsewhere, thefts are more equally split between home and other locations—and in agricultural areas, higher-income modern family

---

[6]Moreover, the smaller theft categories in Table 5.2 cannot be very reliably broken down by ACORN group.

areas, and affluent suburbs, when owners *do* experience theft it is more likely to occur when their cars are somewhere other than around their home. This will signify the relatively greater safety of the places in which they live, and the fact that they may drive more outside their own area: commuting into work, or travelling further away for their social activities—perhaps, indeed, to the ACORN neighbourhoods where risks are high.[7]

Table 5.4

Relative risks of theft involving cars (car owners)

Inner city	155	Local car ownership[1]	
Non-inner city	90	Lower	140
ACORN risk group		Medium	105
High	135	Higher	85
Medium	115	Risky parking at night[2]	150
Low	90	Other night parking	85
Dwelling type		Household income[3]	
Other houses and flats etc	125	Higher	125
Detached houses/semis	85	Medium	100
Renters etc	125	Low	80
Owner occupiers	95	Household consumer durables[4]	
SEG of household head		'Consumerist'	110
Manual	100	Other	90
Non-manual	100	Council areas[5]	115
		Other areas	95

Notes:

1. 'Lower' car-owning areas have about 45% of households owning cars; medium about 65%; high about 85%.
2. Based on where the main household car is parked at night; 1988 BCS data. It covers streets near home, other streets, and estate car parks.
3. Higher income households, £20,000 per annum household income or more; medium, £10,000 to under £20,000; lower, under £10,000.
4. 'Consumerists' are those who owned three or more of five items: a portable colour TV, a VCR, a CD player, a personal computer, or a car radio/cassette. Based on 1988 BCS data.
5. Council areas are those defined by ACORN as having the highest percentage of council tenants (ACORN categories G, F and E).
6. Source: Combined 1988 and 1992 BCS (weighted data), except for household consumer durables and parking factors, where the data are from half the 1988 sample. All thefts of and from cars, including attempts.

---

[7] As Hope (1987) notes, a somewhat crude measure of differences in driving patterns (and one which will reflect differences in car ownership anyway) is the proportion of people in different ACORN areas who walk or use public transport to work. Figures from the 1981 Census show that more people walk to work or use public transport in high-risk areas, presumably leaving their cars unattended at home for longer periods during the day.

Aside from area differences, risks co-vary with other factors. Table 5.4 shows differences in risks for all thefts involving cars, based on data from the 1988 and 1992 surveys. Risks are higher than average, for instance, for those who have to park at night in more vulnerable places (streets near home, other streets, and estate car parks), and for those in terraced houses and flats who will be less likely to have garages. Those who live in areas where car ownership is relatively low are more prone to theft. There are also greater risks for higher-income households (no doubt because of the types of cars they own). The BCS is unable to measure very effectively the attractiveness of cars to thieves, but an indicator from the 1988 survey of consumer durables in the home shows that those who have more 'higher-tech' items were more prone to having their car stolen or broken into. This is consistent with data that shows more expensive 'sporty' cars are particularly vulnerable to being targeted by thieves (Houghton, 1992).

What best explains the pattern of risk?

Many of the risk factors in Table 5.4 will be interrelated. For instance, renters will be more likely to live in council areas, where garage parking is less available. Multivariate analysis was used to assess the independent importance of any one particular factor. The multivariate approach taken was a series of logistic regression models which looked, variously, at whether or not owners had been a victim of any theft involving cars, home-based theft, and theft away from home in relation to a number of variables which bivariate analysis (ie, simple two-way tables) suggested were implicated in risks. (Appendix C explains the approach and gives detailed results.) Data from half the 1988 sample was used as this provided measures of parking and consumer durables. The factors which emerged as most important are summarised in Table 5.5.

Table 5.5
Risk factors related to theft involving cars (1988 BCS)

All thefts involving cars	Thefts around the home	Other thefts
Living in an inner city	Living in an inner city	Living in an inner city
Higher income		Higher income
'Consumerist'	'Consumerist'	'Consumerist'
Flats/terraced houses	Flats/terraced houses	
Living in an area of low car ownership	Living in an area of low car ownership	
Street parking at night	Street parking at night	

What, then, are the main risk-inducing aspects of car ownership?

a) **Inner city residence**. The risk of having your car stolen or broken into is higher in inner city areas even when other factors are taken into account. The variation in risks in different ACORN neighbourhoods shown earlier appears secondary to inner city residence *per se*. This may suggest that the density of vehicles on the road is important (Mayhew, 1990).

b) **Higher income**. Taking account of other factors, the better-off are more at risk, quite probably because their cars are more attractive to thieves. (Income was less important for thefts around the home.)

c) **Household consumer durables**. Those who have up-to-date 'higher-tech' equipment in the home—and therefore those likely to have better equipped cars—face higher risks. Ownership of these consumer durables is important independent of income.[8]

d) **Dwelling type**. Those in terraced houses and flats are more at risk, net of other effects. They will be less likely to have garages. Not surprisingly, dwelling type and the other 'home location' variables—where cars are parked at night, and local car ownership—were not associated with autocrime occurring *away* from the home, taking other factors into account.

e) **Lower car ownership**. In areas where there are fewer car owners, the more susceptible they seem to be to having their cars picked out by thieves. This result is somewhat surprising given that those in inner cities are more at risk and that other research has shown that at country or regional level theft risks are generally higher when there *are* more targets available (Mayhew, 1990). It is difficult to be certain whether it is the relative number of targets which is operating as a causal factor here, or whether low car ownership is 'standing in' as an indicator of social disadvantage.

f) **Street parking at night**. Those who have to, or choose to park in more vulnerable places at night (streets near home, other streets, and estate car parks) face higher risk, taking account of other factors.

Multiple victimisation

Chapter 4 took up the degree of multiple (or repeated) victimisation among burglary victims, showing that some 18% of burglary victims had been burgled more than once in a period of about 14 months. Table 5.6 shows how the picture compares for thefts involving cars. The data are from the 1984, 1988 and 1992 sweeps of the survey; thefts from all locations are considered, but the pattern of multiple victimisation is similar for thefts around the home.

---

[8] One of the items was a car radio or cassette. Risks were higher for those with a radio or cassette, but in multivariate tests this was not by itself independently important, probably because most cars had one or other. Adding together the number of consumer durables gave a better measure.

Table 5.6
Multiple victimisation of thefts involving cars: 1984, 1988 and 1992 BCS

	% respondents	% victims	% incidents
Number of thefts			
None	83	—	—
One	13	75	54
Two	3	17	25
Three or more	1	8	22
TOTAL	100	100	100
Unweighted N	22,883	5,822	4,156

Notes:
1. Columns do not necessarily add to 100% because of rounding.
2. Source: 1984, 1988 and 1992 BCS (weighted data). Based on all thefts of and from cars, including attempts.

More theft victims were repeatedly victimised in 1991 than one would expect if bad luck was evenly distributed. And more were repeatedly victimised than is the case for burglary. A quarter experienced more than one incident accounting for just under half of all the incidents recalled, and an unfortunate 8% of victims accounted for 22% of the incidents measured in the three surveys. Another question from the BCS measures experience of thefts *of* vehicles in the four years prior to the recall period. Those who had vehicles taken in 1991 were more likely than others to have similar thefts earlier: 12% of those victimised in the previous four years were a victim again in 1991, as against 3% of those not victimised over the longer period. This corresponds to a similar finding for burglary victims.

When and where thefts occur

In analysing the timing and setting of car crime there were few differences between thefts *of* cars, thefts *from* them, and attempts. In this section therefore we have combined the categories.

Figure 5.2 shows that more than half of thefts occurred around the home, usually in the evening or at night. A quarter of thefts took place in car parks, or on private or semi-private work-sites. The single most likely time and location is a street near to home at night, accounting for a third of incidents; another fifth were home-based thefts at night, when cars were parked in carports, drives and in estate car parks. (Table A5.1 in Appendix A shows further details.)

That thefts are more common during the evening or at night will reflect the fact that cars remain unmoved for longer, and darkness will provide more cover.

Figure 5.2
Location and time of thefts involving cars

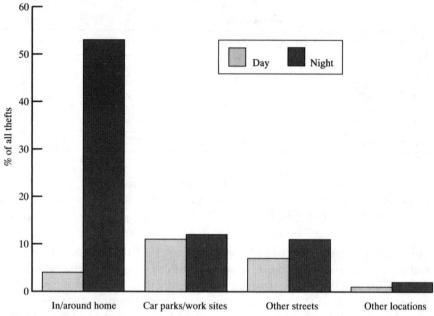

Based on 1982, 1984, 1988 and 1992 BCS

Seventy eight per cent of all theft offences when the time was known by victims occurred between 6pm to 6am, and only slightly less than this were known to have been committed when it was dark.[9]

The main locations of theft change between day and night. Reflecting obvious differences in parking patterns, less autocrime happens near home during the day (16% of daytime offences). In the evening and at night—when most people park near to where they live—more incidents occur in the home environment: 68% of nighttime offences took place near home.

While Figure 5.2 shows the common and less common locations of theft, it does not provide a true measure of the *risks* in different places. For this, one needs to take into account the number of cars parked in different places at different times, or 'parking exposure'. Most cars are parked for most of the time at their owners' homes, and it is unsurprising that the greatest number of thefts occur here. In

---

[9]Some 28% of 1991 victims were able to pinpoint their thefts as occuring between 6pm and midnight, while 40% said it was between midnight and 6am; but some 9% knew only that the theft occurred between 6pm and 6am. These figures are based on victims who had some idea of when the theft had occurred; about 10% of victims had no idea.

terms of thefts per hours at risk, the BCS nonetheless suggests that car parks may pose a disproportionately high risk (cf Webb *et al*, 1992).[10]

Security

Among victims in the 1992 BCS who knew how entry to their car was made, 6% said that thieves had got in through an unlocked door or open window. With increasing publicity about the need to keep cars secure, owners may possibly be more reluctant to admit to lax security now than in the past. But the BCS provides no evidence to attribute the recent increase in theft involving cars to driver carelessness. As with burglary, fewer victims in 1991 (9%) than in 1984 (16%) admitted that the household was in any way to blame (by leaving the car unlocked for instance). Moreover, the figure of 6% of entries into unlocked cars compares with 11% in 1988. The decrease in cars being left unlocked may testify to the success of publicity campaigns, or to a sharper sense among car owners of the increasing risks of autocrime, whether based on their own or friends' experience.[11] At the same time, the increasing prevalence of good locking systems—such as central locking or remote control devices—may also be a factor. The drop in the figure may also signify that the very easy opportunities presented by unlocked cars are not particularly sought by thieves interested in high performance cars, and who consistently claim to researchers that they can overcome locks easily (eg, Light *et al*, 1993).

When cars were stolen in 1991, the most common method of entry was by forcing the lock (Figure 5.3). For thefts *from* cars, however, over half involved a broken window. The picture from the 1988 survey is fairly similar, though the proportion of victims who said a key had been used was higher (21% for all thefts in 1987, as against 8% in 1991). This may indicate some improvement in the design of locks and increasing difficulty in cutting duplicate keys.

---

[10]The 1988 BCS can provide a rough 'parking exposure' base over which thefts can be placed, and this and other sources of information are currently being examined to assess better the risks of theft in different locations.

[11]Half the 1992 BCS sample were asked about security precautions when they parked their cars. (One question was: "When you park the car, even if just for a short time, in the street or in a car park to which there is public access, do you <u>ever</u> leave any of the doors or the boot unlocked?" A second question referred to leaving windows open.) Some 12% of drivers admitted to sometimes leaving doors unlocked, and 9% to leaving windows open.

Figure 5.3
Means of entry (1992 BCS)

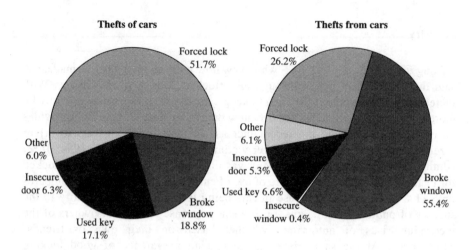

Thefts of cars   Thefts from cars

Forced lock 51.7%
Other 6.0%
Insecure door 6.3%
Used key 17.1%
Broke window 18.8%

Forced lock 26.2%
Other 6.1%
Insecure door 5.3%
Used key 6.6%
Insecure window 0.4%
Broke window 55.4%

The impact of theft involving cars

Financial costs

The BCS asks victims to assess both the value of any property which was stolen or damaged, and *net* losses, taking into account the value of recovered property, loss of earnings, insurance repayments or other compensation. Most victims of car theft in 1991 placed their losses at more than £1,000 (see Table A5.2, Appendix A). As well as losses from theft, many victims sustained damage to their cars, either in the process of the theft itself or through crash damage or mishandling when the stolen vehicle was being driven. Assessments of losses through damage were generally smaller than losses through theft, although nearly a quarter of thefts from cars involved damage losses of at least £100, and as many as a third of attempted thefts incurred costs of this order (Table A5.2, Appendix A).

By no means all victims with financial losses were insured, and not all those who were made a claim. Victims always claimed when their car did not reappear, and seven out of ten whose car was recovered did so—the rest presumably not claiming because they recovered their vehicles in a state which did not justify a claim (and a lost 'no-claims' bonus). When property was stolen *from* cars it was rarely seen again: only 5% of owners recovered anything. Even so, only 43% of insured victims of thefts from cars made a claim, and 36% of insured victims of attempts.

74

Net losses were significant for thefts of cars, whether or not the vehicle was recovered. Two-thirds of those who did not get their cars back reckoned they were out of pocket by £500 or more, as did a quarter of those whose cars were recovered (Table 5.7). This must partly reflect insurers' conditions that owners carry a proportion of any loss themselves, and partly differences between victims' and insurers' valuation. Net losses were lower for thefts from cars and attempts. A tiny proportion said that they were better off in the end, presumably having made a profit on the insurance claim.

Grossing up BCS estimates to represent victims in the general population in 1991, net losses to victims of thefts of cars were in the region of £375m, and to victims of thefts from cars, £340m. The loss from attempts was £60m. The points made in relation to the gross costs of burglary are as pertinent here (see page 61): eg, estimates will be least accurate for more minor incidents; and they take no account of the cost of insurance or security. Again, assessing criminal justice costs for thefts involving cars to be 5-10% of total costs, the figure would be £440m-£890m for 1991/92.

Table 5.7
Net losses from theft involving cars

	Thefts of cars (recovered)	Thefts of cars (not recovered)	Thefts from cars	Attempts	Total
Net losses	%	%	%	%	%
Less than £100	41	20	60	77	61
£100 - £499	34	16	34	22	31
£500 or more	25	64	6	1	8
TOTAL	100	100	100	100	100
Mean	£560	£1530	£140	£70	£190
Unweighted N	151	35	893	322	1412

Notes:
1. Victims were asked to assess the value of property stolen and damaged, and total costs after recovery and insurance payments. Net losses are the sum of property and damage losses, and loss of earnings, taking into account property recovered or compensated for. Mean loss figures are rounded. The total theft figures include a small number of thefts of cars for which information on recovery was missing. Cases are excluded where the victim had not yet made an insurance claim, or did not know whether the property was insured or a claim made.
2. Percentages may not add to 100% because of rounding
3. Source: 1992 BCS (weighted data).

THE 1992 BRITISH CRIME SURVEY

Summary

This chapter has focused on thefts of cars, theft from them and attempts. In summary:

* In 1991, thefts involving cars comprised a quarter of the offences mentioned in the BCS, and a similar proportion of recorded offences. If vandalism to cars is included, cars become the target in over one in three BCS crimes.

* The BCS estimate of thefts *of* cars is similar to those from police statistics as most offences are reported by victims. But the number of thefts *from* cars is about three times higher than those recorded by the police as by no means all are reported to or recorded by the police. The number of *attempts* is a full seven times larger.

* Thefts *from* cars are the major problem: there were nearly five incidents for every car driven away. There were two attempts for every car driven away.

* Since 1981, attempts have risen by a factor of about four according to both the BCS and police figures. Offenders seem to be more active, but owners' security, or better car design, is at least thwarting them in being successful. Police figures show a sharper rise in thefts from vehicles since 1981 than the BCS and increased reporting may play a part.

* Three-quarters of cars stolen in 1991 were recovered according to BCS figures. It is generally assumed that recovered cars will have been taken for 'joyriding'. The proportion of stolen cars recovered has declined since 1981 indicating that stealing cars for other purposes (stripping, resale, export etc) is on the rise more.

* One is slightly more likely to have a car taken from around the home than elsewhere, and this is very much more likely to happen at night. A third of all thefts took place in the street near home at night, and a fifth from other home parking places.

* In one in twenty thefts in 1991 thieves got into a car through an unlocked door or window. This figure is lower than in previous surveys, perhaps indicating more driver care or the increasing prevalence of central locking.

* Over half of thefts *from* cars involved thieves breaking windows; a quarter forced the lock—the method of entry in half of thefts *of* cars.

* The main factors that increase risks of theft for owners are: living in an inner city or an area in which levels of car ownership is relatively low; being in a higher-income group; and parking at night on the street or in estate car parks. Those who live in flats and terraced houses (who are less likely to have garages) are also more at risk. The indications from the BCS are, too, that having a car that is better fitted makes it more attractive to thieves.

*   Even after insurance claims, net losses from thefts of car were appreciable. Two-thirds of those who did not get their cars back said they were out of pocket by £500 or more. *Aggregate* net losses to victims of all types of thefts involving cars may even so be in the region of £775m, excluding insurance and security costs.

6 Violence

This chapter presents findings on the risks of violent crime. First the correlates of violent victimisation in aggregate are described. Then a typology of violent crime is presented and the salient characteristics of each type of violence are discussed and some findings on risks presented. The following types of crime have been taken as constituting violence: wounding; common assault; and robbery and snatch thefts (the latter being combined as 'mugging').[1]

Sexual offences are excluded, largely because these are poorly measured by the survey. So too are 'frightening threats'. Such incidents are problematic when 'crime' is defined as incidents which can be prosecuted, and which victims and the police consider should be.[2] Many threats uncovered by the survey fall outside this definition, though there is undoubtedly an argument for including them in the BCS count. They are salient enough to their victims to be reported in a survey about 'crime', and they may well constitute one example of the type of everyday interpersonal abuse that may very well need to be accounted for in aligning high levels of fear of crime with low survey-measured risks of violence, especially among women (eg, Painter, 1992). Incidents of sexual and racial harassment are other examples. These have been addressed in the BCS, but have been excluded in this analysis of 'violence'.

Measuring violence

Crime surveys measure violence less well than property crimes, for several reasons. Some incidents of violence may be on the margins of what people regard as 'criminal' (for instance, fights and pub brawls). Also, it is likely that those most involved in fights, for instance younger people, may be harder to contact (eg because they are more likely to be out when the interviewer calls) or harder to persuade to be interviewed. Other incidents will remain hidden because of their nature: for example, violence between household members and close friends, and incidents for which the victim feels in some way responsible. Apart from such undercounting, some people may be more willing than others to talk about what happened to them, and changing attitudes to violence may lead to an

---

[1] 'Snatch theft' is a sub-category of theft from the person; police statistics do not have a comparable 'mugging' category.

[2] See footnote 1 to page 11.

increase in willingness to report violence to survey interviewers (as well as to the police), thus compromising trend comparisons.

For these reasons, the BCS cannot be taken as providing hard and fast figures on the extent of different types of violence. Nonetheless, it offers a complementary count to that from the police in covering incidents not reported to, or not recorded by them. It also covers a fuller range of incidents than in the notifiable offences series, which excludes common assaults. The BCS, too, provides a better—if far from complete—count of incidents which involve offenders known to victims. These are substantially under-reported to the police as Chapter 3 showed.

Predictors of risk

Table 6.1 shows factors associated with risks of violence. The data are from the 1988 and 1992 surveys, with the national average incidence risk indexed at 100. The table shows, for example, that risks are about two and a half times the average for those aged 16 to 29, and for those who are single. Of course being young and being single overlap. So too do other risk-related factors. For instance, those who go out frequently will be younger, and will probably frequent pubs more; being married, too, is likely to go along with having children.

As in the previous two chapters, several logistic regression analyses were done to identify the most salient risk factors. The category of violence subsumed a much more heterogeneous set of incidents than burglary or car theft, and we therefore divided the sample into four sub-groups: attacks on males by strangers; those on males by non-strangers; those on women by strangers; and those on women by non-strangers.

Logistic regression models were generated for each sub-group, and full results are in Appendix C. With the exception of stranger attacks on women, the factor most strongly associated with risk was age: the older people were, the less at risk they were. The reason for the lack of association with age for stranger attacks on women was that a large portion of these are muggings, and middle-aged women are mugged no less frequently than younger ones. In all four models, people who rated their neighbourhood as disorderly were at greater risk than others. Being married, rather than single, separated or divorced, was associated with a lower risk of violence;[3] but for violence involving offenders who are

---

[3]With respect to spouse/partner abuse, it may be that respondents are less willing to talk about assaults by current partners than ex-partners, leading to an understatement of these risks by married or cohabiting respondents. While the reasons for this may be diverse, one (testable) factor is whether or not the partner is present during the interview (assuming that interviews conducted alone are least constrained). Overall, the pattern of risk by marital status for interviews conducted alone was similar to that for all interviews.

Table 6.1
Relative factors in the risks of violence[1]

ACORN risk group		Inner city	130
Low	75	Non inner city	95
Medium	130		
High	160	Number of adults in household	
		One	125
Number of evenings out in last week*		Two	65
None or one	65	Three or more	150
Two or three	125		
Four or more	200	Drinking behaviour*	
		None	75
Visited pub in last week*		A little	70
Yes	195	Moderate/heavy	140
No	95		
		Incivilities scale[2]	
Children under 16 in household		Low	85
Yes	130	High	335
No	85		
		Household income[3]	
Age		Higher	70
16-29 year olds	280	Medium	105
30-59 year olds	60	Lower	115
60+ year olds	10		
		Married	50
Male	130	Single	270
Female	75	Separated/divorced	210
		Widowed	15
Men, aged			
16-29 years	360	White	95
30-59 years	70	Black	160
60+ years	15	Indian/Pakistani/Bangladeshi	100
Women, aged			
16-29 years	200		
30-59 years	50		
60+ years	10		

Notes:

1. Rates are indexed at the pooled rate for the full 1988 and 1992 BCS samples, except those marked * which were not asked of the full 1988 and 1992 samples.

2. For five aspects of social disorder, respondents were asked how much of a problem/how common they were in their area. These included noisy neighbours, teenagers on the streets, drunks or tramps, rubbish and litter, vandalism and graffiti. Respondents in areas with 'high' incivilities rated these as more common, or more of a problem.

3. Higher income households, £20,000 per annum household income or more; medium, £10,000 to under £20,000; lower, under £10,000.

4. Risks were slightly higher for those in households where the head was in manual work (105). But the logistic regression analysis showed that, when other characteristics were controlled for, the risk of stranger violence was lower for men in such households.

5. Source: 1988, 1992 BCS (weighted data).

known, having children was associated with increased risk. There is no clear explanation for this but it may be that children increase levels of financial and emotional stress. Alternatively, those with children may get involved in incidents on their behalf.

In general the logistic models identified rather few factors associated with risk; only one model—for incidents against males committed by strangers—succeeded in generating any recognisable profile of the sort of person most at risk: young men in disorderly urban areas (particularly ACORN groups G, H and I) who go out frequently and particularly to the pub.

A typology of violence

The grouping of violence used in the previous section was relatively crude and masked much heterogeneity within sub-categories. We therefore developed a fuller typology of violence, which employs seven sub-categories. This builds on factor analysis carried out on data from previous sweeps of the BCS which led to an earlier typology (Davidoff & Dowds, 1989).[4] It matches closely another typology from research on violent crime, based on an analysis of police records (Genders, 1991). Ideally, we would have validated the typology by demonstrating through logistic regression analysis that each sub-group had its own distinctive set of risk factors; but in practice, the numbers in each group are too small to allow this. This section of the chapter, then, simply provides descriptive information on the salient characteristics of the typology's different sub-groups. These are:

Domestic   Incidents involving partners, ex-partners, household members and other relatives, irrespective of location. On this definition, domestic violence nearly always took place in or just outside the victim's home, or sometimes at the home of a friend, relative or perhaps the offender him/herself.

Home-based   Incidents in or immediately outside the home (including on the street near home) *other than those* involving partners, ex-partners and household members and relatives. Over a third involved neighbours; another third were friends or acquaintances.

Street   Incidents taking place on the street, on public transport, and in other public places.[5]

---

[4]The typology is slightly different from that used by Davidoff and Dowds, principally because they excluded offences involving *relatives* from the domestic assault category and included incidents occurring in and around home, not involving partners etc. In the present typology, the latter are called 'home-based'.

[5]In total, over a third of assaults were said to have taken place 'in the street' but those that happened near home, outside a pub/club or involved mugging are categorised in those respective categories.

Pubs/clubs   Incidents in and around pubs and clubs (discos etc), but excluding public entertainment centres (eg, cinemas) where alcohol is less likely to be served. Pub/club violence most often involved strangers or those known casually or just by sight.

Work-based   Incidents at the workplace, including incidents in work car parks, but excluding incidents in the street near work. Roughly a quarter were incidents involving workmates; most of the rest involved members of the public who came into contact with workers in the course of their job.

Mugging   All robbery and snatch thefts (a sub-set of thefts from the person), irrespective of location.

Other assaults   A residual set of incidents not falling into other categories. They include incidents at sporting events, schools, shops and leisure centres.

Men and women as victims

Figure 6.1 shows a breakdown of the number of incidents of different types in 1991, distinguishing between offences involving men and women. (Table A6.1 in Appendix A shows more detailed figures.) The most numerous type of assaults uncovered by the BCS were incidents of 'domestic violence'. Eight out of ten of these incidents were against women. In fact nearly half of the assaults mentioned by women in the survey were of this type. Grossed-up survey figures would imply 530,000 incidents in England and Wales in 1991—although as the survey is likely to undercount many such incidents, this figure should be regarded as a minimum. Street assaults are nearly as common as domestic assaults, amounting to about 510,000 incidents in 1991; eight out of ten involved men. There were an estimated 420,000 assaults in pubs and clubs—again eight out of ten against men—and some 260,000 incidents of 'mugging'. Muggings were evenly split between male and female victims, though women were more often subject to snatch theft and men to robbery—the two constituent elements of mugging. This difference becomes important in interpreting some later results. For a further discussion of the nature of mugging see Barker *et al* (1993).

Figure 6.1
Types of violence, 1991

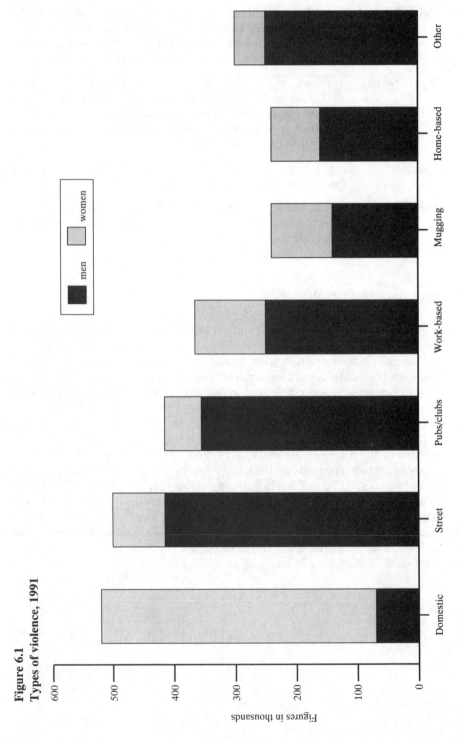

The age of victims

Those aged 16 to 29 were overwhelmingly the most frequent victims of all types of assault. The elderly were rarely victims, although 10% of muggings involved those aged 60 or over, as did 10% of home-based incidents. Details are in Figure 6.2 (see also Table A6.2 in Appendix A).

Figure 6.2
Age breakdown of victims in different types of violent crime

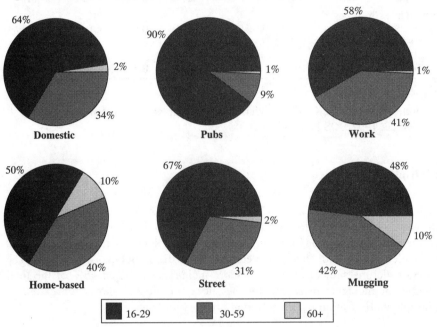

Risks of different types of violence in 1991

Risks can be expressed in terms of *prevalence* rates (the number of *victims* per head of population), or in terms of *incidence* rates (the number of *crimes* per head). Prevalence risks are necessarily lower than those for incidence as some people are victims more than once over the year. Prevalence rates by age and gender are shown in Table 6.2. (Incidence rates are shown in Table A6.3 in Appendix A.) Just under 1% of women said they had been a victim of domestic assault in 1991, but double that number of young women. Except for domestic violence, men are more at risk, though the difference for mugging is slight.

85

Table 6.2
Risks of violence by age and sex: percentage of individuals victimised once or more in 1991

	Domestic	Home-based	Street	Pub/club	Work-based	Mugging	Other assault
Men							
16-29	0.4	1.2	3.8	2.1	1.5	1.5	2.5
30-59	0.2	0.6	1.1	0.3	0.6	0.3	0.4
60+	0.1	0.1	0.2	0.1	—	0.2	—
Total	**0.3**	**0.6**	**1.6**	**0.7**	**0.7**	**0.6**	**0.7**
Women							
16-29	2.2	0.8	1.0	1.1	0.6	0.9	0.4
30-59	0.7	0.4	0.2	0.1	0.3	0.4	0.1
60+	0.1	0.1	0.1	—	—	0.3	—
Total	**0.9**	**0.4**	**0.3**	**0.3**	**0.3**	**0.5**	**0.1**

Notes:
1. Rates based on the first three victim forms completed by respondents
2. Source: 1992 BCS (weighted data).

Multiple victimisation

Being a repeated victim is more likely in relation to violence than it is for most property crime. Thus, for instance, while 83% of burglary victims in 1991 fortunately had only one break-in, some 33% of violence victims were involved in incidents more than once, often cutting across different types of violence. The 17% of victims subject to three or more incidents generated 45% of the total number of incidents measured by the survey. Table 6.3 shows the extent of multiple victimisation *within* different types of violence .

Table 6.3
Levels of multiple victimisation

	Domestic violence[1]		Street		Pub/club		Work-based		Mugging		All violence	
	% victims	% inc	% victims	% inc	% victims	% inc	% victims	% inc	% victims	% inc	% victims	% inc
No. of victimisations												
1	49	20	77	55	61	36	68	35	87	70	68	38
2	16	14	14	20	27	31	9	9	7	12	16	17
3+	35	66	9	25	12	33	23	56	6	19	17	45

Notes:
1. Offences against women only.
2. Based on combined data from 1988 and 1992 BCS, for all incidents over full recall period (ie, the number of times adults were victimised in the year prior to the survey and in early months of the survey year).

Women are particularly likely to be repeat victims of domestic violence: half experienced more than one offence within the survey period. Victims of assaults in and around work and of pub fights were also more likely to be repeatedly victimised. Mugging is more usually a one-off event.

Ethnic origin and risks

Table 6.4 suggests that Afro-Caribbeans are more at risk of domestic violence than whites or Asians. Whether this is because these three groups are differentially reticent is hard to say. Home-based incidents were also more common among Afro-Caribbeans and Asians, as was mugging. Analysis of the 1988 survey showed that the higher risks for both minority groups of violent crime and other household property theft were in part rooted in demographic, social and area factors known to be related to greater vulnerability to crime; this was particularly so for Afro-Caribbeans (Mayhew *et al*, 1989).

Table 6.4
Risks of violence by ethnicity: proportion of individuals victimised once or more in 1991

	Domestic	Home-based	Street	Pub/club	Work-based	Mugging	Other assault
Whites	0.6	0.4	0.9	0.5	0.4	0.4	0.4
Afro-Caribbeans	1.2	1.0	1.3	0.3	0.4	1.7	0.3
Asians	0.1	1.1	1.0	0.1	0.6	1.5	0.3

Notes:
1. Rates based on the first three victim forms completed by respondents.
2. Source: 1992 BCS core sample and ethnic boost (weighted data).

Asians and Afro-Caribbeans often reported that there was a racial element in violent incidents against them (Table 6.5). Asians were particularly likely to see assaults around the home as racially-based. Rather more Afro-Caribbeans than Asians cited a racial element in assaults at the workplace and in pubs—possibly because Afro-Caribbeans work and socialise more in mixed ethnic settings.[6]

---

[6]Victims were asked why they believed the incident had been racially motivated. Seven out of ten mentioned the use of racist language, three out of ten said it was because it had happened before, and six out of ten stated they knew it was *because* they were black or Asian. Further analysis on this will explore in more detail perceived racial motivation and multiple victimisation.

Table 6.5

Extent of racial motivation in violent incidents against Afro-Caribbeans and Asians

	Afro-Caribbeans	Asians
	% incidents thought to be racially motivated	
Domestic	11	—
Home-based	18	64
Street	58	53
Pubs/clubs	24	5
Work-based	34	7
Mugging	5	12
Other assaults	33	52
All violent incidents	27	37
Unweighted N	156	116

Note:
1. Source: 1988 and 1992 BCS core and ethnic minority booster samples (weighted data).

Relationship between offender and victim

Over half of incidents involved assailants the victim knew, at least casually or by sight, and in a further third victims knew the offender(s) well. Figure 6.3 shows the proportion of each type of violence involving offenders who were strangers, known casually or by sight, or known well to the victim. In total, some 43% of violent incidents were committed by strangers. This was most common in muggings, followed by street assaults (just over two-thirds involved strangers). In contrast, nearly half of pub assaults involved offenders who were known at least to some degree, and this was the case for seven out of ten work assaults.

Victims who knew their offender at least by sight were asked the nature of their relationship. A third of domestic assaults against women involved a current husband or partner, a fifth a current boyfriend, and a third a former husband or partner. One in ten involved some other household member, or a relative. Six out of ten domestic assaults against men on the other hand were by non-partner relatives or non-partner household members.

When violence occurs

Violent incidents are particularly likely to occur at the weekend: half of all incidents took place between 6pm on Friday and 6am on Monday. Pub violence, not surprisingly, most often took place on Friday and Saturday nights, but over half of domestic violence also happened during the weekend.

Figure 6.3
Stranger and non-stranger breakdown in different types of violent crime

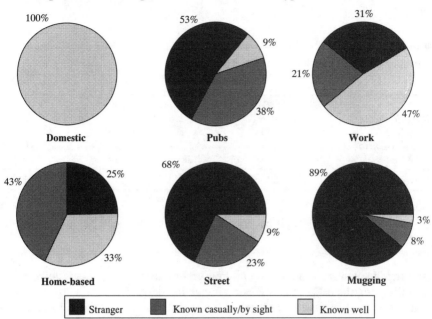

Most violence occurred in the evening between 6pm and midnight, particularly pub violence (80%). Women were more likely to be mugged during the day than men (51% as against 18%). Overall, about one in ten incidents of violence took place at night (between midnight and 6am), probably representing a comparatively high risk for those still up and about (see Table A6.4 in Appendix A).

Offender characteristics

Although violence between those who know each other well was usually one-to-one, nearly half of stranger and casual acquaintance violence involved more than one assailant. A fifth of home-based assaults, four out of ten pub assaults, and a third of street attacks were reported to have involved four or more offenders. The majority of muggings were carried out by groups: muggers worked alone in only a third of the incidents in which the victim could say something about the offender.

The number of assailants involved varied by race of victim (see Table 6.6). Most attacks against white and Afro-Caribbean victims involved only one offender but three-quarters of Asian victims were involved in incidents where more than one offender operated; a full 28% were subject to incidents involving groups of four or more.

Table 6.6
Number of assailants by race of victim

	One	Two	Three	Four plus
	%	%	%	%
Race of victim				
White	63	9	8	19
Afro-Caribbean	65	17	9	10
Asian	34	26	12	28
Unweighted N	639	157	95	191

Note:
1. Source 1988 and 1992 BCS core and ethnic minority boost samples (weighted data).

The involvement of school age children in violent crime against adults is rare according to the BCS: just 4% of violent incidents were said to have been committed by those under 16. Work-based assaults were most likely to have been committed by those under 16 (8% were), suggesting that some people come into contact with troublemakers as part of their work. Most offenders were judged to have been between 16 and 25. Assaults between those who knew each other well more often involved older offenders. In over half of domestic and work-based incidents the offender was 26 or older. (Table A6.5 in Appendix A shows details.)

Most violence is perpetrated by men, whether directed against men or women (Table 6.7). Nine out of ten assaults against men involved male attackers. Three-quarters of female victims were assaulted by men, although the proportion was considerably higher in domestic assaults.

Men are only infrequently assaulted by women—though a quarter of domestic assaults against men involved women (Table 6.7). Female victims, however, are more frequently on the receiving end of violence from other women. One in five incidents against women were committed by other women, and a further 6% by men and women acting together. More than half of pub incidents against women involved other women, and a third of home-based and street assaults. Female offenders however were less likely to inflict much injury.

Table 6.7
The sex of offenders in violent crime

	% incidents: male offenders	% incidents: female offenders	% incidents: both sexes
Male victims			
Domestic	66	26	8
Home-based	89	6	3
Street	87	0	12
Pubs/clubs	92	1	1
Work-based	94	5	2
Mugging	94	0	0
Other assault	90	1	2
All violence	89	3	5
Female victims			
Domestic	92	7	1
Home-based	55	33	9
Street	60	35	3
Pubs/clubs	28	56	16
Work-based	68	22	9
Mugging	65	12	12
Other assault	55	23	19
All violence	72	20	6

Notes:
1. Percentages do not always sum to 100% as there were some incidents for which the victim did not give the sex of the assailant. These included, for instance, 11% of muggings against women, and 6% of assaults in pubs/clubs against men.
2. Source: 1988 and 1992 BCS (weighted data).

For violent incidents generally, the vast majority of white victims reported that white offender(s) had been involved (see Table 6.8). Afro-Caribbeans were much more likely than whites to have been assaulted by other Afro-Caribbeans (43% were as against 6% of white victims). Asians were more likely than whites to say Afro-Caribbeans were responsible (they were cited in 21% of incidents against Asians). It was unusual for Asians to be mentioned except in the case of Asian victims. The pattern of these results may reflect the fact that Afro-Caribbean and Asian victims are more likely to encounter an offender from the same minority group because of a higher proportion of minorities in areas where they live.

For muggings, only half of cases involving white victims were said to be by a white offender. A third were said to be by black offenders, although black offenders were even more likely to be involved in mugging for Afro-Caribbean and Asian victims (however, the number of incidents is small). These findings should be interpreted with care: not all victims were able to give information about their offender(s), and not all of those that did so may have given correct information. Home-based assaults on Asians were mainly by white offenders, and, as noted earlier, such assaults were particularly likely to be seen as racially motivated.

Table 6.8
Ethnic origin of offender by ethnic origin of victim 1987 & 1991

	White victims %	Afro/Caribbean victims %	Asian victims %
Home-based			
White offender	88	24	67
Black offender	2	32	5
Asian offender	1	—	6
Other/mixed group	6	41	22
Unknown	3	4	—
	100	100	100
Unweighted N	90	22	19
Mugging			
White offender	49	16	20
Black offender	32	58	55
Asian offender	1	—	10
Other/mixed group	8	13	8
Unknown	10	13	9
	100	100	100
Unweighted N	103	30	41
Violence excluding above			
White offender	88	51	62
Black offender	3	42	11
Asian offender	1	1	19
Other/mixed group	5	3	7
Unknown	3	3	1
	100	100	100
Unweighted N	628	108	59

Note:
1. Source 1988 and 1992 BCS core and ethnic minority boost samples (weighted data).

In four out of ten incidents of violence in the 1988 survey, the victim said the offender was drunk (the question was not asked in the 1992 survey). Not surprisingly, assaults in pubs most frequently involved a drunken assailant (86% did so), though alcohol was also likely to be a contributory factor in disputes in and around the home against men, and in street attacks. Four out of ten women implicated a drunken offender in domestic violence (see Figure 6.4). Violence involving female offenders was less likely to be influenced by alcohol: only a quarter were judged to have been drinking, compared to 47% of male assailants.

Figure 6.4
Percentage of offenders said to be drunk (1988 BCS)

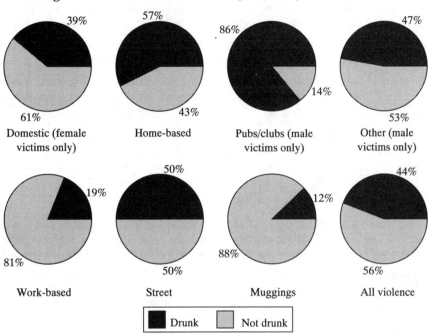

39% / 61%	57% / 43%	86% / 14%	47% / 53%
Domestic (female victims only)	Home-based	Pubs/clubs (male victims only)	Other (male victims only)
19% / 81%	50% / 50%	12% / 88%	44% / 56%
Work-based	Street	Muggings	All violence

■ Drunk ▨ Not drunk

Methods and impact

Of all violent incidents, a fifth involved something the offender threatened to use or actually used as a weapon.[7] The involvement of weapons varied by type of violence. In half the incidents of mugging against men the offender had a weapon (most commonly a stabbing implement such as a knife or screw driver), but this was rarely the case for women (16% of incidents) among whom there were more 'snatch thefts'. Assaults at work were also likely to involve weapons (27%), especially for women. A weapon was involved in 16% of incidents of domestic assault against women. Of pub violence, 14% involved a weapon. Not surprisingly this was most often a bottle or glass.

Being punched or slapped was the most common type of assault (two-thirds of all incidents), followed by being grabbed or pushed (half). In nearly a third of attacks the victim had been kicked and in one in ten they had actually been struck with a weapon. (Victims could specify more than one method of attack.)

---

[7]This analysis, and that on injuries, excludes 6% of incidents in which no one was aware of what happened.

A third of incidents resulted in minimal injury. Victims of muggings were the least likely to be injured (59%) presumably because they handed over their money or valuables to avoid a physical attack or because the offender was mainly intent on getting away.[8] Women were less likely to be hurt during mugging than men, again reflecting more snatch thefts. Those most likely to be injured were victims of domestic assaults followed by victims of pub/club assaults.

The most common result was some bruising or a black eye, particularly for women (63% of all incidents). About one in five resulted in the victim receiving cuts, while in 15% they had scratches, and in 5% they suffered broken bones.

Relatively few victims saw a doctor (16%). Male victims of mugging and assault around the home were the most likely to seek medical help, as were women subject to domestic assault (about a quarter in each case saw a doctor). Incidents involving weapons were far more likely to require medical attention (37%). (Table A6.7 in Appendix A shows details.)

Physical injury apart, many victims not surprisingly experienced emotional reactions ranging from shock, anger and fear to difficulty sleeping and depression.[9] Women were more likely to report such reactions than men, and elderly women in particular (though the numbers are small). Domestic assaults and muggings upset them most, though men were even more affected by muggings than women (more than half reporting they were 'very much affected'). The higher proportion of robberies would explain this. Victims were, if anything, more upset by attacks from those they knew than by strangers. (Table A6.6 in Appendix A shows the percentage of male and female victims who said they were 'very much' emotionally affected by their experience.)

Overall, women regarded violent incidents rather more seriously than men (see also Pease, 1988). The relatively small number of home-based incidents against women were considered most serious, followed by incidents of domestic violence against women (see Figure 6.5). Any notion that victims will take a rather indifferent attitude to pub brawls is somewhat belied by the data; they were viewed as of at least average seriousness. Assessments of seriousness by and large reflected other indicators of the consequences of different types of victimisation such as injury and emotional upset.

Some victims felt that they were responsible in some way for what had happened. This was the case in a quarter of domestic assaults, and in 13% of violent incidents overall. (Table A6.7 in Appendix A shows details.) The degree of self-blame was very much higher for incidents involving those who knew each other well.

---

[8]In half of incidents, cash was taken; in 18%, jewellery was stolen; in 15% of incidents victims lost wallets and a quarter a purse or handbag; 4% involved loss of cheque books and/or cards. Muggers failed to steal anything in nearly a quarter of incidents.

[9]Anger was the most common reaction for both male (44%) and female (58%) victims, followed by shock (25% of male victims, 47% of female).

Figure 6.5
Mean 'seriousness' scores for different types of violence

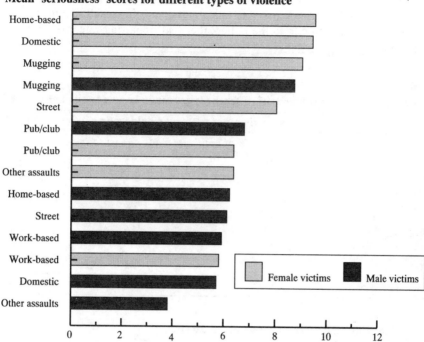

Nearly a quarter involved in domestic incidents said they thought they had provoked the attack, as did one in ten victims of pub violence. The small proportion of mugging victims who felt in some way to blame regretted leaving possessions insecurely guarded. For most types of violence (pub assaults were the exception), male victims more often felt they were to blame in some way than did women.

Reporting to the police

According to the 1992 survey, mugging and offences in and around the home were most likely to become known to the police (47%). About a third of work-related incidents, street and pub/club assaults came to police attention (Table 6.9). There was more variation in reporting across types of violence among women than men. Women were more likely than men to report cases of mugging and assaults in and around the home than men, but less likely to report domestic and street assaults.

One in five of the domestic assaults mentioned in the survey by women were said to have been reported to the police, compared to two-fifths of those experienced by men. The decision to bring in the police will, of course, rest on different considerations for men and women, given that the types of domestic assaults experienced by them differ (eg, in the level of spouse abuse). It may also be that women who were prepared to talk about domestic assault to interviewers were more prepared to talk to the police; the 'real' reporting rate, then, may be much lower.

Table 6.9
Percentage of violent offences of different types made known to the police, 1991

	Male victims	Female victims	Total
	% of incidents made known to the police		
Domestic	40	21	23
Home-based	38	62	47
Street	38	22	35
Pub/club	32	27	31
Work-based	39	30	36
Muggings	41	56	47
Other assaults	18	34	21
All violence	34	31	33
Unweighted N	238	199	437

Note:
1. Source: 1988 and 1992 BCS (weighted data).

The pattern of these results indicates that when victims know their offender(s) they are less likely to bring in the police. For violent crime in general in 1991, some 41% of incidents committed by strangers became known to the police, but only 20% of incidents in which the offender was well known to the victim. In other words four out of five cases are shielded from police view even though firm identification of the offender would have allowed action to be taken. Chapter 3 has previously taken up this issue.

Trends in violence 1981 to 1991

The indications from the BCS are that domestic assaults have increased significantly in number between 1981 and 1991, as have those occurring in and around work see Figure 6.6 (and Table A6.1 in Appendix A). Other types of assault have shown less change, or in the case of street assaults and pub brawls, a slight decrease.

Whether there are now actually more domestic incidents or whether victims are becoming more willing to admit to such incidents is a moot point. On the basis of earlier BCS results, it was argued that the increasing acceptability of admitting domestic incidents to interviewers may have underpinned the BCS increase in domestic assaults between 1981 and 1987—especially as there was an apparent parallel increase in reporting to the police (Davidoff and Dowds, 1989). (The *number* of incidents of domestic violence recorded by the police certainly increased between 1985 and 1987.) In 1981, about a fifth of women who experienced domestic assaults said they had reported them to the police, while in 1987 half said they had. Figures from the 1992 survey, however, suggest the level of reporting in 1987 was unusually high: according to the 1992 survey, only 21% of women brought in the police—very close to the levels in other survey years.

Figure 6.6
BCS: Violence in different circumstances: 1981 and 1991

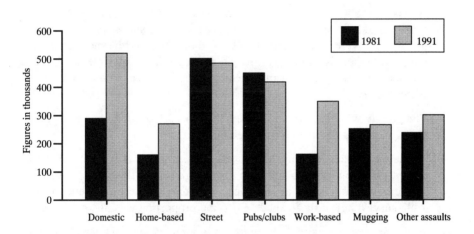

The increase in assaults at work is not readily explained. However, a much higher proportion of incidents were reported to the police in 1991 (36%) than in 1981 (17%), which may suggest some shift in perceptions about the criminal nature of work-related incidents. (The Health and Safety Executive and trade unions have been involved in raising the saliency of this issue.) Between 1987 and 1991, 'mugging' increased to a similar extent to other types of violence. However, there was a steeper rise in snatch thefts than in robbery.

Summary

*   The BCS count of 'actual' violence is unlikely to be a full one. For a number of reasons, many incidents will go unmentioned in interview. Offences involving people who know each other are particularly likely to be undercounted.

* Categorising violent incidents, the largest number (estimated at 530,000 in 1991) were domestic assaults, involving partners, ex-partners and other relatives and household members. Nearly half of assaults mentioned by women in the survey were of this type.

* Street assaults were nearly as common as domestic assaults, amounting to about 510,000 incidents. Male victims were involved in over eight out of ten of them. There were about 420,000 assaults in pubs and clubs, again with over eight out of ten victims men.

* There were about 260,000 incidents of 'mugging' (robberies and snatch thefts), fairly evenly split between male and female victims. The number of robberies against men was higher than against women, and 'snatch thefts' were higher for women.

* Age is strongly related to violent victimisation with younger people facing higher risks. Areas with higher levels of social disorder produced more people who were victimised. Men who go out frequently, especially to the pub, run higher risks. Married people run lower risks of violence, but for offences involving known offenders, having children is associated with increased risk.

* The elderly were infrequent victims, though 10% of muggings and home-based incidents involved those aged 60 or over.

* Women were considerably less at risk than men of all types of violence except domestic assaults and mugging. Slightly less than one per cent of women overall reported at least one incident of domestic violence in the 1992 survey, but of those aged 16-29, the proportion was just over 2%.

* Afro-Caribbeans reported more domestic violence than whites or Asians. Whether this is because the ethnic groups are differentially reticent is hard to say. Home-based incidents and muggings were higher among both minority groups.

* About a third of incidents against Afro-Caribbeans and Asians were felt to be racially motivated. More than a half of street assaults were said to be. Asians also said race was involved in two-thirds of incidents around the home, usually citing white offenders.

* Victims of violent crime are more likely to be repeatedly victimised than is the case with most property crimes. Half of female victims of domestic assault had experienced more than one incident in 1991. For violent crime as a whole, some 17% of the sample accounted for 45% of the incidents involved.

* About five out of ten pub brawls involved people known to the victim in some degree; and this was even more often the case with violence at work. Mugging was most likely to involve strangers, followed by street assaults.

* The vast majority of pub assaults involved offenders said to be drunk. But many other incidents of violence were also committed by drunken offenders.

* One in five incidents of violence against women were committed by other women, and a further 6% by men and women acting together. The highest proportion of woman-on-women violence took place in pubs. But women offenders caused less injury.

* Some victims felt that they were responsible in some way for what happened. This was the case in nearly a quarter of domestic assaults, and in 13% of violent incidents all told.

* Muggings and offences around the home were most likely to be reported to the police: about half were. About a third of work-related, street and pub assaults were reported. Reporting of domestic assaults was low: only one in five women brought in the police. Offences involving strangers were more frequently reported.

* Domestic assaults and other home-based assaults against women were regarded most seriously by their victims, despite low reporting. Many pub assaults against men were considered serious by their victims.

* On the definition of violent crime used here, the number of offences measured in the survey has risen by 24% between 1981 and 1991, and by 15% since 1987. The number of domestic assaults reported to BCS interviewers has risen by 79% since 1981, though greater willingness to talk about these cannot be ruled out. The number of assaults at work has more than doubled since 1981, but as more are now being reported to the police, changing perceptions about their criminality may be implicated. There was no statistically significant change in the number of muggings, street assaults, and pub assaults.

7 Conclusions

This report has presented results from the fourth (1992) British Crime Survey, which interviewed a representative 'core' sample of 10,059 people in England and Wales, and a 'booster' sample of 1,654 Afro-Caribbeans and Asians. They were asked about their experience of crime in 1991 and about various other crime-related topics. The survey's findings are summarised elsewhere in this report. Here, we discuss some of their main implications:

*   what the BCS contributes to our understanding of recent trends in crime;

*   what pointers the results offer for tackling crime;

*   how the police should deal with victims of crime.

Trends in crime

The BCS now provides a measure of crime trends spanning eleven years. It demonstrates clearly that police statistics are an unreliable guide both to the extent of crime and to crime trends—since there can be changes both in the propensity of victims to report to the police, and in police recording practices. For crimes that can be compared with police figures, the survey shows an increase of nearly 50% between 1981 and 1991, about half that of comparable police statistics. The police figures show a steeper increase, because a larger proportion of crimes are now reported to the police. Since 1987, the survey showed a 14% rise in crime, compared with 39% in police figures. The BCS confirms that there has been a large growth in crime over the last decade, but it also shows that the size of the increase has been overstated by police figures.

The pattern of change over the 1980s has not been consistent across all types of crime. The rise in crimes of violence and vandalism has been amplified by police statistics and this is the main source of the higher *overall* increase in police figures since 1981. Police statistics for acquisitive crimes are in line with those of the BCS, both sources of data showing that levels of theft and burglary have doubled since 1981. However, over a longer period, from 1972, the BCS combined with findings from the General Household Survey shows for burglary at least—the evidence is not available to look at other crimes—a much shallower increase than police figures.

Whether and how far police figures will continue to overstate the increase in crime remains to be seen. They may well do so. Despite the increase in reporting, two out of three BCS offences still remain unrecorded by the police. There is thus ample 'headroom' for more crimes to be recorded even if offending rates remain unchanged.

The reasons behind the increase in reporting cannot be gauged for certain. People may be becoming increasingly intolerant of some types of crime, and more ready to define incidents as ones which *ought* to be dealt with by the police. The evidence for this is discussed in Chapter 2. Whether levels of reporting continue to increase must depend at least in part on the quality of the police response—a point discussed below. One factor which has clearly led to higher reporting rates is the growth of insurance cover, as claimants are—or feel—under an obligation to notify the police. Rising insurance premiums may in the future stem the growth in insurance cover, but between 1987 and 1991 it can be roughly estimated that wider cover and the fact that insured victims are more likely to report, may have accounted for about a fifth of the extra incidents of theft and damage which the police had available to them to record.

The potential of police statistics to paint a misleading picture of crime has led some to suggest that they should be dispensed with (eg, *The Times*, 27th September 1990; 30th October, 1992). We do not support this. On the one hand police statistics provide a useful—and fairly accurate—index of that part of police workload to do with crime; and in any case, crime surveys are unable to cover a wide range of commercial and 'victimless' crimes. On the other, the increasing ease of analysing police statistics at local level provides the police with effective strategic and tactical information about the nature of criminal work they have to tackle.

Tackling crime: pointers from the British Crime Survey

The BCS serves largely to *describe* crime problems, and in the main *prescriptions* flow only indirectly from its results. However, the four sweeps conducted to date cumulatively provide many pointers about the nature of crime and how to tackle it.

Mapping the contours of the crime problem

The first step in the formation of social policy is to define the problems which need addressing, and the BCS can make a significant contribution here by saying which sorts of people are at risk of what sorts of crime and to what extent it maps the contours of crime. Perhaps the clearest example of this is the way in which the BCS has quantified the very large proportion of crimes involving motor vehicles (see Figure 2.1 on page 12). Another example can be found in crimes of violence. Successive sweeps of the survey have filled out our knowledge about the main forms of violence, their settings and the context in which they occur (see, for example, Figure 6.1 on page 84). The survey has also provided a great deal of information about the impact of crime on its victims. Information of this sort does not always suggest specific solutions to different forms of crime, but it helps in assessing the nature and severity of the problem they present.

The BCS is now the main source of information about the distribution of crime risks across the population in England and Wales. The current report in particular has highlighted how risks are unevenly distributed between the sexes, across age groups, and between urban and rural areas. The range of risks evidenced in the survey clearly limits the usefulness of presenting statistically average risks— though national rates obviously have their place. The results have shown where risks are highest within cities, and what lifestyles are associated with risk. At first sight, the results may simply serve to underscore the fact that offending rates are highest amongst young males in poor areas of conurbations, and that anyone who falls within their ambit is particularly at risk. But the consequences of this uneven distribution of risk are marked. The BCS has shown that risks of a wide range of crimes are two to three times the national average in the following three of the eleven ACORN neighbourhoods:

Group H: mixed inner metropolitan areas

Group I: high status non-family areas

Group G: poorest council estates.

Nor is crime evenly distributed within the ACORN area types which make up these three groups. In practical terms, this means that although most people face *some* level of crime risk, crime represents for some households an endemic and relentless problem.

Developing preventive strategies

The BCS illustrates graphically the very small proportion of crime which results in detection and punishment. The national clear-up rate for crimes recorded by the police in 1991 stood at 29%; for the sub-group of crime which can be compared with the BCS, the figure was lower, at 24%. If crimes cleared up are expressed as a percentage not of recorded crimes, but of offences estimated by the BCS, the figure falls to well under 10%. The proportion of crimes resulting in conviction is lower still, at 3% (Barclay, 1993). These figures underline the limitations of the formal criminal justice system as a mechanism for controlling crime, and emphasise the need to look beyond it to other approaches.

In its nature, the BCS yields little information about offenders, and thus carries few pointers for ways of tackling crime by reducing the motivation to offend. It can say a fair amount, by contrast, about approaches which emphasise the reduction of criminal opportunities. The implications are clearest for thefts involving cars and burglary.

THE 1992 BRITISH CRIME SURVEY

Cars and theft

The main pointers from the BCS are:[1]

* The BCS clearly shows that the greatest crime-preventive gains, simply in numerical terms, are to be made in relation to crimes involving cars. Over a third of crimes against individuals and their private property involve motor vehicles.

* Thefts from cars are much more numerous than thefts of cars, and concentrating effort on these will have most impact on the number of recorded offences. Thefts of cars may occupy more police time and cause greater distress and loss for victims, but action to reduce thefts *from* cars— in particular design improvements to make it harder for thieves to get into cars—may often be such as to reduce thefts *of* them too.

* In dealing with thefts *of* cars, preventive action will have most effect on crime levels if focused on 'joyriding'. Although thefts for other reasons appear to be increasing more rapidly, thefts for the purpose of joyriding still comprise the vast majority of incidents.

* Given present levels of security, encouraging owners to be more careful about locking their cars is unlikely to pay large dividends in terms of crime reduction, although continuing publicity effort to maintain security awareness could be valuable. Most owners already lock up, and in less than one in ten incidents in 1991 might owner negligence have had a part to play. Moreover, several studies have shown that locked cars can be easily entered by thieves (eg, Light *et al*, 1993). The conclusion of almost all preventive reviews has been that bigger gains will come from improving the 'in-built' security of cars. The technology exists to make cars much harder to break into, and much harder to drive away.

* There is probably limited scope for relying on the vigilance of householders in spotting car thieves and intervening. About three-quarters of thefts are committed when it is dark, and many of these occur after people have gone to bed. The fact that a substantial proportion of incidents involve breaking windows hardly indicates that offenders feel very wary of the risks of being heard.

* The finding that most thefts of and from cars occur outside the owners' homes is one which has been given insufficient attention in preventive advice. It also underscores the need to consider solutions for the areas in which thefts most often occur. There has been a tendency to see the protection of cars as a separate enterprise from the protection of other

---

[1] The full range of possible strategies are not rehearsed here, for which see, eg, Clarke, 1991; Clarke and Harris, 1992; Webb and Laycock, 1992.

domestic property and the needs of high-crime areas (Hope, 1987). At the very least, then, when publicity is directed at owners to secure their cars more, this should emphasise the higher risks at home. Also, given the higher risks for those who have to park on the streets, more can be done when new estates and residential areas are designed (or old ones re-built) to provide car owners with more secure off-street parking facilities.

Burglary

The preventive priority which different types of crime should receive is not just a function of their prevalence. Burglaries may be much rarer than thefts from car, but their consequences are much further-reaching, and are a widespread source of anxiety. What does the BCS suggest in relation to burglary?

* The results provide properly grounded information about the risks of burglary which can help people—householders and local authorities— make informed judgements about the crime preventive measures worth taking. It can also offer practical advice about the most likely entry-points that burglars will target, and thus the most efficient parts of the house to 'target harden'.

* The results provide support for the value of 'target hardening' in reducing risks (pages 55-57). Those with more security devices faced a smaller chance of being burgled, and although there is truth in the view that 'a burglar will get in if he really wants to', better security succeeds in deflecting some burglars, as measured by the proportion of attempts at entry which fail. There will, however, be limits to solving burglary simply by persuading people to be more assiduous about security. Burglary has gone up despite the fact that security consciousness has improved over the decade and many people will not be able to afford high quality security hardware, leaving ample easy opportunities for offenders.

* Apart from improving the quality of security in homes by targeting preventive advice and advertising on householders, there may be gains to be made by providing householders with incentives to upgrade their security, through insurance discounts, for example. There is also room for encouraging builders to 'design out' opportunities for crime and persuading them not to cut corners when choosing the specification of doors and windows. Setting up and seeing through initiatives of this sort is a complex and fragile process, but continuing progress needs to be made.

Multiple victimisation

One unintended consequence of strategies of encouraging improved security is that risks may be progressively displaced from those who can afford to make improvements, onto those who cannot. One solution advanced is to target crime preventive attention on recent victims (Barr and Pease, 1992; Farrell, 1993; Farrell and Pease, 1993). The grounds for doing so are partly those of efficiency, in that those who have been burgled, for example, are demonstrably at risk of burglary; but analysis of both police statistics and survey findings also suggest that those who have been victims run a heightened risk of re-victimisation in the period immediately after the first incident. The extent to which this occurs, and the reasons for it need further examination, as do other issues surrounding multiple victimisation. For instance, more needs to be known about how far it is confined to particular groups or areas. Little is also known about the degree of 'cross-offence' repeat victimisation and how far this might stem from victims' behaviour and lifestyles, and how far simply from their proximity to offenders. Nonetheless, the preventive implications of multiple victimisation already seem considerable.

The police treatment of victims

Reporting a crime is one of the most frequent ways in which contact is made with the police according to the BCS (Skogan, forthcoming). The way in which the police deal with victims inevitably shapes the demand for their services and public confidence in, and satisfaction with, the police. Both the Victim's Charter and the police's own Quality of Service initiative have emphasised the need for victims to receive efficient and fair service from the police.

The 1992 BCS shows that many victims have no complaint on this score: on a general measure of satisfaction, 65% were very or fairly satisfied. This is slightly lower than in 1984 (68%) but higher than 1988, when satisfaction dipped to 60%. Nine out of ten victims in the 1992 survey felt that the police were polite, and three-quarters felt that the time taken to attend calls was reasonable. The interest the police took in what they reported was also judged good enough by two-thirds of victims. However, the BCS provides ample evidence that various groups are over-represented amongst the dissatisfied—the young, those from ethnic minorities, and manual workers, for example.

The BCS identifies two main ways in which victims felt badly served by the police: first, that the police had failed to make enough effort; and second, that they should have kept victims better informed. A little needs saying about each.

Police effort

More than a third of BCS victims who had called the police felt they had made insufficient effort. The survey cannot say whether or not their assessments were justified. But the finding raises the issue of whether public expectations of the police are unrealistic, and if so, how to deal with this. The best way is probably to *explain* operating procedures unequivocally and to tell victims what to expect. It is clear that initiatives intended to manage the demands on police resources, such as graded response and case-screening, stand no chance of being acceptable to victims unless they are clearly explained. Without proper explanation, strategies of this sort are likely to erode public confidence in the police. The issues involved here bear consideration not least because if the trend in increased reporting continues, this will both increase police workload and draw into it a larger proportion of the less serious offences about which the police can probably do least.

Victims' sense that the police had taken insufficient trouble over their case was shown to be to be strongly related to whether there was face-to-face contact with an officer—an important point given that the number of BCS victims having face-to-face contact with the police has fallen since 1987 (Skogan, forthcoming). But feeling that too little had been done may often stem less from police actions—or omissions—than from their demeanour. Incidents which victims experience as intrusive and very upsetting are often from the police perspective routine, mundane events about which they can do little. The more that the victims are made to sense this, the less satisfied they will be. The evidence is that victims do not necessarily expect the offender to be 'brought to book', but rather want sympathy, reassurance, and due attention given to the 'rituals' of investigation as recognition that something untoward has occurred (eg, Newburn and Merry, 1990). There may be scope for better training in the social skills needed for dealing with upset victims, in the techniques for providing emotional support, and in the provision of practical advice. Consideration has already been given in this country to specialised victim 'after-care' units (offering a more accessible information point, speeding the return of stolen property and easing some practical problems), and these are judged successful in Canada (Waller, 1982). Maintaining links with outside agencies would also help, and this endorses the current police practice of automatically referring certain types of victim to Victim Support schemes.

Feedback of information

Four out of ten victims who reported their crimes felt that the police had failed to keep them well-enough informed. The remainder were either happy with the information they had received or—more often—were realistic enough to see that there was unlikely to be much news to pass on. The demand for better feedback from the police is a consistent finding from the BCS and other studies (see Mayhew, 1985, for a review).

There are obvious obstacles to improvement: often the information which victims want is held, not by the police, but by the courts or the Crown Prosecution Service; for many offences the police may have little information to pass on; and where they do, there is an inevitable cost in passing this on, whether by

107

follow-up visits, letters or phone calls. Nevertheless, better and well-enforced procedures for relaying information—or the lack of information—would clearly help allay victims' sense of dissatisfaction. A standard letter, or a brief telephone call may be cheapest, but the BCS indicates that having face-to-face contact with the police soon after reporting a crime improves ratings of police performance, including perceptions of the adequacy of information given. Hard judgments have to be made in deciding the extent to which scarce police resources should be earmarked for improving feedback to victims. Doing so promises to improve public satisfaction with, and confidence in, the police; but in the short term at least, the police will see little tangible return on the investment.

Questions of public satisfaction must bear on whether the police should encourage victims to report *more often*. There would be strong grounds for doing this if many of the extra incidents reported were amenable to detection. There are additional arguments for encouraging fuller reporting, in that the uniformed police are gatekeepers to other services such as crime prevention advice, victim support and compensation. In all probability, victims of unreported *property* crimes are generally quite accurate in their judgement about the scope for catching the offender (cf Skogan & Antunes, 1979). Clearly, it would be desirable to encourage selective reporting of crimes which *could* be cleared up— but it is hard to see what this would entail. In relation to *violent* crimes— especially those committed by non-strangers—the issue is less whether unreported crimes could be detected than whether it is practical or desirable to take formal action against the offender (Cretney *et al*, forthcoming). Many incidents of violence are best resolved without recourse to official action; on the other hand, there are some categories of violence such as spouse abuse, where there may be a positive declaratory value in making it clear that such incidents are 'police business'. The worst outcome, obviously, would be for the police to stimulate demand for their services by encouraging victims to report, and to be overwhelmed as a result by large numbers of intractable cases and dissatisfied victims.

The future

The BCS has now been placed on a biennial cycle, with an enlarged sample size to improve the reliability of results. The fifth sweep will take place early in 1994, and like the last two, it will carry a 'booster' sample of ethnic minorities. A significant technical development will be the use of Computer Assisted Personal Interviewing (CAPI). Interviewers are equipped with lap-top computers onto which the questionnaire is pre-programmed. CAPI is being found increasingly useful for large surveys in facilitating use of complex questionnaires. By simplifying the process of data preparation, it also offers quicker results.

As with previous sweeps of the survey, the 1992 data-set will be deposited in the Economic and Social Research Council's Data Archive to allow for secondary analysis. British criminologists have now carried out a fair amount of such analysis, though greater use has still been made by American researchers. We are keen to see increased academic use of the BCS in this country. The four sweeps conducted to date represent one of the largest, most varied and most flexible data-sets available to social researchers. It affords considerable scope for substantive new research. It is now possible, for example, to combine data-sets from different sweeps to conduct the sorts of multivariate analysis which cannot always be supported by the sample size of a single sweep. The BCS could also serve as an invaluable teaching resource.

This report has by no means covered all the material in the 1992 BCS. A large component of the questionnaire focused on people's contacts with the police, and results have been analysed by Skogan (forthcoming). Reports are planned on a range of other topics, including:

*   drug misuse,

*   teenagers' experience of crime,

*   ethnic minorities' experience of crime,

*   fear of crime,

*   multiple victimisation,

*   women's experience of obscene telephone calls.

Appendix A
Supplementary tables

Table A2.1

Number of offences in England and Wales, 1981, 1983, 1987 and 1991: BCS estimates

Figures in 000s	Numbers of BCS offences				% diff 87-91	% diff 81-91
	1981	1983	1987	1991		
COMPARABLE WITH RECORDED OFFENCES						
ACQUISITIVE CRIME	3,153	3,823	4,808	6,174	28 **	96 **
VANDALISM	2,715	2,795	2,947	2,730	-7 *	1
VIOLENCE	670	568	743	809	9	21
ALL COMPARABLE	6,538	7,186	8,497	9,713	14 **	49 **
Burglary	750	914	1,186	1,365	15	82 **
Attempts and no loss	376	461	668	660	-1	76 **
With loss	374	454	517	705	36 **	88 **
All vehicle thefts	1,753	2,115	2,916	3,807	31 **	117 **
Theft from motor vehicles	1,287	1,537	2,098	2,400	14	86 **
Theft of motor vehicles	286	284	387	517	34 **	81 **
Attempted thefts of/ from vehicles	180	294	430	890	107 **	395 **
Bicycle theft	216	288	389	564	45 **	161 **
Theft from the person	434	505	317	439	39 *	1 n.a.
Vehicle vandalism	1,558	1,708	1,629	1,669	2	7
Household vandalism	1,155	1,089	1,317	1,063	-19 **	-8
Wounding	507	423	566	626	11	23
Robbery	163	145	177	183	4	13
OTHER BCS OFFENCES						
Other household theft	1,518	1,543	1,515	1,838	21 *	21
Other personal theft	1,588	1,730	1,794	1,744	-3	10
Common assault	1,402	1,429	1,493	1,757	18	25
ALL BCS OFFENCES	11,045	11,888	13,000	15,052	13 **	36 **

Notes:

1. **Acquisitive crime**: burglary, thefts of and from vehicles (including attempts), bicycle thefts, theft from the person. **Vandalism**: household property and vehicles. **Violence**: wounding and robbery.

2. Attempted motor vehicle thefts are not easily classifiable as attempts from or of vehicles, and they have previously been counted as 'other household thefts' in the BCS.

3. Numbers of 1991 offences were derived by multiplying offence rates by 20,131,000 households in England and Wales (household crimes) and 40,661,000 adults (personal crimes). Multipliers for earlier years differ slightly from ones used previously, so some figures differ from previous results.

4. The statistical significance of changes is calculated on the basis of rates taking population change into account. Double-starred differences are statistically significant at the 5% level (2-tailed). Single-starred differences are significant at the 10% level (2-tailed). Percentage changes based on unrounded numbers. Tests on the 1981-1991 differences for theft from the person have not been carried out as classification changes make the two measures incomparable.

5. Source: 1982, 1984, 1988, 1992 BCS (weighted data).

Table A2.2

Rates of victimisation in England and Wales in 1981, 1983, 1987 and 1991: BCS estimates

Rates per 10,000 households/individuals	BCS offence rates				% diff 87-91		% diff 81-91	
	1981	1983	1987	1991				
COMPARABLE WITH RECORDED OFFENCES								
ACQUISITIVE CRIME	1,604	1,910	2,396	2,962 ±181	24	**	85	**
VANDALISM	1,481	1,504	1,521	1,356 ±119	-11	*	-8	
VIOLENCE	173	145	185	199 ±52	8		15	
ALL COMPARABLE	3,509	3,908	4,403	4,913 ±266	12	**	40	**
Burglary	409	492	612	678 ±90	11		66	**
Attempts and no loss	205	248	345	328 ±55	-5		60	**
With loss	204	244	267	350 ±54	31	**	72	**
All vehicle thefts	955	1,138	1,503	1,890 ±132	26	**	98	**
Theft from motor vehicles	702	827	1,083	1,192 ±104	10		70	**
Theft of motor vehicles	156	153	200	257 ±37	29	**	65	**
Attempted motor vehicle thefts	98	158	222	442 ±65	99	**	351	**
Bicycle thefts	118	155	201	280 ±47	39	**	137	**
Theft from the person	112	129	79	108 ±25	37	*	-4	n.a.
Vehicle vandalism	850	919	841	829 ±83	-1		-3	
Household vandalism	630	586	680	528 ±72	-22	**	-16	
Wounding	131	108	141	154 ±46	9		18	
Robbery	42	37	44	45 ±20	2		7	
OTHER BCS OFFENCES								
Other household thefts	828	830	782	913 ±105	17	*	10	
Other personal thefts	410	442	447	429 ±68	-4		5	
Common assault	362	365	372	432 ±87	16		19	
ALL BCS OFFENCES	5,112	5,577	6,025	6,687 ±338	11	**	31	**

Notes:

1. **Acquisitive crime**: burglary, thefts of and from vehicles (including attempts), bicycle thefts, theft from the person. **Vandalism**: household property and vehicles. **Violence**: wounding and robbery.

2. Rates for 1991 are shown with the range in which they are likely to lie taking sampling error into account.

3. Attempted motor vehicle thefts are not easily classifiable as attempts from or of vehicles, and they have previously been counted as 'other household thefts' in the BCS.

4. The statistical significance of changes is calculated on the basis of rates taking population change into account. Double-starred differences are statistically significant at the 5% level (2-tailed). Single-starred differences are significant at the 10% level (2-tailed). Percentage changes based on unrounded numbers. Tests on the 1981-1991 differences for theft from the person have not been carried out as classification changes make the two measures incomparable.

5. For violence, all comparable offences, theft from the person, wounding, robbery, other personal theft, common assault and all BCS offences, rates are quoted per 10,000 adults. For acquisitive crime, vandalism, burglary, vehicle offences, bicycle thefts and other household thefts, rates are quoted per 10,000 households.

6. Source: 1982, 1984, 1988, 1992 BCS (weighted data).

Table A2.3

Rates of victimisation for vehicle offences in England and Wales in 1981, 1983, 1987 and 1991: BCS estimates

Rates per 10,000 owners	BCS offence rates					% diff 87-91	% diff 81-91
	1981	1983	1987	1991			
VEHICLE OFFENCES							
All vehicle thefts	1,398	1,655	2,126	2,541	±168	20 **	82 **
Theft from motor vehicles	1,025	1,202	1,533	1,600	±139	4	56 **
Theft of motor vehicles	232	224	282	346	±50	23 *	49 **
Attempted motor vehicle thefts	142	229	313	595	±88	90 **	319 **
Vehicle vandalism	1,256	1,325	1,191	1,111	±124	-7	-12
Bicycle theft	282	349	451	653	±107	45 **	132 **

Notes:

1. Attempted motor vehicle thefts are not easily classifiable as attempts from or of vehicles, and they have previously been counted as 'other household thefts' in the BCS.

2. The statistical significance of changes is calculated on the basis of rates taking population change into account. Double-starred differences are statistically significant at the 5% level (2-tailed). Single-starred differences are significant at the 10% level (2-tailed). Percentage changes based on unrounded numbers.

3. Source: 1982, 1984, 1988 and 1992 BCS (weighted data).

Table A2.4

A comparison of British Crime Survey and notifiable offences recorded by the police

	1991 Police	1991 BCS	% rep'd	% rec'd of rep'd	% rec'd of all BCS	% change 87-91 Police	% change 87-91 BCS	% change 81-91 Police	% change 81-91 BCS
Figures in 000s									
COMPARABLE WITH RECORDED OFFENCES									
ACQUISITIVE CRIME	2,264	6,174	60	62	37	40	28 **	95	96
VANDALISM	410	2,730	27	56	15	35	-7 **	105	1 **
VIOLENCE	198	809	48	51	24	34	9 *	93	21 **
ALL COMPARABLE	2,872	9,713	50	60	30	39	14 **	96	49 **
Burglary	625	1,365	73	63	46	29	15	79	82
Attempts and no loss	145	660	53	41	22	35	-1 **	96	76
With loss	480	705	92	74	68	28	36	74	88
All vehicle thefts	1,373	3,807	56	65	36	43	31 **	111	117
Theft from motor vehicles	769	2,400	53	61	32	36	14 **	128	86 **
Theft of motor vehicles	481	517	99	94	93	46	34	68	81
Attempted thefts of and from vehicles	123	890	41	34	14	88	107	336	395
Bicycle theft	225	564	69	58	40	70	45	78	161 **
Theft from the person	41	439	35	27	9	5	39	19	1 n.a.
Vandalism	410	2,730	27	56	15	35	-7 **	105	1 **
Wounding	157	626	48	53	25	33	11	86	23 **
Robbery	41	183	47	48	22	38	4	123	13 **
OTHER BCS OFFENCES									
Other household theft	..	1,838	29	..	..	..	21	..	21
Other personal theft	..	1,744	38	..	..	..	-3	..	10
Common assault	..	1,757	26	..	..	..	18	..	25
ALL BCS OFFENCES	..	15,052	43	..	..	..	13	..	36

Notes:

1. **Acquisitive crime**: burglary, thefts of and from vehicles (including attempts), bicycle thefts, theft from the person. **Vandalism**: household property and vehicles. **Violence**: wounding and robbery.

2. Attempted motor vehicle thefts are not easily classifiable as attempts from or of vehicles, and they have previously been counted as 'other household thefts' in the BCS.

3. Police figures have been adjusted to improve comparability with the BCS. See Appendix F for details.

4. Totals do not sum to sub-totals because of rounding. Percentage changes based on unrounded numbers.

5. The statistical significance of changes is calculated on the basis of rates taking population change into account. Double-starred differences are statistically significant at the 5% level (2-tailed). Single-starred differences are significant at the 10% level (2-tailed). Tests on the 1981-1991 differences for theft from the person have not been carried out as classification changes make the two measures incomparable.

6. Source: 1982, 1984, 1988, 1992 BCS (weighted data). Police figures adjusted from *Criminal Statistics, 1991*.

Table A2.5
Levels of reporting, 1981, 1983, 1987 and 1991: BCS estimates

	Proportion incidents reported				% diff	% diff
	1981	1983	1987	1991	87-91	81-91
	%	%	%	%		
COMPARABLE WITH RECORDED OFFENCES						
ACQUISITIVE CRIME	47.1	49.4	50.9	59.5	17 **	26 **
VANDALISM	22.2	22.0	23.7	27.0	14 *	22 **
VIOLENCE	41.5	54.7	43.4	48.4	12	17
ALL COMPARABLE	36.0	38.7	41.1	49.5	20 **	38 **
Burglary	66.2	67.8	62.8	73.0	16 **	10 **
Attempts and no loss	48.4	50.2	43.7	53.0	21 **	9
With loss	84.7	86.6	86.3	92.2	7 **	9 **
All vehicle thefts	40.8	43.1	46.4	55.9	21 **	37 **
Theft from motor vehicles	30.0	38.2	39.9	52.6	32 *	75 **
Theft of motor vehicles	94.9	96.4	94.9	98.6	4 **	4 **
Attempted motor vehicle thefts	30.7	18.0	33.9	41.2	22 *	35 *
Bicycle thefts	63.9	68.2	62.4	69.0	11	8
Theft from the person	31.3	31.2	33.6	34.6	7	15
Vehicle vandalism	10.3	16.1	21.7	24.5	13	138 **
Household vandalism	36.4	31.6	26.2	30.9	18 *	-15
Wounding	40.2	59.6	43.3	47.7	11	20
Robbery	46.5	39.0	43.9	47.2	13	6
OTHER BCS OFFENCES						
Other household thefts	25.2	21.8	23.7	29.1	23 **	16 *
Other personal thefts	22.7	29.8	31.2	38.0	22 *	67 **
Common assault	25.1	30.5	32.5	25.5	-22	2
ALL BCS OFFENCES	31.1	34.1	36.6	43.0	17 **	38 **

Notes:

1. **Acquisitive crime**: burglary, thefts of and from vehicles (including attempts), bicycle thefts, theft from the person. **Vandalism**: household property and vehicles. **Violence**: wounding and robbery.

2. Question 'Did the police come to know about the matter?'. The table includes incidents which occurred in the full recall period, not the calendar year.

3. The statistical significance of changes is calculated on the basis of rates taking population change into account. Double-starred differences are statistically significant at the 5% level (1-tailed). Single-starred differences are significant at the 10% level (1-tailed). Percentage changes based on unrounded numbers. Tests on the 1981-1991 differences for theft from the person have not been carried out as classification changes make the two measures incomparable.

4. Source: 1982, 1984, 1988 and 1992 BCS (weighted data).

Table A2.6
Levels of recording, 1981, 1983, 1987 and 1991: BCS estimates

| | Proportion of reported incidents recorded by the police | | | |
	1981	1983	1987	1991
	%	%	%	%
COMPARABLE WITH RECORDED OFFENCES				
ACQUISITIVE CRIME	78	69	66	62
VANDALISM	33	37	44	56
VIOLENCE	37	36	46	51
ALL COMPARABLE	62	58	60	60
Burglary	71	70	65	63
Attempts and no loss	41	39	37	41
With loss	87	87	84	74
All vehicle thefts	91	75	71	65
Theft from motor vehicles	88	64	68	61
Theft of motor vehicles	106	104	90	94
Attempted motor vehicle thefts	51	53	45	34
Bicycle thefts	91	73	55	58
Theft from the person	26	21	36	27
Vandalism	33	37	44	56
Wounding	41	37	48	53
Robbery	24	36	38	48

Notes:
1. **Acquisitive crime**: burglary, thefts of and from vehicles (including attempts), bicycle thefts, theft from the person. **Vandalism**: household property and vehicles. **Violence**: wounding and robbery.
2. The estimates of recording levels are calculated by expressing adjusted recorded offence figures as a proportion of the estimated number of BCS offences reported to the police.
3. Estimates are only calculable on the sub-set of offences comparable with those recorded by the police; this table therefore excludes common assault, other household theft and other personal theft. Percentage changes based on unrounded numbers.
4. Source: 1982, 1984, 1988 and 1992 BCS (weighted data).

Table A3.1

Reasons for not reporting, by type of offence: unreported incidents 1992 BCS

	Assault	Robbery/ theft from person	Burglary	Auto theft	Bicycle theft	Other household theft	Other personal theft	Vandalism	All offences
Reasons for not reporting:	%	%	%	%	%	%	%	%	%
Too trivial/no loss	40	53	64	58	55	62	49	63	55
Police could do nothing	11	26	25	36	27	24	27	27	25
Police would not be interested	8	16	9	15	17	13	12	16	13
We dealt with matter ourselves/inappropriate for police	40	10	6	4	14	8	3	61	12
Reported to other authorities	4	8	5	1	2	3	23	2	6
Inconvenient to report	5	5	2	4	1	2	5	2	3
Fear reprisals	9	—	1	—	—	—	—	2	2
Fear/dislike police	3	—	2	<1	1	—	2	<1	1
Other	5	3	9	2	—	4	4	3	4
All 'police-related' reasons	19	39	32	46	41	34	36	39	35
Unweighted N	242	98	187	760	74	529	233	768	2,905

Notes:

1. Based on all incidents not reported to the police. 'Vague/not stated' responses are excluded from the base. More than one answer allowed.
2. 'Police-related' reasons comprise: police could do nothing, police would not be interested, fear/dislike police.
3. Source: 1992 BCS (weighted data). Incident-based analyses.

Table A3.2

Proportion of individuals citing particular reasons for not reporting, by type of offence: 1984, 1988 and 1992 BCS

	Police could do nothing			Police would not be interested		
	84	88	92	84	88	92
Type of offence:	%	%	%	%	%	%
Vehicle thefts	20	28	36	4	13	15
Bicycle thefts	30	21	27	10	9	17
Burglary	16	18	25	11	11	9
Other household thefts	13	19	24	10	11	13
Other personal thefts	19	17	27	2	7	12
Robbery/theft from person	23	32	26	2	12	16
Assault	6	10	11	6	5	8
Vandalism	20	27	27	11	13	16

Notes:

1. All categories include attempts.
2. Source: 1988, 1992 BCS (weighted data).

Table A3.3

Reasons for not reporting, by seriousness and type of crime: 1992 BCS

	Vandalism		Assault		Other offences	
	Least	*Most*	*Least*	*Most*	*Least*	*Most*
	Serious		*Serious*		*Serious*	
Reasons for not reporting:	%	%	%	%	%	%
Police could do nothing	21	38	5	16	24	35
Police would not be interested	13	23	9	14	12	15
We dealt with matter ourselves/ inappropriate for police	7	5	29	37	5	9
Fear reprisals	1	8	—	20	—	<1
Fear/dislike police	—	1	1	1	<1	1
All 'police-related' reasons	29	63	19	29	30	45
Unweighted N	468	96	75	91	995	400

Notes:

1. 'Assault' comprises wounding and common assault.
2. 'Least serious' = scores 0-3; 'most serious' = scores 7-20. Figures for intervening seriousness scores omitted.
3. 'Police-related' reasons comprise: police could do nothing, police would not be interested, fear/dislike police. Not all reasons for reporting are shown.
4. Source: 1988 and 1992 BCS (weighted data). Incident-based analyses.

Table A3.4

Measures of satisfaction with police response, by offence: 1992 BCS

Percentage of incidents in which police:					
	Showed enough interest	*Victim had no/ reasonable wait*	*Showed enough effort*	*Kept victim informed*	*Were very/ fairly polite*
Theft of motor vehicle	69	85	63	56	92
Theft from motor vehicle[1]	60	72	50	22	89
Bicycle theft	69	84	58	30	91
Burglary	68	80	61	30	92
Other household theft	68	72	61	29	93
Other personal theft	58	75	52	25	87
Robbery/theft from the person	71	92	61	33	88
Assault	59	81	53	33	67
Vandalism	63	74	51	24	92
All offences	64	77	55	29	88

Notes:

1. Including attempted thefts of and from vehicles.
2. 'Don't know' responses are included in the analysis. Base: all incidents police came to know about.
3. Sample sizes range from 67 to 551 according to offence, total n = 2470.
4. Source: 1992 BCS (weighted data).

Table A4.1

Relative crime rates for residents of different ACORN neighbourhood groups[1]

	Burglary with entry	Burglary attempts	All
LOW RISK			
A. Agricultural areas	30	10	20
K. Better-off retirement areas	70	65	65
B. Modern family housing, higher income areas	60	70	65
J. Affluent suburban housing	80	55	70
C. Older housing of intermediate status	70	70	70
MEDIUM RISK			
E. Better-off council estates	100	90	95
D. Older terraced housing	115	110	115
F. Less well-off council estates	130	175	150
HIGH RISK			
H. Mixed inner metropolitan areas	205	150	180
I. High status non-family areas	240	200	220
G. Poorest council estates	255	330	285
Low risk	65	60	65
Medium risk	115	130	120
High risk	235	235	235
Indexed national average	100	100	100

Notes:
1. ACORN areas are grouped into low, medium and high risk groups on the basis of the level of all crimes measured in the BCS in the 1984, 1988 and 1992 sweeps (see Appendix H).
2. Source: 1984, 1988 and 1992 BCS (weighted data).

Table A4.2
Burglar's mode of entry for burglaries: 1982, 1988 and 1992 BCS

Mode of entry:	Burglary with entry Day	Burglary with entry Night	Attempted burglary Day	Attempted burglary Night	All Day	All Night
	%	%	%	%	%	%
Force/break lock	38	49	59	60	44	54
Break glass	19	27	27	25	21	26
Door/window unlocked/open	30	17	5	7	23	13
Offender had key	8	1	2	7	6	4
Push past person	3	1	2	—	3	1
False pretences	2	1	2	1	2	1
Other	10	10	11	10	10	10
TOTAL	100	100	100	100	100	100
Unweighted N	262	382	121	228	383	610

Notes:
1. More than one response allowed. 'Don't know' and not answered responses are excluded.
2. Source: 1982, 1988, 1992 BCS (weighted data).

Table A4.3
Burglar's mode of entry by type of accommodation: 1988 and 1992 BCS

Means of entry:[2]	Detached/semi detached houses	Terraced houses	Flats maisonettes (ground/ basement)[1]	Flats maisonettes (1st floor or higher)[1]
	%	%	%	%
Force/break lock	51	57	44	48
Break glass	27	22	24	30
Door/window unlocked/open	15	15	21	8
Offender had key	2	4	9	8
Push past person	1	1	3	1
False pretences	<1	2	1	1
Other	10	9	11	9
TOTAL	100	100	100	100
Unweighted N	504	391	77	113

Notes:
1. This was the floor on which the main living accommodation was situated. It is possible that some first floor flats also had rooms on the ground floor.
2. More than one response is allowed. 'Don't know' and not answered responses are excluded.
3. Source: 1988, 1992 BCS (weighted data).

Table A4.4
Point of entry for burglaries by time of burglary: 1982, 1988 and 1992 BCS

	Burglary with entry		Attempted burglary		All	
	Day	Night	Day	Night	Day	Night
Point of entry:[1]	%	%	%	%	%	%
Front door	48	23	51	28	49	25
Front window	4	14	4	10	4	12
Back door	23	17	23	29	23	22
Back window	20	41	21	27	21	35
Side door	4	3	3	5	4	4
Side window	3	5	2	3	3	4
TOTAL	100	100	100	100	100	100
Unweighted N	187	332	400	525	587	857
Direction:	%	%	%	%	%	%
All front	50	36	54	36	51	36
All back	41	55	39	53	41	54
All side	7	7	5	8	7	7
More than 1 approach	2	2	2	4	2	3
TOTAL	100	100	100	100	100	100

Notes:

1. The small percentage of incidents (4%) involving approach from more than one or an unknown direction are excluded. More than one response is allowed. Not all possible points of entry are shown.
2. 'Don't know' and not answered responses are excluded.
3. Source: 1982, 1988, 1992 BCS (weighted data).

Table A4.5

Point of entry for burglaries by property type: 1982, 1988 and 1992 BCS

	Detached/semi detached houses	Terraced houses	Flats/ maisonettes (ground/ basement)[1]	Flats/ maisonettes (1st floor or higher)[1]
Point of entry:[2]	%	%	%	%
Back door	26	28	15	6
Back window	38	32	25	6
Front door	21	30	46	72
Front window	6	10	12	9
Side door	6	2	1	2
Side window	6	2	3	3
TOTAL	100	100	100	100
Direction:	%	%	%	%
All back	61	58	34	12
All front	24	36	62	77
All side	12	4	5	6
More than 1 approach	3	2	—	5
TOTAL	100	100	100	100
Unweighted N	692	570	138	174

Notes:

1. This was the floor on which the main living accommodation was situated. It is possible that some first floor flats also had rooms on the ground floor.
2. The small percentage (4%) of all incidents involving an approach from more than one or an unknown direction are excluded. More than one response is allowed. Not all points of entry are shown.
3. 'Don't know' and not answered responses are excluded.
4. Source: 1982, 1988, 1992 BCS (weighted data).

Table A4.6

Trends in the level of contact with offender in burglaries: 1982, 1984, 1988 and 1992 BCS

	1982	1984	1988	1992	All
Level of contact:	%	%	%	%	%
No-one at home	57	57	53	62	57
At home, but unaware	21	24	25	23	23
At home, aware but can say nothing of offender	11	8	7	5	8
At home, aware and can speak about offender (no violence or threats)	7	10	12	7	9
Violence or threats used	4	1	3	3	3
TOTAL	100	100	100	100	100
Unweighted N	515	559	613	634	2,321

Notes:
1. 'Don't know' and not answered responses are excluded.
2. Source: 1982, 1984, 1988, 1992 BCS (weighted data).

Table A4.7

Level of contact with offender in burglaries, by time and type of burglary: 1982, 1984, 1988 and 1992 BCS

	Attempts			Entry		
	Day	Night	All[2]	Day	Night	All[2]
Level of contact:	%	%	%	%	%	%
No-one at home	79	24	46	72	54	65
At home, but unaware	5	32	22	17	33	24
At home, aware, but can say nothing of offender	3	23	15	1	4	2
At home, aware and can speak about offender (no violence or threats)	13	19	15	6	5	5
Violence or threats used	<1	2	1	5	4	4
TOTAL	100	100	100	100	100	100
Unweighted N	259	539	914	569	711	1,407

Notes:
1. 'Don't know' and not answered responses are excluded.
2. The 'all' columns include cases for which the time of the incident was unknown (which were mainly when the house was unoccupied).
3. Source: 1982, 1984, 1988, 1992 BCS (weighted data).

Table A4.8
Items stolen, burglaries with loss only: 1992 BCS

Proportion of burglaries involving loss of:	%
Cash (excluding money from meters)	41
Jewellery	41
Video	37
Stereo/hi-fi equipment (excluding car equipment)	23
Television	20
Clothes	14
Handbag/wallet/purse	13
Camera	12
Documents/papers	8
Cheque/credit cards	7
Silverware	6
Tools	4
Money from meter	2
Bicycle	2
Car/van	1
Motorcycle	<1
Car/van parts/accessories	<1
Other	36
Unweighted N	346

Notes:
1. More than one answer allowed. Don't know responses are included in the base.
2. Source: 1992 BCS (weighted data).

Table A4.9
Value of property stolen: 1992 BCS

	Burglary with loss	All
Value of property stolen:		
Less than £50	11	56
£50-£99	6	3
£100-£249	14	7
£250-£499	14	7
£500-£999	20	10
£1,000-£4,999	29	15
£5,000 or more	6	3
Total	100	100
Mean value of property stolen	£1,320	£650
Unweighted N	332	661

Notes:
1. Mean loss figures are rounded. First column based on incidents with loss only.
2. Source: 1992 BCS (weighted data).

Table A4.10
Costs of damage in burglary: 1992 BCS

	Burglary with entry	Attempted burglary	All
Cost of damage:	.		
Less than £50	66	79	71
£50-£99	9	8	8
£100-£249	11	6	9
£250-£499	4	3	4
£500-£999	5	2	4
£1,000-£4,999	5	2	4
£5,000 or more	1	—	1
Total	100	100	100
Mean cost of damage	£260	£70	£190
Unweighted N	380	210	590

Notes:
1. Mean loss figures are rounded.
2. Source: 1992 BCS (weighted data).

Table A5.1
Car theft: location and timing (percentages): 1982, 1984, 1988 and 1992 BCS

	Daytime	Evening/ Night-time	Total
Home:			
Domestic garages	—	1	1
Off-street parking and estate car parks	1	20	22
Street near home	2	32	34
Total home	4	53	57
Elsewhere:			
Work			
Car parks[1]	4	3	6
Street near work	2	1	3
Other			
Car parks	7	10	17
Other street	5	9	14
Other	1	2	2
Total elsewhere	19	24	43

Notes:
1. Including garages, on-site parking and parking "at work" not on the street.
2. Excluding victims who did not know when the offence had happened.
3. Unweighted N = 4,983 (thefts).
4. Source: 1982, 1984, 1988 and 1992 BCS (weighted data).

Table A5.2
Losses from car theft: 1992 BCS

	Thefts of cars (recovered)	Thefts of cars (not recovered)	Thefts from cars	Attempts	Total[2]
Value of property stolen:					
Less £50	see	—	33	n.a.	32
£50-£99	note 1	—	18	n.a.	17
£100-£499		6	41	n.a.	40
£500-£999		8	5	n.a.	5
£1,000 or more		86	3	n.a.	6
Value of property damaged:					
Less £50	39	n.a.	64	44	57
£50-£99	4	n.a.	13	21	14
£100-£499	22	n.a.	20	28	22
£500-£999	11	n.a.	2	5	4
£1,000 or more	24	n.a.	1	1	3
Value of property stolen and damaged:[3]					
Less £50	39	—	27	44	32
£50-£99	4	—	16	21	16
£100-£499	22	6	45	28	37
£500-£999	11	8	9	5	8
£1,000 or more	24	86	4	1	7
Insurance:					
% incidents covered by insurance (involving theft/damage only)	93	98	66	85	74
% insured incidents where claim made	71	100	43	36	46
Unweighted N	158	44	825	337	1,364

Notes:

1. When cars were stolen and recovered, some respondents discounted any loss and failed to say how much the car had been worth before the theft, or said nothing was stolen and therefore missed the questions on value, although items may still have been stolen from the car.
2. The total figures include a small number of thefts of cars for which information on recovery was missing. They exclude those cases described in note 1.
3. For recovered cars, the total cost refers only to the cost of any damage and excludes the cost of items stolen with the car (see note 1).
4. Percentages do not add to 100% because of rounding.
5. Source: 1992 BCS (weighted data).

Table A6.1
Number of assaults of different types, 1991: BCS estimates

	Men (000s)	Women (000s)	Total (000s)	% increase 1981-1991	% male offences	% female offences	% all offences Men	% all offences Women
Domestic	70	460	530	69	4	46	3	17
Home-based	160	100	260	49	10	10	6	4
Street	430	80	510	-8	26	8	16	3
Pub/clubs	350	80	420	-7	21	8	13	3
Work-based	250	110	350	110	15	11	9	4
Mugging	140	120	260	3	8	12	5	5
Other assault	260	40	300	19	16	4	10	1
All violence	1,660	990	2,640	22	100	100	63	38

Notes:
1. Rates for first three victim forms adjusted to reflect five victim form rate.
2. Source: 1992 BCS (unweighted data).

Table A6.2
Age and gender in violent crime: 1988 and 1992 BCS

	Men 16-29	Men 30-59	Men 60+	All Men	Women 16-29	Women 30-59	Women 60+	All Women	Total
	% of incidents against different age groups								
Domestic	9	7	1	**16**	56	27	1	**84**	100%
Home-based	27	17	6	**51**	23	23	4	**50**	100%
Street	57	27	2	**85**	10	4	1	**15**	100%
Pubs/clubs	75	8	1	**84**	15	2	—	**17**	100%
Work-based	37	29	1	**67**	21	12	—	**33**	100%
Mugging	34	13	3	**49**	15	29	7	**51**	100%
Other assault	71	8	1	**80**	13	7	—	**20**	100%
All violence	45	16	2	**62**	23	13	1	**38**	100%

Note:
1. Source: 1988 and 1992 BCS (weighted data).

Table A6.3
Risks of violence by age and sex, incident rates per 10,000, 1991: BCS estimates

Rates per 10,000 adults	Domestic	Home-based	Street	Pub/ club	Work-based	Mugging	Other assault
Men	33	80	212	170	121	71	128
16-29	62	186	471	583	228	193	438
30-59	28	59	174	30	126	34	29
60+	14	9	15	19	0	18	0
Women	210	44	38	37	49	50	18
16-29	580	83	122	151	107	87	37
30-59	140	43	16	6	48	49	19
60+	16	14	8	0	0	20	0

Notes:
1. Rates based on the first three victim forms completed by respondents.
2. Source: 1992 BCS (weighted data).

Table A6.4
Time of day of violence: 1988 and 1992 BCS

	Morning 6am-noon	Afternoon noon-6pm	Evening 6pm-midnight	Night	Not known precisely
	% of incidents at each time of day				
Domestic	11	21	46	8	14
Home-based	11	21	48	9	10
Street/transport	7	23	54	15	2
Pubs/clubs	—	5	82	13	—
Work-based	13	30	45	2	11
Mugging	14	18	58	5	5
Other assaults	8	32	36	11	13
All violence	8	21	54	10	7
Unweighted N	88	211	466	96	45

Note:
1. Source: 1988, 1992 BCS (weighted data).

Table A6.5
Age of offenders: 1988 and 1992 BCS

	Of school age	16-25	Over 25
	% of offenders in each age group		
Domestic	2	40	57
Home-based	5	52	37
Street assaults	7	65	22
Pub/club assaults	—	68	20
Work-based	8	40	51
Mugging	4	67	14
Other assaults	3	64	14
All violence	4	57	32
Unweighted N	38	505	297

Notes:
1. Percentages do not add to 100 where some incidents involved more than one assailant or no information was available. This was the case for 15% of muggings and 18% of 'other assaults'.
2. Source: 1988, 1992 BCS (weighted data).

Table A6.6
Emotional effects and medical help: 1988 and 1992 BCS

	% 'very much' emotionally affected		*% who saw doctor*	
	Men	*Women*	*Men*	*Women*
Domestic	16	40	15	24
Home-based	23	27	27	16
Street	12	28	13	8
Pub/club	23	16	16	10
Work-based	10	17	10	9
Mugging	52	36	28	8
Other assaults	16	29	13	16
All violence	19	32	16	17
Unweighted N	543	366	544	366

Note:
1. Source: 1988 and 1992 BCS (weighted data).

Table A6.7
Percentage of victims who felt responsible in some way for what happened: 1988 and 1992 BCS

	Male victims	Female victims	All victims
	% of incidents in which victims felt a degree of responsibility		
Domestic	38	23	26
Home-based	17	6	11
Street	7	1	6
Pubs/clubs	13	22	14
Work-based	10	6	9
Mugging	0	9	4
Other assaults	21	15	20
All violence	12	15	13
Unweighted N	544	364	908

Note:
1. Source: 1988 and 1992 BCS (weighted data).

Appendix B
Trends in different acquisitive crimes

This appendix discusses trends in different types of acquisitive crime, following on from the more general discussion in Chapter 2. Within the acquisitive crime category, some offences have risen more than others; most have increased more on police figures; and one (bicycle theft) has risen more judged by the BCS.

Burglary

Trends in *burglary with loss* are generally similar according to both the BCS and police figures, although the picture for *attempted burglary* is more complex. This is discussed further in Chapter 4, which also takes up trends in burglary over the last twenty years, made possible by drawing in information from the General Household Survey.

Theft from the person

It is difficult to say much about trends in theft from the person since 1981 as classification in the first two surveys is somewhat different from the later two; this upsets comparability. However, between 1987 and 1991, thefts from the person increased by 39% according to the BCS. This is higher than the increase in police figures (5%)—but the difference is not statistically significant, due to the relatively small numbers of incidents.

Vehicle thefts

Vehicle thefts of all kinds have more than doubled since 1981 according to both sources, although the increase in police figures since 1987 is steeper. *Attempted thefts of and from vehicles* have risen most rapidly since 1981— 395% (BCS statistics) and 336% (police figures). This suggests that not only are car thieves more active, but that cars have become better protected— whether by manufacturers or owners. (Security and car theft are returned to in Chapter 5.) Police figures have shown a sharper rise in thefts *from* motor vehicles than the BCS since 1981, and this is statistically reliable. It is consistent with this that reporting has increased significantly since 1981. The respective trends in thefts *of* vehicles are not statistically distinguishable. Figure B.1 shows details.

Figure B.1
Indexed trends in different offence groups, 1981-1991 (all 1981 numbers = 100)

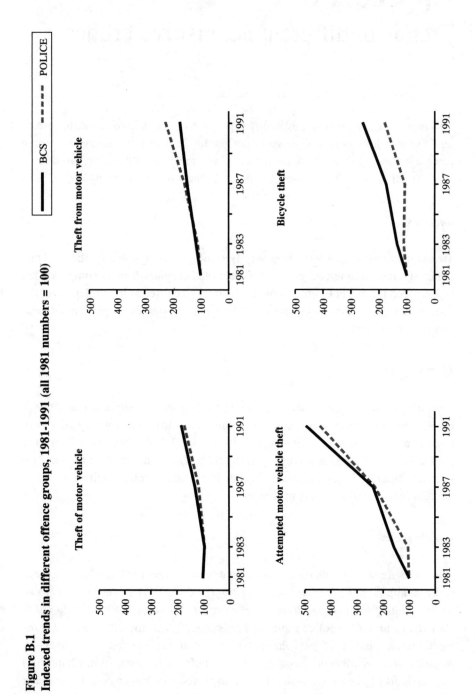

Bicycle theft

Over the full period 1981 to 1991, bicycle thefts have risen by 161% according to the BCS, and by 78% according to police figures—a statistically significant difference (Figure B.1). The sizeable increase evidenced by both sources may be attributable in part to increasing ownership of more valuable types of bikes (eg 'mountain bikes').

However, the pattern of growth according to the two series has differed somewhat. Between the first (1981) and third (1987) surveys, bicycle thefts according to the BCS rose much more than police statistics indicated (80% compared to 5%)—a difference which cannot be accounted for by sampling error. In this period, there was a fall in the reporting of bicycle thefts—which would in part explain this—as well as a fall in the number of reported offences recorded by the police. In the last four years, however, the BCS trend has slowed to below that of police figures (although the divergence between the trends is not statistically significant); and reporting and recording have stabilised.

Insurance issues may underlie the swings in reporting. The earlier part of the 1980s saw insurance companies becoming increasingly inclined to ask for separate cover for bikes. The BCS indicated a drop during this period in the number of insured victims—which is consistent with a fall in reporting, since fewer victims would have felt the need to notify the police for insurance reasons. Since 1987, the proportion of victims with insurance cover has increased, perhaps because cyclists have accepted the need to protect themselves against increasing risks. (Although numbers are fairly small, the indications are that reporting has increased for insured victims of bike theft, while remaining static for non-insured victims.)

Appendix C
Multivariate models for victimisation risks and victims' satisfaction with police

Logistic regression is a multivariate statistical technique which allows one to see whether any independent variable (eg area of residence or age) thought to be related to a dependent variable (eg risk of burglary) is statistically important once possible associations with other variables have been taken into account. For example, dwelling type and area of residence are both related to the risk of being burgled, but they are also related to each other (eg houses are more likely to be found in lower risk areas and flats in higher risk areas). Logistic regression means that one can assess whether dwelling type has a correlation—and by implication a causal link—with risks in its own right and not in a way that is simply explained by its association with area. (The technique of logistic regression is also used to look at which reporting victims thought the police showed sufficient interest in their case (Chapter 3). The model for this is described at the end of the Appendix.)

The following tables look at factors correlated with risks of burglary, car theft and violence. Results for 'main effects' models are presented, although where interactions between effects were found to be significant, these are discussed in the text.[1] For each factor listed in the tables (eg inner city residence), two measures are given:

a)   The coefficient associated with that factor as estimated by the logistic regression model;

b)   An 'estimated change in probability'. This corresponds to the increase in risk that a household with the average risk of being victimised would experience, if it had the specified attribute, all other things being held constant. Thus, for example, the risk for a household outside an inner city who has on other counts an average chance of being burgled —4.7%— would increase by 5.1%—to around 9.8%—if they were located in an inner city area. (All other variables, such as dwelling type and household structure, are held constant in this). It should be noted that these probabilities *cannot* be used to calculate predicted probabilities for particular sub-groups, in that increased probabilities are not straightforwardly additive; thus, the 9.8% risk for the average household in an inner city area will not rise by a precise 4.0% if they have no security devices, though their risks may well rise by some factor.

---

[1]In 'main effects' model, it is assumed that the effect of a factor is the same for all cases. No account is taken of possible variations in how a factor operates for different sub-groups.

135

The models presented here enable us to examine which groups have high risks of victimisation *relative* to the overall average. They cannot be regarded as powerful predictors of victimisation *per se*. Thus, while we are able to say that men are more likely than women to experience assault, it is unlikely that we shall be able to identify any group of men who have more than an evens chance of falling victim to an assault in a year. There are various reasons why the models are not powerful in predicting victimisation *per se*:

a) *The nature of BCS data.* In a survey such as the BCS, it is difficult to capture adequately some of the more idiosyncratic factors affecting risk. For example, the make and model of an owner's car may influence car theft risks, but the survey would not count enough cars of any one type to test this out. Similarly, though living in a bedsit may lead to higher burglary risks, insufficient bedsit residents will be covered to examine differences in their risks.

b) *Omission of influential factors.* Some factors affecting victimisation may have been omitted from the analysis (and may not have been collected in the survey). For example, the present models do not include much about the social dynamics of areas. And in relation to burglary, for instance, the survey collected relatively little information about the specific vulnerability of a dwelling to do with its layout, visibility etc; indeed it would have been difficult to do so.

c) *The nature of crime.* Given that most individuals, even in higher risk groups, are not subject to the crimes covered by the BCS, there may be a degree of genuine element of chance operating in victimisation. This will reduce the predictive strength of the models.

Burglary (Chapter 4)

All burglary

Table C.1 presents the factors associated with being subject to a burglary (with entry or attempts). Area had a strong effect on victimisation risks, as did the lack of security devices.

Table C.1

Significant factors in the risks of all burglary

Significant effects:	Coefficient[1]	Estimated change in probability (%)
ACORN risk:[1]		
High risk	1.03 **	7.4
Medium risk	0.40 **	2.1
Inner city areas	0.79 **	5.1
No security devices	0.66 **	4.0
Flats/maisonettes/rooms	0.36 **	1.9
Only one adult in household	0.35 **	1.8
Spent two or more evenings out in last week	0.25 **	1.3
Constant	-4.37	
Average probability of victimisation		4.7
Number of cases in final model: 8,631		

Notes:

1. ** indicates coefficients significant at the 5% level; * indicates coefficients significant at the 10% level. Significance tests are based on the Wald statistic ($[Coefficient/se(coeff)]^2$). Strictly speaking, such tests should take design effects into acount—therefore factors of marginal significance should be regarded with caution.

2. High risk ACORN neighbourhoods are ACORN groups G (council estates— category III), H (mixed inner city metropolitan areas) and I (high status non-family areas); medium risk ACORN areas are ACORN groups D (older terraced housing), E (council estates—category I) and F (council estates—category II).

3. Other factors tested were: tenure, income, council areas, manual/non-manual status of head of household, sex of head of household, sex of respondent, marital status of respondent, number of calls made by interviewer, presence of children under 16 or under 5, age of household head and ethnic origin of respondent.

4. Source: unweighted data, 1988 and 1992 BCS, households living in their present address on the 1st of January of the preceding year.

Burglary with entry

The model for *burglary with entry* was similar to that for all burglary, except that dwelling type no longer exerted a statistically significant effect on risks. The smaller number of victimisations may explain this. Also, residents in medium risk ACORN neighbourhood types ran similar risks of burglary with entry to those living in low risk ACORN neighbourhood types.

Table C.2
Significant factors in the risks of burglary with entry

Significant effects:	Coefficient	Estimated change in probability (%)
No security devices	0.82 **	3.5
ACORN risk:		
High risk	0.81 **	3.4
Medium risk	0.16	0.5
Inner city areas	0.74 **	3.0
Only one adult in household	0.36 **	1.2
Spent two or more evenings out in last week	0.24 *	0.8
Constant	-4.48	
Average probability of victimisation		2.9
Number of cases in final model: 8,948		

Note:

1. Source: unweighted data, 1988 and 1992 BCS, households living in their present address on the 1st of January of the preceding year.

Attempted burglary

For **attempted burglary** only inner city and ACORN risk group were found to have a significant impact upon risks. It may be that attempted burglary is affected by very different factors from burglary with entry, although the smaller number of victimisations may have made it more difficult to find significant associations.

Table C.3
Significant factors in the risks of attempted burglary

Significant effects:	Coefficient	Estimated change in probability (%)
ACORN risk:		
High risk	0.74 **	2.5
Medium risk	0.56 **	1.7
Inner city areas	0.71 **	2.4
Constant	-4.27	
Average probability of victimisation		2.4
Number of cases in final model: 18,221		

Note:

1. Source: unweighted data, 1988 and 1992 BCS, households living in their present address on the 1st of January of the preceding year.

Interactions

In logistic regression models, it is usual to test for what are called 'interactions' between the main individual risk factors since they may operate differently for particular sub-groups. Such interactions mean that the effect of two individually important variables (eg, area and type of accommodation) can, when taken together, be reduced or enhanced.

In further modelling, three interactions were found for risks of all burglary, and three were found for burglary with entry, one of which was the same as that for all burglary. The interactions were:

a)   *Number of adults and dwelling type (all burglary)*
     Although living in a flat or being a one adult household are individually associated with higher risks (Table C.1), there is less of an household size effect for people in houses, and conversely more of an effect for those in flats. Thus, one adult households in *houses* were not particularly much more at risk (perhaps because of specific features of their neighbourhood or the type of people they are). However, single adult households in 'flats' were at particular risk—maybe because the units concerned are especially insecure accommodation such as bedsits, or non-self-contained flats.

b)   *Occupancy and security devices (all burglary)*
     While having few security devices increased risks, as did leaving the home unoccupied, there was an interaction such that risks for houses with lower security protection were *not* increased by lower levels of occupancy. This could indicate that such households are vulnerable to burglary whether or not they are empty.

c)   *Number of adults and security devices (all burglary and burglary with entry)*
     This interaction operated such that security devices had a stronger impact on reducing risks for households with one adult rather than for those with two or more adults. It may be that larger households pose more of an occupancy barrier to burglars than single adult households, so that security devices are less important in their own right.

d)   *Area type (inner city; ACORN neighbourhood) and occupancy (burglary with entry)*
     The link between lower occupancy and higher burglary risk was weaker *outside* inner cities than within them. This may indicate that other unmeasured factors are at work in reducing the effect of occupancy outside cities. It does not appear to suggest that leaving the house empty in inner cities is a particularly risky activity since—in a rather contrary way—lower occupancy also had a weaker effect on risks *within* higher risk ACORN groups. In particular, in the very highest risk areas (inner city areas within the highest risk ACORN groups), occupancy appeared to have little impact on burglary risks; other factors may well outweigh occupancy levels.

139

Thefts involving cars (Chapter 5)

All thefts

Variables relating to area of residence, income, consumer durables, and parking facilities all emerged as important in risks of all thefts (Table C.4). Consumer durables and higher income will both be tapping the 'attractiveness' of the car; that ownership of 'higher-tech' household consumer durables remains important independent of income suggests that some cars, even those owned by better-off households, provide more tempting opportunities to thieves than others.

Table C.4
Significant factors in the risks of all thefts involving cars

Significant effects:	*Coefficient*[1]	*Estimated change in probability (%)*
Inner city	0.58 **	10.2
Higher household income	0.47 **	8.1
'Consumerist' household[2]	0.41 **	6.9
Flats/terraces	0.37 **	6.2
Low car ownership in area[3]	0.25 **	4.1
Street parking at night	0.21 **	3.3
Constant	-2.21	
Average probability of victimisation		18.4
Number of cases in final model: 2,517		

Notes:
1. See Note 1 to Table C.1.
2. 'Consumerist' households are those which owned three or more of five items: a portable colour TV, a VCR, a CD player, a personal computer, or a car radio or cassette.
3. Lower car-owning areas are those with 65% of household or less owning cars.
4. Other factors tested were: tenure, council areas, manual/non-manual status of head of household and car radio/cassette.
5. Source: unweighted data, 1988 BCS. Based on thefts of and from cars, and attempts at such.

Thefts around the home

Unlike the model of all thefts, only household income did not emerge as also significant for incidents around the home (Table C.5). Not surprisingly, factors connected with the home location (such as where cars were parked at night, dwelling type and level of car ownership in the area) were important.

Table C.5
Significant factors in the risks of thefts involving cars around the home

Significant effects:	Coefficient	Estimated change in probability (%)
Inner city	0.63 **	7.2
Flats/terraces	0.44 **	4.7
Street parking at night	0.44 **	4.6
'Consumerist' household	0.35 **	3.6
Low car ownership in area	0.32 **	3.3
Constant	-2.96	
Average probability of victimisation		9.9
Number of cases in final model: 3,441		

Note:
1. Source: unweighted data, 1988 BCS. Based on thefts of and from cars, and attempts at such taking place in private and semi-private parking places by home, or the streets by home.

Thefts involving cars away from the home

Thefts away from the home were more influenced by the attractiveness of the car, which will be related to income and ownership of consumer durables (Table C.6). However, inner city residence remains important (presumably because 'inner city' covers a large enough area for residents to still be parking their vehicles there when away from home).

Table C.6
Significant factors in the risks of thefts involving cars away from the home

Significant effects:	Coefficient	Estimated change in probability (%)
Higher household income	0.54 **	5.7
Inner city	0.50 **	5.3
'Consumerist' household	0.34 **	3.3
Constant	-2.65	
Average probability of victimisation		9.6
Number of cases in final model: 2,942		

Note:
1. Source: unweighted data, 1988 BCS. Based on thefts of and from cars, and attempts taking place away from home.

Interactions

In further modelling, various interactions were found for risks of theft involving cars. These were:

a) *Levels of car ownership and parking behaviour (all thefts and thefts around the home)*
    This interaction operates such that the reduction in risk for those who park their cars 'safely'—essentially off-street—at night is only found in areas where car ownership is high; it is not noticeable in areas where car ownership is lower. In areas where car ownership is high, then, there may be enough 'good targets' parked in unsafe locations, so those in safer locations are passed over.

b) *Household income and type of accommodation (all thefts)*
    This operates such that the higher risks associated with high income households are only observed for residents of detached/semi-detached houses. It may be that higher-income owners in these types of houses have cars which are more attractive to thieves which are stolen predominantly away from home.

c) *Inner city area and consumer durables (thefts around the home)*
    With this interaction, the higher risks observed for those with more consumer durables operates only outside inner city areas; in inner city areas, ownership of consumer durables has little impact. It is difficult to interpret this, but it may be that offenders in inner city areas are less choosy about the type of cars they target.

Violence (Chapter 6)

Acquaintance violence against men

Demographic factors emerged as important in determining risks, as did the level of incivilities in the area (Table C.7). Younger and unmarried men (particularly those in the 16-29 age group) ran higher risks, although so did men with children under 16 in the household.

Table C.7
Significant factors in the risks of acquaintance violence—men only

Significant effects:	Coefficient[1]	Estimated change in probability (%)
Age		
16-29	2.24 **	14.1
30-59	1.27 **	4.8
Marital status:		
Separated/divorced	1.33 **	5.2
Single	1.18 **	4.3
High incivilities	0.97 **	3.2
Children under 16	0.61 **	1.6
Constant	-6.32	
Average risk		2.0
Number of cases in final model: 9,172		

Notes:
1. See Note 1 to Table C.1
2. Other factors tested were: income per household members, inner city area, manual/non-manual status of head of household, residential mobility, number of adults in the household, drinking behaviour, household income.
3. Source: unweighted data, 1988 and 1992 BCS.

Acquaintance violence against women

The model for acquaintance violence against women mirrored that for men, with the same demographic and area factors being important (Table C.8).

Table C.8
Significant factors in the risks of acquaintance violence—women only

Significant effects:	Coefficient	Estimated change in probability (%)
Age		
16-29	2.37 **	14.9
30-59	1.40 **	5.3
Marital status:		
Separated/divorced	1.72 **	7.7
Single	0.98 **	2.9
High incivilities	1.07 **	3.4
Children under 16	0.63 **	1.6
Constant	-6.63	
Average risk		1.9
Number of cases in final model: 10533		

Note:
1. Source: unweighted data, 1988 and 1992 BCS.

Stranger violence against men

The model here differs. Age of victim and area of residence were still associated with risks of stranger violence (Table C.9). However, lifestyle variables also emerged as important—with higher risks for men going out frequently, and/or to the pub. (Increased risks were only associated with residents of the highest risk ACORN neighbourhood types and those with the highest frequency of going out.)

Table C.9
Significant factors in the risks of stranger violence—men only

Significant effects:	*Coefficient*	*Estimated change in probability (%)*
Age		
16-29	2.76 **	31.4
30-59	1.37 **	8.5
Evenings out		
4+	0.68 **	3.0
2-3	0.17	0.6
High incivilities	0.64 **	2.8
Visited pub	0.54 **	2.2
ACORN risk:		
High risk	0.50 **	2.0
Medium risk	-0.02	-0.1
Non-manual HoH	0.39 **	1.5
Constant	-5.54	
Average risk		3.3
Number of cases in final model: 4,391		

Note:
1. Source: unweighted data, 1988 and 1992 BCS.

Stranger violence against women

Very different models are obtained according to whether or not mugging is included. Mugging accounts for a significant proportion of stranger violence against women, mainly in the form of snatch thefts. These differ from other incidents of violence against women, being committed mostly against older women and very often involving no injury. *Including* mugging, only area of residence and marital status emerged as important (Table C.10). *Excluding* mugging, the model bore more resemblance to that of stranger violence against men, with age, area of residence and lifestyle having significant effects (Table C.11). As with men, only the highest risk ACORN neighbourhood type and highest frequency of going out were significantly associated with higher risks.

Table C.10

**Significant factors in the risks of stranger violence (including mugging)—
women only**

Significant effects:	Coefficient	Estimated change in probability (%)
Marital status		
Single	1.33 **	3.3
Separated/divorced	0.80 **	1.5
High incivilities	1.00 **	2.1
ACORN risk		
High risk	0.94 **	1.9
Medium risk	0.54 **	0.9
Constant	-5.38	
Average risk		1.2
Number of cases in final model: 10,555		

Note:
1. Source: unweighted data, 1988 and 1992 BCS.

Table C.11

**Significant factors in the risks of stranger violence (excluding mugging)—
women only**

Significant effects:	Coefficient	Estimated change in probability (%)
Age		
16-29	2.17 **	5.3
30-59	1.11 **	1.5
ACORN risk		
High risk	1.00 **	1.2
Medium risk	0.61 *	0.6
Evenings out		
4+	0.75 **	0.8
2-3	-0.27	-0.2
Constant	-6.75	
Average risk		0.7
Number of cases in final model: 7,928		

Note:
1. Source: unweighted data, 1988 and 1992 BCS.

Interactions

Further modelling showed interactions in the 'main effects' models for women:

a) *Level of incivilities in the area and age (acquaintance violence against women)*
   This interaction does not affect the interpretation of age differences within

area type—for each, younger women still face higher risks of violence—but serves only to adjust the exact estimates of age effects in each area type.

b) *ACORN neighbourhood type and marital status (stranger violence against women including mugging)*
As above, this interaction has little impact on the interpretation of the effects of marital status and area—single and separated or divorced women remain at higher risk in each area, although there is some indication that the impact of marital status is less in higher risk ACORN areas.

c) *ACORN neighbourhood type and evenings out (stranger violence against women excluding mugging)*
This interaction tended to increase the impact of going out in high risk ACORN areas. Where risks of violence are particularly high, greater exposure (in the form of going out) seems to have a stronger impact.

Ethnic origin and violence

Further tests were carried out to see whether respondents of Afro-Caribbean or Asian (here defined as Indian, Pakistani or Bangladeshi) origin faced significantly different risks to whites once other risk factors had been controlled for. No significant 'ethnic origin' effects were found in any of the models for men. However, in the models for women, it was found that:

a) *women of Indian, Pakistani or Bangladeshi origin were less likely to report incidents of acquaintance violence, after other factors had been controlled for*. This is more likely to reflect under-reporting of incidents to the survey, rather than a genuine difference in risks. (Women of Asian origin are also under-represented in the sample as a whole, which may reflect both a reluctance to take part or English language difficulties.)

b) *women of Afro-Caribbean origin were more likely to report a stranger assault (excluding mugging), after other factors had been controlled for.*

Interest shown by police (Chapter 3)

Having face-to-face contact with the police was most influential in whether victims thought the police had showed enough interest in their case. Measures of whether the police had 'done their job' also had an effect: whether they had found out who had done it, whether property was recovered, and whether the victim had claimed on insurance (the police presumably fulfilling what was required). However, victims were less content with the level of interest shown in incidents where they knew the offender before, and in offences rated more seriously. Victim characteristics (head of household status, age and race) also had an effect.

Table C.12

Significant factors in whether police showed enough interest in what victim had to say

Significant effects:	Coefficient[1]	Estimated change in probability (%)
Had face-to-face contact with police	1.10 **	19.9
Perpetrator identified	0.70 **	14.0
Offender known casually/well	-.50 **	-12.1
Offence perceived as very serious	-.33 **	-7.8
Property recovered	0.34 **	7.4
Non-manual head of household	0.33 **	7.1
Claimed on insurance	0.23 **	5.0
Aged over 30	0.21 **	4.7
Non-white	-.19 **	-4.4
Constant	-.55	

Overall proportion of victims satisfied with interest shown: 64.8%
Number of cases in model = 2,560

Notes:

1. See Note 1 to Table C.1.

2. Other factors tested were: sex of respondent, tenure, employment status, ACORN and type of offence.

3. Source: unweighted data, 1992 core and ethnic minority boost samples, reporting victims.

Appendix D
Survey design and methods

The coverage of the survey

The 1992 British Crime Survey (BCS) aimed not only to estimate crime levels, but to provide a range of extra information on matters related to crime (see Table 1.1 in Chapter 1 for the list of topics covered). To ensure comparability, most questions on victimisation were the same as in previous sweeps of the BCS, as were those on fear of crime. The questions on victim support organisations, security behaviour and household fires were all modified versions of those used in 1988. Questions on Neighbourhood Watch Schemes were a sub-set of those asked in the 1988 BCS. Obscene telephone calls were covered briefly in the 1982 survey, but in more detail in 1992. The sections on attitudes to crime and sentencing, and drug use and awareness, were new. Detailed questions on contacts with the police were also included in the 1988 survey; the questions in 1992, while covering the same ground, were structured somewhat differently, incorporating improvements suggested by 1988 analysis. Questions on the Police Complaints Authority were modified from those used in 1988.

Questions differed for the three samples included in the 1992 BCS: the 'core' sample; the ethnic minority booster sample; and (new to the survey) the sample of 12-15 year olds in households where an adult interview had been obtained. Questions to teenagers focused on their experience as victims at school and in public places. As with the questions on victimisation, those on contacts with the police had necessarily to differ to reflect the younger age involved. More details of the three samples are given later.

Structure of the questionnaire

These were five parts to the adult questionnaire: the *Main Questionnaire*; the *Victim Form*; the *Follow-up Questionnaire*, the *Demographic Questionnaire* and the *Self-completion Questionnaire* (which covered self-reported offending for 16-19 years olds, and the questions about drugs for those aged 16-59). There were two versions of the Follow-up Questionnaire, one of which concentrated almost entirely on the police. The largely attitudinal questions in the two Follow-up Questionnaires did not require the same precision as those in other parts, so the sample could be reduced. Questions on household fires however were included in both Follow-up Questionnaires to increase precision.

149

One adult respondent per selected household completed the Main, Demographic and one or other version of the Follow-up Questionnaire. Victim Forms were completed only by those who said they had experienced a crime since the beginning of 1991. Victims could complete up to five Victim Forms, with the fourth and fifth being a shortened version of the full form (a new procedure).

Adult victims answering all four parts of the questionnaire were interviewed for about an hour on average; non-victims were interviewed for about 40 minutes. The teenage questionnaire, which was usually completed while the adult interview was taking place, was designed to take around 20-30 minutes.

Sampling

Core sample

Most BCS analyses are based either on *households* or *individuals*. The core sample was designed to give, after appropriate weighting, both a representative cross-section of private households in England and Wales, and of individuals aged 16 and over in such households.

Sampling frame

The sampling procedures used in 1992 differed from those in earlier sweeps. Previously, the Electoral Register had been used as a sampling frame, providing a listing of *individuals* for interview. However, for the 1992 BCS, the Postcode Address File (PAF) was used as the sampling frame. The PAF generates a sample of *addresses*, rather than individuals.

The PAF comprises a listing of all addresses in England and Wales. It is divided into 'small' and 'large' users—the former being used for the BCS as it corresponds most closely to private households (the latter corresponds more to businesses and institutions). The correspondence is not perfect, however. Because of this and other reasons, the proportion of ineligible addresses (ie, small businesses or empty/demolished buildings) in PAF samples tends to be higher than that drawn from the Electoral Register.

The main argument for switching to PAF was that it is now a more complete and accessible listing of the population. In particular, the Electoral Register was believed to under-represent young people, the unemployed, ethnic minorities and those in rented accommodation (Todd and Butcher, 1982). Since a major feature of the BCS is to determine *trends* in crime, it is important to distinguish genuine shifts in the rate of crime from differences due to changes in procedures or questioning between surveys. There was reason to believe that a switch to PAF sampling might lead to differences in the sample selected and concomitant shifts in crime rates, ie if groups previously under-represented had different experiences of crime to others. A detailed comparison of PAF and ER sampling was undertaken to assess whether any such 'PAF effect' existed and, if so, what procedures were needed to adjust for it. In brief, there was a PAF effect in the expected direction, although not great enough to merit any adjustments to be made for the change in sampling frame.

Sampling methods

As in previous years, inner city areas were oversampled by a factor of about two. The 1992 definition of inner cities approximates to that used in 1988, and classifies constituencies on the basis of population density, level of owner-occupied tenure and social class profile.

The sample design required selection of 70 inner city, and 219 non-inner city, constituencies (289 in total). Having defined constituencies as inner city or otherwise, the following procedures were used to generate samples of addresses for each group separately. The selection of the inner city constituencies is described in detail; the method for non-inner city constituencies was analogous. There are five steps in the selection of respondents:

i.   Selection of constituencies

Constituencies were sorted:

(a)   by standard region;

(b)   within standard region, by population density;

(c)   population density was divided into three roughly equal bands: then within standard region *and* population density band, constituencies were sorted in increasing order of the percentage of households in Socio-Economic Groups: Professional and Managerial, Other Non-Manual and Skilled Manual.[1]

For inner cities, the count of delivery points was cumulated and then divided by the number of constituencies to be selected (here, 70), to give a sampling interval of, say, s. Taking a random start point (call it r), 70 constituencies were selected by taking those in which the sampling interval fell (ie the first constituency selected was the one containing the rth delivery point on the list, the second containing the $(r+s)$th on the list, then the $(r+2s)$th and so on).

---

[1]Sorting the constituencies in this way prior to selection ensures that the issued sample includes different area types, on the basis of these characteristics.

In counting delivery points, the Multiple Output Indicator (MOI) was taken into account. This shows the number of residential units believed to exist at a delivery point (and equals one for most addresses). A typical situation in which it may be more than one is a house converted into several flats with a communal entrance, each having the same postal address.

ii. Selection of postcode sectors

Two postcode sectors—or 'sample points'—were selected per constituency, a total of 576.[2] Within constituencies, postcode sectors were listed in alphanumeric order and the delivery points cumulated. Taking a random start point, two sectors were selected with a sampling interval of half the total number of delivery points (using a method like that described in i. above).

iii. Selection of addresses and dwelling units

Each sample point was divided into four equal-sized 'segments' (in terms of delivery points). A segment was chosen at random and a starting address identified. Further addresses were identified at a fixed interval, designed to yield a gap of about 30 delivery points between each interview. (This design allows for other segments of the same sectors to be used in future BCS sweeps.) In inner city areas, 28 or 29 addresses were selected per sample point; in non-inner city areas, 25 addresses were selected per point. Sample points were randomly distributed between SCPR and BMRB interviewers.

Interviewer workloads consisted of addresses from two sample points in the same constituency. A total of 14,890 addresses were issued, of which 3,990 (26.8%) were in inner city areas. Addresses which were (wholly) institutional or non-residential were not identified at this point, and would be eliminated by the interviewer on arrival at the address.

iv. Selection of dwelling units (households) at addresses

On the PAF file, a sampled address corresponds to a 'delivery point' (i.e. letterbox). In a very small minority of cases (2%), the generated 'address' actually covered more than one household (even after the MOI had been taken into account). Where this occurred, interviewers had to select a household for interview at random.

To select a dwelling unit, the households were listed in a fixed order, and one selected using a random selection grid. This consisted of one row of numbers running from 1 to 12, for each of which a corresponding random number was provided. If the interviewer listed, say, five flats (dwelling units) at an address, the random number (call it r) printed under the '5' identified the rth on the list as the selected unit.

---

[2]The postcode sector is the first half of the postcode and the number in the second half: eg NW5 2.

v.   Selection of respondents aged 16 and over

Once the selected household had been determined, an individual was selected at random (except in the 30% of households with only one adult aged 16 or over). The procedure used was similar to that for dwelling units. Within each selected household, the interviewer listed the number of adults aged 16 or over, in alphabetical order of Christian names, and selected one using the random number grid. No substitution was permitted, and if necessary the interviewer made further visits to contact the selected adult.

This respondent identification process represents the main difference from the interviewer's point of view between an ER and a PAF sample. (On previous BCS sweeps using the ER, interviewers had a copy of the relevant part of the register which identified the respondent in advance—at least if the composition of the household was the same as on the ER.)

From a sampling point of view, the practical differences are broadly summarised as follows. In the PAF sample, each household has an equal chance of selection, but, as only one adult is interviewed per selected household, the chance of an individual being interviewed is *inversely* related to the number of adults (eg in a two-person household an adult has a 50% chance of being picked; in a four-person household, an adult has a 25% chance). The unweighted PAF sample therefore provides a 'typical' slice of households, but a sample of individuals which *under*-represents those in larger households. Conversely, in ER samples, electors (individuals) are selected with equal probability. A household with n electors in has n chances of being picked, so the chance of a household being selected increases with the number of electors. The unweighted ER sample therefore consists of a broadly typical slice of individuals, but a sample of households that *under*-represents smaller households.

To represent private households and individuals aged 16 and over living in private households, corrections had to be made to the sample at the data-processing stage to correct for:

i.   the oversampling of inner city areas;

ii.   cases where more than one household was covered by an entry on the PAF file;

iii   the selection of one individual at multi-person household (the majority of cases)

Further details of weighting are given later.

Ethnic minority booster sample

As in 1988, the sample of ethnic minority respondents was enlarged, using the process of 'focused enumeration'. This involves screening the addresses three doors to the left and right of the 'core sample' address to identify ethnic minority adults. (Field tests conducted in the early 1980s suggested that three addresses on either side is the limit for reliable information *(Focused Enumeration: the Development of Sampling Ethnic Minority Groups, SCPR, 1984)*.) Specific instructions were devised for situations where it was difficult to identify six 'adjacent' addresses (eg, blocks of flats with fewer than seven dwellings on the same floor).

If core address residents said that there were no ethnic minority members in the addresses either side, interviewers could accept this; but if in doubt they had to visit each address and ask whether any of the adult occupiers considered themselves to be *'Black or of Asian origin . . . by Asian we mean someone whose family comes originally from India, Pakistan or Bangladesh'*. If there was an ethnic minority adult at an adjacent address, the interviewer attempted to carry out an interview (in the same way as for a core sample address).

Within the booster sample, 'Blacks' cover Afro-Caribbeans or Africans. Asians are those who classified themselves as Indian, Pakistani or Bangladeshi. (In the event, a small number of booster sample respondents put themselves into the category of 'Chinese', 'other Asian', or 'other'; these have been omitted from analysis, as they would not necessarily be representative of these groups.) All respondents in the booster sample completed Follow-Up A questionnaires (to allow for sufficient numbers in examining differences in attitudes between ethnic groups).

Young Person 12-15 year old booster sample

At each 'core' and 'ethnic boost' sample address where an adult interview was obtained, permission was also sought to interview any 12-15 year olds in the household. All 12-15 year olds in a household were eligible for the questionnaire (rather than one picked at random). This maximised the number of teenagers, as a relatively high proportion of 12-15 year olds would be in households with more than one child in this age group (18% of completed questionnaires were multiple forms from the same household).

Fieldwork

Of the issued sample of 14,890 addresses in the core sample, 1,773—or 11.9%—were empty, demolished, or ineligible for interview for other reasons. The remaining 13,117 addresses yielded 10,059 achieved interviews, a response rate of 76.7%. At 10.9% of eligible addresses, the selected respondent refused to be interviewed, and at 5.3% of addresses, no information was forthcoming about the household; non-contact accounted for most of the other failures (4.2%). Table D.1 presents details of response rates, and a comparison with previous sweeps.

Table D.1
Response rates (percentages)

	1992	1988	1984	1982
Core sample	76.7	77.4	77.3	80.8
Inner cities[1]	71.0	71.3	72.6	72.7
Elsewhere	78.5	79.4	79.8	81.2
Ethnic minority boost	63.6	59.8	—	—
Teenage boost[2]	77.9	—	—	—

Notes:
1. The 1982 definition of inner city is not exactly comparable with those used in subsequent surveys.
2. Based on core and ethnic minority booster samples.

A total of 315 interviewers worked on the 1992 BCS. Addresses were allocated randomly between the two survey companies. Around 77.5% of successful interviews with those in the core sample had taken place by the end of February, 1992; 15.2% took place in March, and 6.8% later than this. A small number of interviews were undated.

Representativeness of the samples

In general, the sample was a fair representation of the population in England and Wales (see SCPR, 1993, for further details). After weighting to correct for unequal selection probabilities, however, the sample contained a higher proportion of women aged 34-59, at the expense of fewer elderly women, and younger men (Table D.2).

Table D.2
Age-sex distribution: BCS and population estimates

	16-34	35-59	60+	All men	16-34	35-59	60+	All women	All
BCS	17.1	19.0	11.5	47.6	17.0	21.9	13.5	52.4	100.0
OPCS mid-year 1991	18.1	19.0	11.1	48.2	17.6	19.0	15.2	51.8	100.0
Difference	-1.0	0.0	+0.4	-0.6	-0.6	+2.9	-2.3	+0.6	

Notes:
1. OPCS figures are mid-year estimates for the 1991 England and Wales population aged 16 or more, based on early 1991 Census estimates.
2. BCS: weighted data; unweighted n = 10,059. Source: 1992 BCS core sample.

Table D.3 shows the BCS age and sex distribution of people of Afro-Caribbean or Asian origin, as compared with the population estimates from the 1991 Census. The BCS picked up fewer black men aged 30-59 than the population distribution would suggest, and more black women aged 30-59. On the other hand, Asian women were under-represented, particularly those in the 30-59 age bracket.

Table D.3
Ethnic minority age-sex distribution: BCS and population estimates

	16-29	30-59	60+	All men	16-29	30-59	60+	All women	All
Afro-Caribbeans									
BCS	19.2	20.6	5.9	45.7	21.1	28.7	4.5	54.3	100.0
Census	19.3	22.9	5.7	47.9	22.3	25.4	4.5	52.1	100.0
Asians									
BCS	19.0	29.7	5.3	54.0	18.7	23.6	3.7	46.0	100.0
Census	18.0	28.0	4.7	50.7	19.0	26.5	3.8	49.3	100.0
Afro-Caribbeans/Asians									
BCS	19.1	26.1	5.5	50.7	19.6	25.6	4.0	49.3	100.0
Census	18.5	25.9	5.1	49.6	20.3	26.0	4.1	50.4	100.0

Notes:
1. Estimates from the 1991 Census (OPCS).
2. BCS: weighted data; unweighted n = 2,013. Source: 1992 BCS core and ethnic booster samples.

Weighting

Data from the survey were weighted in a number of ways at the data processing stage. Weighting served two main purposes: to correct imbalances introduced in sampling; and to correct imbalances created by the design of the interview. Weights were applied to correct for the following:

i.   The inner city imbalance: taking actual contact rates into account, inner city areas were effectively oversampled by a factor of around two (so that weighting reduced the contribution of such interviews by the inverse of this factor).

ii.   The dwelling unit weight: this is to correct for cases where more than one household was covered by an entry on the PAF file. Interviews were weighted by a factor proportional to the number of dwelling units at an address (one, in most cases).

iii. The individual weight: as the PAF file generated a sample of *addresses*, this meant that in the unweighted sample, *individuals* living in larger households were under-represented (as the chance of an adult being selected for interview was inversely related to the number of adults in that household). When doing individual-based analyses, interviews had to be weighted up by the number of adults in the household (which, in most cases, was greater than one).

iv. Victim incidents: where it is necessary to produce tabulations for victim incidents in general (ie, both personal and household crimes), personal victim incidents were weighted by i-iii. above and household victim incidents by i-ii. above. (This was different from earlier sweeps when an extra weight had to be applied to *household* crimes to correct for the fact that larger households had a disproportionately *high* chance of selection.)

v. Series offences: for series offences (see below), only one Victim Form was completed. In the analysis of victim incidents, these forms were weighted by the number of incidents involved, with an arbitrary top limit of five.

Series victimisations

When a person is victim of a number of very similar offences, it is not always possible for him/her to separate them into discrete events. In an already lengthy interview, it is also very demanding for respondents to report on all the incidents separately. Offences of this kind are usually called *series incidents*. In the BCS, interviewers could treat incidents as a series provided that they were all very similar in type, were done under the same circumstances and probably committed by the same person(s).

For crimes classified as series offences, full details were collected only about the most recent incident. In calculating offence rates for 1991, series incidents were given a score equal to the number of incidents in the series occurring in 1991, with an arbitrary top limit of five.

Classifying and counting incidents

The rules for classifying incidents reported to interviewers in the BCS were drawn up in consultation with the Home Office Statistical Department and statistical officers of a number of police forces, so as to enable comparison with statistics of offences recorded by the police. In 1992, a computer program was written based on the 1988 coding instructions. This generated an initial classification for a Victim Form. Independently, coders also classified Victim Forms. The computer-suggested classification was then compared with the coder classification to identify Victim Forms which needed further inspection. In a number of cases where there was doubt about accurate classification, Victim

Forms were referred to the Home Office Research and Planning Unit, who then often consulted with the police.

A number of Victim Forms (7%) which were completed for incidents in the survey were not included in any of the analyses of offences, for instance, because they fell outside the survey's coverage (eg, burglary of business premises) or because there was insufficient evidence that an offence had occurred. Victim Forms were completed for incidents of threatening behaviour though, for the most part, these have not been included in analyses of offences in this report; threats comprised 11% of 'legitimate' BCS incidents.

Respondents were interviewed in early 1992, and asked about incidents which had happened since 1 January 1991. In calculating offence rates for 1991, all incidents occurring in 1992 were excluded, as were offences which occurred outside England and Wales.

Appendix E
Sampling error

A sample is a small-scale representation of the population from which it is drawn. Survey estimates of characteristics of the population are subject to imprecision because of both sampling and non-sampling error. For example, an estimate of household income might be inaccurate because the sample failed to reflect the parent population adequately (sampling error) or because respondents provided inaccurate information to interviewers (a form of non-sampling error). Various sorts of non-sampling error have been discussed in Chapter 1.

The estimates in this report are based on a sample of the population in England and Wales aged 16 or over. The sample tended to over-represent older age groups (particularly women) at the expense of younger people (particularly men under 35): compared to 1991 Census estimates, the unweighted sample had 3.6% fewer men aged under 35 and 2.9% more women aged 60 or over; there were 3.4% more women in the sample than in the population. (It should be noted that the age-sex distribution of the sample, when weighted to account for differing selection probabilities, was much closer to that of the Census.) Institutionalised respondents were not covered by the survey. Both younger people and those in institutions may be disproportionately victimised.

This apart, the sample may well produce estimates which differ slightly from figures which would have been obtained if the whole population had been interviewed. One measure of the likely difference is given by the standard error, which indicates the extent to which an estimate might have varied by chance because only a sample was interviewed. The chances are about 68 in a 100 that a sample estimate will differ by less than one standard error from the figure which would have been obtained in a complete census of the population, and about 95 in a 100 that the difference would be less than two standard errors.

Tables E.1 and E.2 present sampling errors for a selection of BCS statistics for the 'core' and 'booster' samples respectively. Simple Random Sample (SRS) standard errors are estimates of the sampling error which a simple random sample of the size of the BCS would have achieved. The BCS did not employ a simple random sample however, but used a stratified multi-stage sample as described in Appendix D (using weighting to adjust for differing selection probabilities). The complex standard errors take account of these factors. Deft (or √deff) is the ratio of the complex standard error to the SRS standard error. Defts were calculated by SCPR, using Taylor's Expansion method.

The numbers of various offences in England and Wales, used in Chapter 2, are derived by multipying rates per 10,000 by the number of households (for household offences) and by the population over the age of 16. The multipliers, respectively, were 2013.1 and 4066.1 (see Appendix F for further details). The range within which the number of offences lies can be calculated from the statistics in Table E.1 (eg, with 95% certainty the number of incidents of vandalism will fall between 1,237,000 and 1,475,000).

Table E.1
Sampling errors for selected BCS statistics: 'core' sample

	Rate	SRS st. error	Complex st. error	'Deft' (√deff)
COMPARABLE OFFENCE RATES				
Vandalism	1,356	54	60	1.10
Violence	199	23	26	1.14
Burglary	678	36	45	1.26
Attempts and no loss	328	23	28	1.19
With loss	350	23	27	1.14
Theft from vehicle	1,192	45	52	1.15
Theft of vehicle	257	17	19	1.09
Attempted vehicle theft	442	26	33	1.26
Bicycle theft	280	20	23	1.19
Theft from the person	108	11	12	1.08
Motor vehicle vandalism	829	40	42	1.04
Household vandalism	528	35	36	1.04
Wounding	154	20	23	1.15
Robbery	45	9	10	1.17
OTHER BCS OFFENCE RATES				
Other household theft	913	42	52	1.25
Other personal theft	429	28	34	1.20
Common assault	432	37	43	1.19
OWNER-BASED RATES				
Theft from vehicle (owners)	1,600	61	69	1.14
Theft of vehicle (owners)	346	23	25	1.09
Bicycle theft (owners)	653	47	54	1.15
OTHER RATES				
Police knew about matter (victims)[2]	41.3%	0.63%	0.81%	1.30
Feel "very unsafe" out alone	12.4%	0.33%	0.47%	1.42
Burglary screen = 1+ (Q29)	3.0%	0.24%	0.25%	1.07
Had fire in last 2 years	4.3%	0.20%	0.27%	1.32
H'hold in Neighbourhood Watch area	27.4%	0.44%	1.02%	2.28

Notes:
1. Incidence rates are those in Appendix A, Tables A2.2 and A2.3, for which design effects were calculated.
2. Based on V92 for all offences, including threats.
3. Weighted data; unweighted n = 10,059, or slightly less for 'other rates' where there are missing values. Source: 1992 BCS, core sample.

Table E.2
Sampling errors for selected BCS statistics: 'booster' sample

	Rate	SRS st. error	Complex st. error	'Deft' (√deff)
COMPARABLE OFFENCE RATES				
Vandalism	1,623	168	225	1.34
Violence	347	27	23	0.84
Burglary	1,312	120	148	1.23
Attempts and no loss	533	83	97	1.16
With loss	630	75	90	1.19
Theft from vehicle	1,283	117	130	1.11
Theft of vehicle	304	46	51	1.12
Attempted vehicle theft	418	74	75	1.02
Bicycle theft	258	43	54	1.25
Theft from the person	179	39	47	1.23
Motor vehicle vandalism	944	113	143	1.26
Household vandalism	679	117	157	1.34
Wounding	205	56	47	0.83
Robbery	142	36	31	0.88
OTHER BCS OFFENCE RATES				
Other household theft	673	92	102	1.12
Other personal theft	436	88	116	1.31
Common assault	224	54	61	1.13
OWNER-BASED RATES				
Theft from vehicle (owners)	1,858	170	190	1.11
Theft of vehicle (owners)	440	67	74	1.11
Bicycle theft (owners)	838	144	171	1.19
OTHER RATES				
Burglary screen = 1+ (Q29)	5.9%	0.59%	0.68%	1.15
Had fire in last 2 years	4.0%	0.49%	0.62%	1.27
H'hold in Neighbourhood Watch area	17.5%	0.96%	1.83%	1.92
Police knew about matter (victims)	42.7%	1.35%	1.79%	1.32
Feel "very unsafe" out alone	12.4%	0.83%	1.34%	1.62
Classified as Afro-Caribbean	50.6%	1.26%	3.07%	2.44
Classified as Asian	49.4%	1.26%	3.07%	2.44

Notes:

1. Weighted data; unweighted n = 1,583, or slightly less for 'other rates' where there are missing values.
2. Source: 1992 BCS, booster sample. The table excludes 71 booster sample respondents who described their ethnic origin as other than black or Asian.

Appendix F
Comparison between the BCS and Criminal Statistics

Some offence groups can be compared using BCS information and offences recorded by the police as shown in *Criminal Statistics, England and Wales, 1991* (see Home Office, 1992). For each of these, details are presented below on the precise offence categories which were compared. (The *Criminal Statistics* (CS) classification numbers are shown below in brackets after each relevant offence group.)

Survey offence rates for 1991 were grossed up to yield the number of offences likely to have been experienced in England and Wales in that year. To do this, household rates were multiplied by a factor of 2013.1: 1991 household estimates from the Department of Environment, divided by 10,000. Personal rates were multiplied by a factor of 4066.1: 1991 estimates for the number of persons over the age of 16 in England and Wales from the 1991 Census, divided by 10,000. While personal multipliers for previous sweeps remain the same, the household multipliers used to derive numbers of offences in earlier sweeps differ slightly from those used in the presentation of previously published results (see Hough and Mayhew, 1983: 45; Hough and Mayhew, 1985: 85, Mayhew *et al*, 1988: 111). The base of present household multipliers is more consistent with those available in 1991. The multipliers used are: for 1981, 1833.4 household, 3872.4 personal; for 1983, 1858.7 household, 3914.9 personal; for 1987, 1937.4 household, 4013.7 personal.

Various adjustments were made to the CS categories of offences recorded by the police to account, for instance, for the fact that crimes against people under 16 appear in official records, but will not have been picked up in the survey. These adjustments were largely the same as those made for comparisons between results from earlier surveys and offences recorded by the police. The 1991 adjustments were decided on the basis of information sent by 40 of the 43 police forces in England and Wales (considerably more than replied for the 1988 results) and are estimates only. In 1992, a slightly different adjustment was made for vandalism and bicycle thefts. Attempted thefts of and from motor vehicles are included in the comparison for 1991, having been excluded from comparisons in previous years. Sexual offences and theft from a dwelling are not included in the comparison for 1991 as the small number of offences picked up by the BCS and questionnaire changes give rise to unreliable trends.

THE 1992 BRITISH CRIME SURVEY

1. VANDALISM

Survey categories: Arson

Criminal damage to motor vehicle, £20 or under

Criminal damage to motor vehicles, over £20

Criminal damage to the home, £20 or under

Criminal damage to the home, over £20

Criminal Statistics: Arson (56)

Criminal damage endangering life
(excluding arson) (57)

Other indictable offences of criminal damage:
    Value over £20 (58a)
    Value £20 and under (58b)

Adjustments: i.   The CS total of 819,489 is reduced by a half to 409,745 to exclude offences committed against institutions and organisations.

2. THEFT FROM MOTOR VEHICLE

Survey categories: Theft from car/van

Theft from motorbike, motorscooter or moped

Criminal Statistics: Theft from vehicle (45)

Adjustments: i.   The CS total of 913,276 is reduced by 86,302—the number of nil-value thefts from motor vehicles—to exclude attempted thefts, yielding 826,974.

    ii.   The adjusted total of 826,794 is then reduced by 7% to 769,086 to exclude thefts from commercial vehicles.

Notes: i.   No adjustment has been made to allow for the very small proportion of thefts from bikes etc. recorded under the CS classification 45/11 (the average reduction from the 1991 force returns came out as 0.5%).

3. THEFT OF MOTOR VEHICLE

Survey categories: Theft of car/van

Theft of motorbike, motorscooter or moped

Criminal Statistics: Theft and unauthorised taking of motor vehicle (48)

Adjustments: i.   The CS total of 581,901 is reduced by 47,270—the number of nil-value thefts of motor vehicles—to exclude attempted thefts, yielding 534,631.

    ii.   The figure of 534,631 yielded by i. has been reduced by 10% to exclude thefts of commercial vehicles, which would not have been covered by the BCS. The adjusted total is 481,168.

4. ATTEMPTED THEFTS OF AND FROM MOTOR VEHICLES

Survey categories: Attempted theft of/from car/van
Attempted theft of/from motorbike, motorscooter or moped

Criminal Statistics: Theft from vehicle (45)
Theft and unauthorised taking of motor vehicle (48)

Adjustments: i. Attempted thefts of and from motor vehicles are approximated by the number of nil-value thefts of and from vehicles.

ii. The CS number of nil-value thefts from motor vehicles, 86,302, is reduced by 7%, to exclude attempted thefts from commercial vehicles, to 80,261. The CS total of nil-value thefts of motor vehicles, 47,270, is reduced by 10%, to exclude attempted thefts of commercial vehicles, to 42,453. The sum of these adjusted totals—122,084—is then taken.

Notes: i. The 'nil-value' categories in thefts of and from vehicles consist largely of attempted thefts. In the 1991 CS, nil-value thefts of vehicles comprised 8% of all thefts of vehicles and nil-value thefts from vehicles comprised 9% of all thefts from vehicles.

5. BURGLARY IN A DWELLING

Survey categories: Burglary in a dwelling (nothing taken)
Burglary in a dwelling (something taken)
Attempted burglary

Criminal Statistics: Burglary in a dwelling (28)
Aggravated burglary in a dwelling (29)

Adjustments: None

Notes i. Comparisons are made on the basis of incidents with and without loss. In 1991, 23% of the total of CS burglaries were "nil value" thefts. The CS categories include attempts (where an offender does not gain entry), and it is estimated that these comprise around 7% of recorded residential burglaries.

6. BICYCLE THEFT

Survey category:	Theft of pedal cycle
Criminal Statistics:	Theft of pedal cycle (44)

Adjustments i.   Most police forces record incidents of bicycle theft as such, subsequently deleting or 'no crime-ing' the record if the bicycle is recovered. There is some doubt as to whether forces follow this procedure with any uniformity. The CS total of 212,169 is increased by 6% to include unauthorised takings recorded by the police and subsequently 'no-crimed' after the cycle's recovery. The adjusted total is 224,899. This adjustment is lower than the 11% used for CS figures for 1988.

7. WOUNDING

Survey categories: Serious wounding
Other wounding
Serious wounding with sexual motive
Other wounding with sexual motive

Criminal Statistics: Wounding or other act endangering life (5)
Other wounding, etc (8)

Adjustments: i.   British Transport Police (BTP) keep their own crime statistics; these do not overlap in most cases with CS, but crimes for which there were prosecutions and very serious crimes tend to be included in the statistics maintained by local police forces. Thus, the 1,160 cases of wounding which were recorded by the BTP but not cleared up are added to the CS total of 183,653 to make 184,813.

        ii.   To exclude cases where the victim was under 16, the figure of 184,813 has been reduced by 15% to make 157,091.

8. ROBBERY

Survey categories:		Robbery
		Attempted robbery
Criminal Statistics:		Robbery (34)
Adjustments:	i.	The 1,128 cases of robbery which were recorded by the BTP but not cleared up are added to the CS total of 45,323 to make 46,451.
	ii.	To exclude cases where the victim was under 16, the figure of 46,451 has been reduced by 12% to 40,877.
Notes:	i.	Attempted robberies are classified by the police as robberies. They seem to amount to around 15%-20% of the total
	ii.	About 25-30% of robberies recorded by the police involve business property—ie. post offices, banks, off-licences; an unknown proportion of these will have more than one victim. As the BCS assumes that there can be only one victim per robbery, there will be a slight tendency for the survey to overestimate the number of robberies—minimal enough to be disregarded. (It is assumed that virtually all robberies involving private property had single victims.)

9. THEFT FROM THE PERSON

Survey categories:		Snatch theft from the person
		Other theft from the person
		Attempted theft from the person
Criminal Statistics:		Theft from the person of another (39)
Adjustments:	i.	The 8,224 cases of theft from the person which were recorded by the BTP but not cleared up are added to the CS total of 35,432 to make 43,656.
	ii.	To exclude cases where the victim was under 16, the total of 43,656 has been reduced by 5% to 41,473.
Notes:	i.	Attempted thefts from the person are classified by the police as thefts from the person, and probably amount to around 5-10% of the total.

Appendix G
Household burglary: comparing the BCS, the General Household Survey and offences recorded by the police

The General Household Survey (GHS) is an annual sample survey conducted by the Office of Population Censuses and Surveys of about 10,000 households in England and Wales. In 1972, 1973, 1979, 1980, 1985, 1986 and 1991, the GHS included questions, asked of the head of the household, to estimate the number of households which had been burgled in the last 12 months (see for example OPCS, 1993). The main question was: *"During the last 12 months (while you've been living here) has anyone got into this house/flat etc. without your permission and stolen or attempted to steal something?"*. Comparisons of GHS and BCS burglary trends during 1972-1980 have previously been reported in Home Office Statistical Bulletin No 11/82 (Home Office, 1982), and updated in Hough and Mayhew (1985: 16), Elliott and Mayhew (1988) and Mayhew *et al* (1989).

Comparison of BCS and GHS burglary rates is not straightforward, for the following reasons:

i.   The BCS definition of household burglary includes unsuccessful attempts to gain entry. The 1991 GHS (and the surveys carried out before 1985) asked only about incidents where the burglar effected entry, defining attempts as incidents where nothing was stolen. (In 1985 and 1986, the GHS included some questions on attempted burglary, though for various technical reasons the comparison between GHS and BCS attempts was rather unsound.)

ii.   In the GHS, victims of burglary were taken to be those who answered in the affirmative to the question given above. There were no supplementary questions to check that the incident, as described by the respondent, met any specified criteria of burglary. In the BCS, the 'screen' question which was similar to the GHS question was used only to identify people who should be administered a Victim Form; incidents were then classified according to information given in the Victim Form. There may therefore be definitional differences in addition to i. above.

iii.   Analysis of the GHS burglary questions excluded those who had moved to their home less than twelve months before interview.

The best comparison to make is between the GHS burglary rate (excluding incidents where nothing was taken, and in 1985 and 1986 attempts) and the response rate to the main burglary 'screen' questions in the BCS. In 1982 this was Question 22b of the Main Questionnaire, in 1984 Question 32, and in 1988 and 1992 Question 29. However, the following adjustments had to be made to BCS data to enable valid comparison :

i.   Excluded from analysis were those who had moved to their present home after the beginning of the respective recall period (eg, 1st January 1991 in the case of the 1992 survey). The BCS shows that movers have higher burglary rates than others, so the burglary figures presented below are underestimates. 'Movers' comprise about 10% of survey respondents.

ii.   Any responses to the screen question which, according to the victim form, referred to incidents where nothing was taken were excluded.

iii.   The relevant screen question was preceded by others concerned with theft and damage to cars, motorcycles and bicycles; a few incidents which triggered responses to these screen questions were subsequently classified as burglaries, some of which would probably have triggered responses to the burglary screen, had this come first. Therefore, an arbitrary 50% of these incidents were added to the number of responses to the main burglary screen.

In 1992, the BCS sample was from the Postcode Address File (PAF), as opposed to the Electoral Register (ER), which had been used in previous years. Extensive checks were made to ascertain whether this made any substantial changes to the observed rates and sample, but none were detected. No adjustment was therefore made to the 1992 BCS data because of the change in sampling frame. Similarly, no adjustment is made here to the GHS figures (the GHS moved over from ER sampling to PAF sampling in 1985).

With the above adjustments made, estimates of the number of burglaries with loss from the 1991 GHS and from the BCS for 1987 and 1991 are given below. In grossing up survey rates, mid-year OPCS estimates for the number of households in England and Wales have been used as a multiplier. (Figures will differ from those previously published as the 1988 BCS analysis used the Inland Revenue's figure for the number of domestic rateable hereditaments in England and Wales as a multiplier, but this series was discontinued with the advent of the community charge.) The comparison must be regarded as tentative; not only are both figures subject to sampling and non-sampling error, but it is always problematic to compare findings from surveys with even small differences in design.

The number of burglaries with loss estimated by the surveys since 1981, after the adjustments described above were made, are:

	BCS 1981	BCS 1983	BCS 1987	BCS 1991	GHS 1991
Burglary with loss	391,000 ±81,000	420,000 ±74,000	422,000 ±98,000	612,000 ±87,000	606,000 ±99,000

Note: The range of error for the BCS figures are approximate.

Burglaries with loss recorded by the police, with which BCS and GHS figures are compared in Figure 4.1 (Chapter 4), are all residential burglaries, minus nil-value cases. In years for which a GHS measure is given (eg, 1979), recorded offences refer to the average of the year of the survey and the previous year (eg 1979/78). This is because GHS respondents are interviewed over the survey year so that the 'recall period' for burglary will span the two years. (Figures shown in Hough and Mayhew, 1985: 17, differ slightly as an average was not used.) In other years, police figures relate to the calendar year. The 1991 BCS estimate is used in Figure 4.1.

In some comparisons of burglary as measured by the GHS and police recorded figures the latter included 'theft in a dwelling' (see Home Office, 1982). The rationale for this was that the GHS question, although designed to identify burglary victims alone, may have picked up some incidents actually committed by non-trespassers. However, the BCS burglary screen question which corresponds most closely to the GHS question elicits very few incidents which, on the basis of Victim Form information, are subsequently classified as theft in a dwelling. Here therefore, as in previous comparisons of GHS and BCS results, police and BCS figures refer only to burglaries in a dwelling.

Appendix H
The ACORN system of neighbourhood classification

ACORN stands for 'A Classification of Residential Neighbourhoods'. It is a system of classifying households according to the demographic, employment and housing characteristics of their immediate neighbourhood. It was produced by CACI, a market and policy analysis consultancy, by applying the statistical technique of cluster analysis to variables from the 1981 Census. (ACORN based on 1991 Census data was not available for the present report, although it is envisaged that this will eventually be added to the data set.) ACORN is now used for planning and marketing by a wide range of commercial and public sector organisations, and is being employed increasingly in social research.

There are 38 ACORN neighbourhood types, these aggregating to 11 groups. Each of the 130,000 enumeration districts (EDs) in Great Britain (an average ED comprises about 150 households) has been assigned to an ACORN neighbourhood type on the basis of its scores on 40 selected Census variables. As CACI have matched postcodes to enumeration districts, any household in the country can be given an ACORN code provided its full postcode is known.

The principle of ACORN is that people who live in the same neighbourhood share characteristics of class, income and lifestyle. Naturally, there will be differences between individual EDs within the same ACORN classification, and between households within the same ED—particularly in heterogeneous areas such as those in inner cities. Nevertheless, ACORN is a useful way of determining the immediate social environment of different households, and can be more illuminating for some purposes than individual characteristics such as income or class. For instance, ACORN will show what types of targets for crime different neighbourhoods offer and what risks their residents face compared to those living nearby.

As was the case with the 1984 and 1988 surveys, each respondent in the 1992 BCS was allocated to an ACORN neighbourhood type on the basis of the postcode for their address. The 11 neighbourhood groups are used in this report mainly to analyse rates of victimisation. (Previous work looked at other crime-related variables in relations to ACORN (eg fear of crime and membership of Neighbourhood Watch schemes).) The BCS sample size is insufficient to make much use of the fuller 38 neighbourhood types. The 11 ACORN groups are shown in Figure A, with the percentage of the 1991 England and Wales population in each group.

Table H.1 shows that the distribution of households in the BCS sample across the different ACORN neighbourhood groups closely matches CACI's updates of the England and Wales figures for 1991. BCS respondents are slightly under-represented in Group A (agricultural areas), E (council estates—category I) and G (council estates—category III). They are slightly over-represented in ACORN groups I (high status non-family areas) and J (better-off retirement areas).

Table H.1

Percentage of households in ACORN neighbourhood groups:
1991 England and Wales households, and 1992 BCS core sample

	1991 England and Wales households	1992 BCS core sample
	%	%
A. Agricultural areas	3.3	2.8
B. Modern family housing, higher incomes	16.3	16.7
C. Older housing of intermediate status	18.9	18.2
D. Older terraced housing	4.4	4.3
E. Council estates—Category I	12.6	11.3
F. Council estates—Category II	9.6	9.7
G. Council estates—Category III	6.4	4.1
H. Mixed inner metropolitan areas	3.4	3.5
I. High status non-family areas	4.6	5.8
J. Affluent suburban housing	15.9	17.7
K. Better-off retirement areas	4.6	4.6
Unclassified	0.0	1.2

Notes:
1. Estimates of 1991 England and Wales households in different ACORN neighbourhood groups supplied by CACI Market Analysis.
2. Source: 1992 BCS core sample (weighted data). Unweighted n = 10,059.

A AGRICULTURAL AREAS

1. Agricultural villages
2. Areas of farms and smallholdings

3.3% *OF GB POPULATION*

B MODERN FAMILY HOUSING, HIGHER INCOMES

3. Post-war functional private housing
4. Modern private housing, young families
5. Established private family housing
6. New detached houses, young families
7. Military bases

16.8% *OF GB POPULATION*

E COUNCIL ESTATES – CATEGORY I

15. Council estates, well-off older workers
16. Recent council estates
17. Better council estates, younger workers
18. Small council houses, often Scottish

12.7% *OF GB POPULATION*

F COUNCIL ESTATES – CATEGORY II

19. Low rise estates in industrial towns
20. Inter-war council estates, older people
21. Council housing, elderly people

9.0% *OF GB POPULATION*

I HIGH STATUS NON-FAMILY AREAS

30. High status non-family areas
31. Multi-let big old houses and flats
32. Furnished flats, mostly single people

4.7% *OF GB POPULATION*

J AFFLUENT SUBURBAN HOUSING

33. Inter-war semis, white collar workers
34. Spacious inter-war semis, big gardens
35. Villages with wealthy older commuters
36. Detached houses, exclusive suburbs

17.7% *OF GB POPULATION*

C

OLDER HOUSING OF INTERMEDIATE STATUS

8. Mixed owner-occupied and council estates
9. Small town centres & flats above shops
10. Villages with non-farm employment
11. Older private housing, skilled workers

17.8% *OF GB POPULATION*

D

OLDER TERRACED HOUSING

12. Unmodernised terraces, older people
13. Older terraces, low income families
14. Tenement flats lacking amenities

4.2% *OF GB POPULATION*

G

COUNCIL ESTATES – CATEGORY III

22. New council estates in inner cities
23. Overspill estates, higher unemployment
24. Council estates with some overcrowding
25. Council estates with greatest hardship

6.1% *OF GB POPULATION*

H

MIXED INNER METROPOLITAN AREAS

26. Multi-occupied older housing
27. Cosmopolitan owner-occupied terraces
28. Multi-let housing in cosmopolitan areas
29. Better-off cosmopolitan areas

3.4% *OF GB POPULATION*

K

BETTER-OFF RETIREMENT AREAS

37. Private houses, well-off older residents
38. Private flats, older single people

4.2% *OF GB POPULATION*

Appendix I
Publications on the British Crime Survey

The main results of the 1982, 1984 and 1988 surveys are reported in, respectively:

Hough, M. and Mayhew, P. (1983). *The British Crime Survey: first report.* Home Office Research Study No. 76. London: HMSO.

Hough, M. and Mayhew, P. (1985). *Taking Account of Crime: key findings from the 1984 British Crime Survey.* Home Office Research Study No. 86. London: HMSO.

Mayhew, P., Elliott, D. and Dowds, L. (1989). *The 1988 British Crime Survey.* Home Office Research Study No. 111. London: HMSO.

Preliminary results from the 1992 survey have appeared in:

Mayhew, P. and Aye Maung, N. (1992). *Surveying Crime: findings from the 1992 British Crime Survey.* Research Findings No. 2. London: Home Office Research and Statistics Department.

Some of the other main publications which deal with results from the British Crime Survey, or draw heavily on them, are listed below. They cover results from all three previous surveys. Results on the survey in Scotland are listed separately.

Publications currently available

Barr, R. and Pease, K. (1992). 'A place for every crime and every crime in its place'. In, Evans, D.J., Fyfe, N.R. and Herbert, D.T. (Eds.), *Crime, Policing and Place: essays in environmental criminology.* London: Routledge.

Block, R. (1987). 'A comparison of victimisation, crime assessment and fear of crime in England/Wales, the Netherlands, Scotland and the United States'. Paper presented at American Society of Criminology Meeting, Montreal, November 1987.

Box, S., Hale, C. and Andrews, G. (1988). 'Explaining fear of crime'. *British Journal of Criminology*, 28, 340-356.

Clarke, R.V.G. (1987). 'The contribution of crime surveys to criminological theory'. Paper presented at the British Criminology Conference, Sheffield, July 1987.

Clarke, R.V.G., Ekblom, P., Hough, M. and Mayhew, P. (1985). 'Elderly victims of crime and exposure to risk'. *Howard Journal of Criminal Justice,* 24, 81-89.

Davidoff, L. and Dowds, L. (1989). 'Recent trends in crimes of violence against the person in England and Wales'. *Research Bulletin*, No. 27. London: Home Office Research and Planning Unit.

Davidson, R. N. (1992). *Crime in your Neighbourhood.* Report to the Home Office. Hull: University of Hull.

Davidson, R. N. (1989). 'Micro-environments of violence'. In, Evans, D.J, and Herbert, D.T., *The Geography of Crime.* London: Routledge.

Elliott, D. and Mayhew, P. (1988). 'Trends in residential burglary: an update'. *Research Bulletin*, No. 25. London: Home Office Research and Planning Unit.

Farrell, G. (1992). 'Multiple Victimisation: its extent and significance'. *International Review of Victimology*, 2, 85-102.

Farrell G. (1993). 'The measurement of repeat victimisation probabilities'. In, M.Tonry and N.Morris (Eds.), *Crime and Justice*. Vol. 29. Chicago: University of Chicago press.

Gottfredson, M.R. (1984). *Victims of Crime: the dimensions of risk.* Home Office Research Study No. 81. London: HMSO.

Hale, C., Peck, P. and Salked, J. (1994). 'The structural determinants of fear of crime: an analysis using Census data and crime survey data from England and Wales'. *International Review of Victimology*, 3.

Hope, T. (1984). 'The first British Crime Survey: current and future research'. *Research Bulletin*, No. 18. London: Home Office Research and Planning Unit.

Hope, T. (1984). 'Building design and burglary'. In, Clarke, R.V.G. and Hope, T. (Eds.), *Coping with Burglary.* Boston, Mass.: Kluwer-Nijhoff.

Hope, T. (1986). 'Council tenants and crime'. *Research Bulletin*, No. 21. London: Home Office Research and Planning Unit.

Hope, T. (1987). 'Residential aspects of autocrime'. *Research Bulletin*, No. 23. London: Home Office Research and Planning Unit. London: HMSO.

Hope, T. (1988). 'Support for Neighbourhood Watch: a British Crime Survey analysis'. In, Hope, T. and Shaw, M. (Eds.), *Communities and Crime Reduction.* London: HMSO.

Hope, T. and Hough, M. (1988). 'Area, crime and incivilities: findings from the British Crime Survey'. In, Hope, T. and Shaw, M. (Eds.), *Communities and Crime Reduction.* London: HMSO.

Hough, M. (1984). 'Residential burglary: findings from the British Crime Survey'. In, Clarke, R.V.G. and Hope, T. (Eds.), *Coping with Burglary.* Boston, Mass.: Kluwer-Nijhoff.

Hough, M. (1985). 'The impact of victimisation: findings from the British Crime Survey'. *Victimology: an International Journal*, 8, 488-497.

Hough, M. (1986). 'Victims of violent crime'. In, Fattah, E. (Ed.), *Reorienting the Justice System: from crime police to victim policy.* London: Macmillan.

Hough, M. (1987). 'Developing a new index of crime: the British Crime Survey'. In, Bradley, U. (Ed.), *Applied Marketing and Social Research.* (2nd Edition). London: Van Nostrand Reinhold.

Hough, M. (1987). 'Offenders' choice of target: findings from victim surveys'. Journal of *Quantitative Criminology*, 3, 355-370.

Hough, M. (1988). 'Public attitudes to sentencing'. In, Harrison, A. and Gretton, J. (Eds.), *Crime UK 1988*. Newbury: Policy Journals.

Hough, M. (1990). 'Threats: findings from the British Crime Survey'. *International Review of Victimology*, 1, 169-180.

Hough. M. (1990). 'Crime surveys and the measurement of crime'. In, Bluglass, R. and Bowden, T. (Eds.), *Principles and Practice of Forensic Psychiatry*. Edinburgh: Churchill Livingstone.

Hough, M. and Lewis, H. (1986) 'Penal hawks and penal doves: attitudes to punishment in the British Crime Survey'. *Research Bulletin*, No. 21. London: Home Office Research and Planning Unit.

Hough, M. and Lewis, H. (1989). 'Counting crime and analysing risks: findings from the British Crime Survey'. In, Evans, D.J. and Herbert, D.T., *The Geography of Crime*. London: Routledge.

Hough, M. and Mo, J. (1986) 'If at first you don't succeed: findings on attempted burglary from the British Crime Survey'. *Research Bulletin*, No. 21. London: Home Office Research and Planning Unit.

Hough, M. and Moxon, D. (1985). 'Dealing with offenders: popular justice and the views of victims'. *Howard Journal of Criminal Justice*, 24, 160-175.

Hough, M., Moxon, D. and Lewis, H. (1987). 'Attitudes to punishment'. In, Pennington, R. and Lloyd-Bostock, S. (Eds.), *The Psychology of Sentencing*. Oxford: Centre for Socio-Legal Studies.

Hough, M. and Sheehy, K. (1986). 'Incidents of violence: findings from the British Crime Survey'. *Research Bulletin*, No. 20. London: Home Office Research and Planning Unit.

Lewis, H. and Mo, J. (1986). 'Burglary insurance: findings from the British Crime Survey'. *Research Bulletin*, No. 22. London: Home Office Research and Planning Unit.

Litton, R. (1987). 'Crime and insurance'. *The Geneva Papers on Risk and Insurance*, 12, 198-225.

Litton, R. (1990). 'Aspects of moral hazard'. *Journal of the Society of Fellows* (The Chartered Insurance Institute), 5, 2-15.

Maguire, M. and Corbett, C. (1986). *The Effects of Crime and the Work of Victim Support Schemes*. Cambridge Studies in Criminology, 56. Aldershot: Gower.

Mawby, R.I. (1988). 'Women and crime: from victimization rates to crime experience'. Paper presented to 10th International Congress of Criminology, Hamburg 1988.

Mawby, R.I. (1988). 'Age, vulnerability and the impact of crime'. In, Maguire, M. and Pointing, J. (Eds.), *Victims of Crime: A New Deal*. Milton Keynes: Open University Education Enterprises.

Mawby, R.I. (1991). 'Responding to crime victims'. Final report to the Home Office. Plymouth: Plymouth Polytechnic.

Mawby, R.I. and Firkins, V. (1986). 'The victim/offender relationship and its implications for policies: evidence from the British Crime Survey'. Paper presented to World Congress of Victimology, Orlando, July 1986.

Mawby, R.I. and Gill, M.L. (1987). *Crime Victims: needs, services and the voluntary sector.* London: Tavistock.

Maxfield, M.G. (1984). *Fear of Crime in England and Wales.* Home Office Research Study No. 78. London: HMSO.

Maxfield, M.G. (1987). 'Household composition, routine activity, and victimization: a comparative analysis'. *Journal of Quantitative Criminology*, 3, 301-320.

Maxfield, M.G. (1987). 'Lifestyle and routine activity theories of crime: empirical studies of victimization, delinquency and offender decision-making'. *Journal of Quantitative Criminology*, 3, 275-282.

Maxfield, M.G. (1987). *Fear of Crime: findings from the 1984 British Crime Survey.* Home Office Research and Planning Unit Paper No. 43. London: Home Office.

Maxfield, M.G. (1988). 'The London Metropolitan Police and their clients: victim and suspect attitudes'. *Journal of Research in Crime and Delinquency*, 25, 188-206.

May, C. (1990). *Household fires: findings from the British Crime Survey 1988.* Research and Planning Unit Paper No. 57. London: Home Office Research and Planning Unit.

Mayhew, P. (1984). 'Target-hardening: how much of an answer?'. In, Clarke, R.V.G. and Hope, T. (Eds.), *Coping with Burglary.* Boston: Kluwer-Nijhoff.

Mayhew, P. (1987). *Residential Burglary: a comparison of the US, Canada and England and Wales.* National Institute of Justice. Washington, DC: Government Printing Office.

Mayhew, P. (1987). 'How are we faring on the burglary front? A comparison with the US and Canada'. *Research Bulletin*, No. 23. 1987. London: Home Office.

Mayhew, P. (1993). 'Measuring the effects of crime in victimisation surveys'. In, Bilsky, W., Pfeiffer, C. and Wetzels, P. (Eds.), *Criminal Victimisation and Fear of Crime among the Elderly – Survey Research: Past, Present and the Future.* Stuttgart: Enke Verlag.

Mayhew, P. (1993). 'Reporting crime to the police: the contribution of victimisation surveys'. In, Bilsky, W., Pfeiffer, C. and Wetzels, P. (Eds.), *Criminal Victimisation and Fear of Crime among the Elderly – Survey Research: Past, Present and the Future.* Stuttgart: Enke Verlag.

Mayhew, P. and Elliott, D. (1988). 'Trends in residential burglary in England and Wales: an update'. *Research Bulletin*, No. 25. London: Home Office Research and Planning Unit.

Mayhew, P. and Elliott, D. (1990). 'Self-reported offending, victimization, and the British Crime Survey'. *Victims and Violence*, 5, 83-96.

Mayhew, P. and Hough, M. (1982). 'The British Crime Survey.' *Research Bulletin*, No. 14. London: Home Office Research and Planning Unit.

Mayhew, P. and Hough, M. (1983). 'A note on the British Crime Survey.' *British Journal of Criminology*, 23, 394-295.

Mayhew, P. and Hough, M. (1988). 'The British Crime Survey: origins and impact'. In, Maguire, M. and Pointing, J. (Eds.), *Victims of Crime: A New Deal.* Milton Keynes: Open University Education Enterprises.

Mayhew, P. and Hough, M. (1991). 'The British Crime Survey: the first ten years'. In, G. Kaiser *et al* (Eds.), *Victims and Criminal Justice*. Freiburg: Max-Planck Institute for Foreign and International Penal Law. Reprinted in: *Journal of the Market Research Society*, 32, 23-38.

Mayhew, P. and Smith, L.J.F. (1985). 'Crime in England and Wales and Scotland: a British Crime Survey comparison'. *British Journal of Criminology*, 25, 148-159.

Miethe, T.D. and Meier, R.T. (1990). 'Opportunity, choice and criminal victimization: a test of a theoretical model'. *Journal of Research in Crime and Delinquency*, 27, 243- 266.

Mott, J. (1985). 'Self-reported cannabis use in Great Britain in 1981'. *British Journal of Addiction*, 80, 37-43.

Moxon, D. and Jones, P. (1984). 'Public reactions to police behaviour: some findings from the British Crime Survey'. *Policing*, 1, 49-56.

Osborn, D., Trickett, A. and Elder, R. (1992). 'Area characteristics and regional variates as determinants of property crime levels.' *Journal of Quantitative Criminology*, 8, 265-285.

Pease, K. (1986). 'Obscene telephone calls in England and Wales'. *Howard Journal of Criminal Justice*, 24, 275-281.

Pease, K. (1988). *Judgements of crime seriousness: evidence from the 1984 British Crime Survey*. Home Office Research and Planning Unit Paper No. 44. London: Home Office.

Pease, K. (1992). 'Individual and community influences on victimisation and their implications for Crime Prvention.' In, Farrington, D.P, Sampson, R.J. and Wikstron, P-O, (Eds.), *Integrating Individual and Ecological Aspects of Crime*. Stockholm: National Council on Crime Prevention.

Riley, D. (1984). 'Drivers' beliefs about alcohol and the law'. *Research Bulletin*, No. 17. London: Home Office Research and Planning Unit.

Riley, D. (1986). 'Drinking drivers: the limits to deterrence?'. *Howard Journal of Criminal Justice*, 24, 241-256.

Sampson. R.J. (1987). 'Personal violence by strangers: an extension and test of the opportunity model of predatory victimization'. *Journal of Criminal Law and Criminology*, 78, 327-356.

Sampson, R.J. (1988). 'Local friendship ties and community attachment in mass society: a multilevel systemic model.' *American Sociological Review*, 53, 766-779.

Sampson, R.J. and Groves, W.B. (1989). 'Community structure and crime: testing social disorganization theory'. *American Journal of Sociology*, 94, 774-802.

Sampson, R.J. and Wooldredge, J.D. (1987). 'Linking the micro and macro-level dimensions of lifestyle-routine activity and opportunity models of predatory victimization'. *Journal of Quantitative Criminology*, 3, 371-393.

Shah, R. and Pease, K. (1992). 'Crime, race and reporting to the police'. *Howard Journal of Criminal Justice*, 31, 192-200.

Skogan, W.G. (1990). *The Police and Public in England and Wales: a British Crime Survey Report*. Home Office Research Study No. 117. London: HMSO.

Skogan, W.G. (1993). *Contacts between Police and Public: findings from the 1992 British Crime Survey.* Home Office Research Study No. 133. London: HMSO.

Smith, S.J. (1987). 'Fear of crime: beyond a geography of deviance'. *Progress in Human Geography*, 11, 1-23.

Smith, S.J. (1987). 'Social relations, neighbourhood structure and the fear of crime in Britain'. In, Evans, D.J. and Herbert, D.T., *The Geography of Crime.* London: Routledge.

Southgate, P. (1984). 'Crime and attitude surveys as an aid to policing'. *Research Bulletin*, No. 18. London: Home Office Research and Planning Unit.

Southgate, P. and Ekblom, P. (1984). *Contacts between Police and Public: findings from the British Crime Survey.* Home Office Research Study No. 77. London: HMSO.

Trickett, A., Osborn, D., Seymour, J. and Pease, K. (1992). 'What is different about high crime areas'. *British Journal of Criminology*, 32, 81-89.

Walker, M. (1983). 'Self-reported crime studies and the British Crime Survey'. *Howard Journal of Criminal Justice*, 22, (3), 168-176.

Walker, N. and Hough, M. (Eds.) (1988). *Public Attitudes to Sentencing.* Farnborough: Gower.

Widom, C.S. and Maxfield, M.G. (1984). 'Sex roles and the victimization of women: evidence from the British Crime Survey'. Paper presented at the Annual Meeting of the American Society of Criminology, Cincinnati, November, 1984.

Worrall, A and Pease, K. (1986). 'Personal crimes against women: findings from the 1982 British Crime Survey'. *Howard Journal of Criminal Justice*, 25, 118-124.

Forthcoming publications

Aye Maung, N. and Mirrlees-Black, C. (Forthcoming). *Racial crimes and harassment against ethnic groups: a British Crime Survey analysis.* Home Office Research and Planning Unit Paper. London: Home Office.

Mayhew, P. (Forthcoming). *Household fires: results from the 1992 British Crime Survey.* Home Office Research and Planning Unit Paper. London: Home Office.

Mott, J. and Mirrlees-Black, C. (Forthcoming). *Self-reported drug misuse in England and Wales in 1991: findings from the 1992 British Crime Survey.* Home Office Research and Planning Unit Paper. London: Home Office.

Pease, K. (Forthcoming). 'Obscene telephone calls in England and Wales: a 1992 British Crime Survey analysis. Final Report to the Home Office. Manchester: University of Manchester.

Trickett, A., Osborn, D. and Ellingworth, D. (1993). 'Simple and repeat victimisation: the influences of individual and area characteristics'. Manchester: University of Manchester. (1993). (Submitted for publication).

Scotland

Allen, M.A. and Payne, D. (1991). *Crime Prevention in Scotland: findings from the 1988 British Crime Survey.* A Scottish Office Central Research Unit Paper.

Chambers, G. and Tombs, J. (Eds.). (1984). *The British Crime Survey: Scotland.* A Scottish Office Social Research Study. Edinburgh: HMSO.

Curren, J. (1987). *The Police and the Public in Scotland (The 1982 British Crime Survey).* Central Research Unit Paper. Edinburgh: Scottish Office.

Kinsey, K. and Anderson, S. (1992). *Crime and the Quality of Life: public perceptions and experiences of crime in Scotland.* Central Research Unit Paper. Edinburgh: Scottish Office.

Payne, D. (1992). *Crime in Scotland: findings from the 1988 British Crime Survey.* Central Research Unit Paper. Edinburgh: Scottish Office.

Technical reports

Details of the design of the surveys can be found, respectively, in:

SCPR. (1993). *The 1992 British Crime Survey Technical Report.* London: Social and Community Planning Research.

NOP/SCPR. (1989). *1988 British Crime Survey Technical Report.* London: NOP Market Research Limited/SCPR.

NOP Market Research Limited. (1985). *1984 British Crime Survey Technical Report.* NOP/9888. London: NOP Market Research Limited.

Wood, D.S. (1983). *British Crime Survey: Technical Report.* London: Social and Community Planning Research.

For a user manual on analysing the 1982 BCS, see:

Hall, J.F. and Walker, A.M. (1985). *User Manual for the first British Crime Survey, 1982.* London: Survey Research Unit, Polytechnic of North London.

Glossary of terms

ACORN—A classification of areas developed by CACI on the basis of selected 1981 Census variables. The eleven ACORN neighbourhood *groups* have been used in this report. Appendix H gives further details.

Acquisitive crime—A sub-set of BCS crimes that can be compared with offences recorded by the police. It includes burglary, thefts of and from vehicles (including attempts), bicycle thefts, and theft from the person.

Afro-Caribbeans—Used to cover one of the two ethnic minority groups covered in the 1992 'booster' sample. They are people who described themselves as 'Black-Caribbean', 'Black-African' or 'Black-other'.

Asians—Used to cover one of the two ethnic minority groups covered in the 'booster' sample. They are people who described themselves as from India, Pakistan or Bangladesh.

Attempted burglary—Burglaries where there is clear evidence that the offender made an attempt to gain entry, but did not actually enter the house. The term 'attempted burglary' is also used occasionally in the report to cover attempts and burglaries with entry which did not involve any loss. See also **Burglary**.

Bicycle theft—Theft of pedal cycles. Thefts of cycles from inside the house by a trespasser are counted as 'burglary'. The survey covers thefts of bicycles belonging to the respondent or any member of the household.

Booster sample—see **Ethnic minority booster sample**.

Burglary—Entering a dwelling as a trespasser with the intention of committing theft, rape, grievous bodily harm, or unlawful damage, whether the intention is carried through or not. Entry may be by force, through an insecure door or window, or by impersonating a workman, meter reader etc. The dwelling is a house, flat or any outhouse or garage linked to the dwelling via a connecting door. Temporary residences (hotel rooms, holiday cottages etc) also count as targets for burglary. Burglaries of other premises (eg shops, warehouses) are not covered in this report, although the police record these. Attempted burglaries (see above) are included with burglaries in this report, unless otherwise specified.

Common assault—Assault or attempted assault where there was no or negligible injury. Common assaults are summary offences in law and are not treated by the police as 'notifiable offences'.

Comparable sub-set—Some 65% of BCS offences fall into categories which can be compared with crimes recorded by the police. This sub-set excludes common assaults, and 'other household thefts' and 'other personal thefts'. Various adjustments are made to recorded crime categories to maximise comparability with the BCS (see Appendix F for details). The comparable sub-set of offences is used to compare trends in police and BCS figures, and to identify the amount of crime that goes unrecorded by the police.

Core sample—The main 1992 BCS sample of 10,059 respondents which, after appropriate weighting, is both a representative cross-section of private households in England and Wales and of individuals aged 16 and over living in such households. See Appendix D for details of sampling.

Crimes of violence—See **Violent offences** below.

Criminal damage—Usually referred to as vandalism in this report—see **vandalism** below.

Domestic burglary—See **Burglary**.

Domestic violence—A component of the typology of violence used in Chapter 6. It includes incidents involving partners, ex-partners, household members and other relatives, irrespective of location.

Ethnic minority booster sample—The additional sample of 1,654 respondents interviewed in the 1992 BCS who were: Afro-Caribbean/African, Indian, Pakistani, or Bangladeshi. See Appendix D for details of sampling procedures.

Home-based violence—A component of the typology of violence used in Chapter 6. It includes incidents in and around the home, including on the street near home, *other than those* involving partners, ex-partners, household members and relatives.

Household—Defined as all people living at the same address, having meals prepared together. Members of a household are not necessarily related by blood or marriage. The BCS covers only private households, not people living in hostels, institutions, hotels etc.

Household offences—For household offences all members of the household can be regarded as victims; the respondent answers on behalf of the whole household. This applies to the following BCS offence categories: bicycle theft, burglary, theft in a dwelling, other household thefts, thefts of and from motor vehicle, and vandalism to household property and motor vehicles.

Household theft—A survey category of household offences covering thefts and attempts from domestic garages, outhouses, sheds, etc not directly linked to the dwelling, and thefts from outside the dwelling (excluding thefts of milk bottles from the doorstep). A small number of attempted thefts of or from motor vehicles were included in the survey category of 'other household thefts' in 1988 but are here counted as vehicle thefts. Thefts in a dwelling were considered as a separate offence category in 1988 but are included in household thefts here. (These include thefts committed inside a home by someone who is entitled to be there at the time of the offence—eg party guests, workmen etc).

Incidence rates—Incidence rates show the total number of victimisations based on the number in the sample. This takes account of the fact that some people experience more than one victimisation.

Manual—A social class classification of the head of household based on the Standard Occupation Classification (SOC). See also **Non-manual** below.

Motor vehicles—Unless otherwise specified, these cover cars, vans, motorcycles, scooters, mopeds etc either owned or regularly used by anyone in the household.

Motor vehicle thefts—These cover three categories: (i) theft or unauthorised taking of a vehicle (where the vehicle is driven away illegally, whether or not it is recovered); (ii) theft from motor vehicles (ie theft of parts, accessories and contents); and (iii) attempts. No distinction is made between attempted thefts *of* and attempted thefts *from* motor vehicles because it is often very difficult to distinguish these. If parts or contents are stolen as well as the vehicle being moved, the incident is classified as theft *of* a motor vehicle.

Mugging—A popular rather than legal term. Used in the typology of violence to include all robbery and 'snatch theft', irrespective of where they occurred. (Snatch theft is a sub-category of theft from the person.)

Non-manual—A social class classification of the head of household, based on the Standard Occupation Classification. See also **Manual** above.

Non-white—A term used to refer to respondents who were in the ethnic groups which the booster sample was meant to pick up (ie, Black-Caribbean/African, Indian, Pakistani or Bangladeshi). See also **White** below.

Notifiable offences—Currently used in *Criminal Statistics for England & Wales* to refer to offences which before 1979 were called 'indictable' and then (briefly)

187

'serious' offences. They relate to the type of offences recorded by the police the totals of which are notified to the Home Office for the compilation of *Criminal Statistics*.

Other personal theft—A survey category referring to theft of personal property away from the home property (eg handbags from offices), where there was no direct contact between the offender and victim. Only the respondent can be the victim of this crime category.

Personal offences—For personal offences, the respondent reported only on his/her experience. This applied to the following BCS offence categories: assaults, sexual offences, robbery, theft from the person, and other personal theft. Information was also collected on threats, but few of these meet the criteria of any notifiable or non-notifiable offence and are therefore not included in the count of survey offences in Chapter 2 or the Chapter 6 on violence.

Prevalence rates—Prevalence rates show the percentage of the sample who were a victim once or more of an offence. Unlike incidence rates they take no account of the *number* of victimisations experienced by each person or household.

Pub/club violence—A component of the typology of violence used in Chapter 6. It includes incidents of violence taking place in pubs, clubs, discos etc but excluding places of entertainment where alcohol is less likely to be served.

Racially motivated crime—incidents in which the ethnic minority victim believed the incident to be 'racially motivated'.

Recall period—This is the time between 1st January 1991 and the date of the interview at which respondents were asked to report offences they had experienced. As most interviews took place between January and March 1992, the average recall period was around 14 months. Only those incidents occurring in 1991 are counted when computing annual rates. Other information about victims and their experiences is usually derived from incidents occurring over the full recall period.

Robbery—Completed or attempted theft of personal property or cash directly from the person, accompanied by force or the threat of force. Robbery should be distinguished from other thefts from the person which involve speed or stealth rather than force or threat.

Street assault—A component of the violence typology used in Chapter 6. It includes incidents of violence taking place on the street, on public transport and in other public places.

Teenager booster sample—In the 1992 survey, 1,051 12 to 15 year olds living in the core sample households, and 299 from the ethnic boost households, answered a self-completion questionnaire which included questions about their experience of crime and use of drugs. This report does not cover results.

Theft from motor vehicles—See **Motor vehicle thefts** above.

Theft from the person—Thefts or attempted thefts of a purse, wallet, cash etc by speed or stealth directly from the person of the victim, but without force or the threat of force. One component of theft from the person is 'snatch theft'. This is added to robbery to create a category of 'mugging'.

Theft in a dwelling—Theft committed *inside* a home by someone who is entitled to be there at the time of the offence (eg party guests, workmen, etc). In previous years, thefts in a dwelling have been treated as comparable with the police statistics category. Here they are included with 'other household thefts' as numbers are small and trends thus unreliable.

Theft of motor vehicles—See **Motor vehicle thefts** above.

Threats, threatening behaviour—Verbal threats or intimidating behaviour. The BCS collected information on threats or intimidation to the respondent or threats made to others against the respondent, treating these as personal offences. (If threats or intimidation took place in the course of other offences, they were subsumed by these.) Threats have not been included in the report as few of them meet the criteria of any notifiable or non-notifiable offence.

Vandalism—Intentional and malicious damage to household property and vehicles —equated with the *Criminal Statistics* category of criminal damage. Vandalism ranges from arson to graffiti. Cases where there is nuisance only (eg letting down car tyres) are not included. Where criminal damage occurs in combination with burglary, robbery or violent offences, these take precedence.

Vehicle thefts around the home—Thefts of and from cars (and attempts) taking place in private or semi-private parking places by the home, or the streets by the home.

Violent offences—In Chapter 2 this term is used to refer to the offences of wounding and robbery which can be compared to the equivalent offences recorded by the police. (In contrast to 1988, sexual offences are excluded.). In Chapter 6 violent offences include: wounding, common assault and mugging.

Weighted data—Raw data from the survey adjusted in various ways at the data processing stage to correct for imbalances introduced in sampling and by the design of the interview. The weights applied are listed in Appendix D.

White—A term used to refer to respondents who said they were white. See also **Non-white** above.

Work-based violence—A component of the violence typology used in Chapter 6 covering incidents of violence at the work-place, including incidents in work car parks, but excluding those in the street near work.

Wounding—A category of violence that includes 'serious wounding' involving severe injuries intentionally inflicted; and, 'other wounding', which involves less serious injury or severe injuries unintentionally inflicted.

References

Anderson, S., Grove-Smith, C., Kinsey, R. and Wood, J. (1990). *The Edinburgh Crime Survey: first report.* Central Research Unit Paper. Edinburgh: Scottish Office.

Barclay, G. (Ed.). (1993). *Digest 2: Information on the Criminal Justice System in England and Wales.* London: Home Office Research and Statistics Department.

Barker, M., Geraghty, J., Webb, B. and Key, T. (1993). *The Prevention of Street Robbery.* Crime Prevention Unit Paper No. 44. London: Home Office.

Barr, R. and Pease, K. (1992). 'A place for every crime and every crime in its place'. In, Evans, D.J., Fyfe, N.R. and Herbert, D.T. (Eds.), *Crime, Policing and Place: essays in environmental criminology.* London: Routledge.

Bennett, T.W. and Wright, R. (1984). *Burglars on Burglary: prevention and the offender.* Farnborough: Gower.

Biderman, A.D., Johnson, L., McIntyre, J. and Weir, A. (1967). *Report on a Pilot Study in the District of Columbia on Victimisation and Attitudes to Law Enforcement. US President's Commission on Victimisation and Administration of Justice, Field Studies I.* Washington, DC: Government Printing Office.

Blumstein, A., Cohen, J. and Rosenfeld, R. (1991). 'Trend and deviation in crime rates: a comparison of UCR and NCS data for burglary and robbery'. *Criminology,* 29, 237-263.

Block, C.B. and Block, R.L. (1984). 'Crime definition, crime measurement and victim surveys'. *Journal of Social Issues,* 40, 137-160.

Bottoms, A.E., Mawby, R.I. and Walker, M. (1987). 'A localised crime survey in contrasting areas of a city'. *British Journal of Criminology,* 27, 125-154.

Chambers, G. and Tombs, J. (Eds.). (1984). *The British Crime Survey: Scotland.* A Scottish Office Social Research Study. Edinburgh: HMSO.

Clarke, R. (1991). *Preventing Vehicle Theft: a policy oriented review of the literature.* Central Research Unit Paper. Edinburgh: Scottish Office.

Clarke, R. and Harris, P.M. (1992). 'Auto Theft and its Prevention'. In, Tonry, M. (Ed.), *Crime and Justice: a review of research.* Vol. 16. Chicago: University of Chicago Press.

Crawford, A., Jones, T., Woodhouse, T. and Young, J. (1990). *The Second Islington Crime Survey.* Centre for Criminology. Middlesex: Middlesex Polytechnic.

Cretney, A., Davis, G., Clarkson, C. and Shepherd, J. (Forthcoming). 'The victim's decision to report a crime'. In, Gottfredson, M.R. and Gottfredson, D.M. (Eds.), *Decision Making in Criminal Justice.* London: Plenum Press.

Davidoff, L. and Dowds, L. (1989). 'Recent trends in crimes of violence against the person in England and Wales'. *Research Bulletin,* No. 27. London: Home Office Research and Planning Unit.

Davidson, R. N. (1992). *Crime in your Neighbourhood.* Report to the Home Office. Hull: University of Hull.

Dodge, R. and Lentzner, H. (1984). 'Patterns of personal series victimizations in the National Crime Survey'. In, Lehnen, R.G. and Skogan, W.G. (Eds.), *The National Crime Survey: Working Papers.* Vol II: Methodological Studies. Bureau of Justice Statistics, US Department of Justice. Washington, DC: Government Printing Office.

Durant, M., Thomas, M. and Willcock, H.D. (1972). *Crime, Criminals and the Law.* London: HMSO.

Elliott, D. and Mayhew, P. (1988). 'Trends in residential burglary: an update'. *Research Bulletin,* No. 25. London: Home Office Research and Planning Unit.

Ennis, P.H. (1967). *Criminal Victimisation in the United States. A Report of a National Survey. US President's Commission on Victimisation and Administration of Justice, Field Studies II.* Washington, DC: Government Printing Office.

Farrell, G. and Pease, K. (1993). *Once Bitten, Twice Bitten: repeat victimisation and its implications for crime prevention.* Report to the Home Office Crime Prevention Unit. Manchester: University of Manchester.

Farrell, G. (1993). 'Preventing revictimisation'. In, Tonry, M. and Farrington, D. (Eds.), *Crime and Justice: a review of research.* Vol. 18. Chicago: University of Chicago Press.

Farrington, D.P. and Dowds, E.A. (1985). 'Disentangling criminal behaviour and police reaction'. In, Farrington, D.P. and Gunn, J. (Eds.), *Reaction to Crime: the public, the police, courts, and prisons.* Chichester: John Wiley.

Forrester, D., Chatterton, M. and Pease, K. (1988). *The Kirkholt Burglary Prevention Project, Rochdale.* Crime Prevention Unit Paper No. 13. London: Home Office.

Genders, E. (1991). *Types of Violent Crime: a report on a study in the West Midlands.* Report to the Home Office. Oxford: Centre for Criminological Report, University of Oxford.

Gottfredson, M.R. (1986). 'The substantive contribution of victimization surveys'. In, Tonry, M. and Morris, N. (Eds.), *Crime and Justice: an annual review of research.* Vol 7. Chicago: University of Chicago Press.

Gottfredson, M.R. and Gottfredson, D.M. (Eds.). (1988). *Decision-Making in Criminal Justice.* Second Edition. Law, Society and Politics, Vol. 3. London: Plenum Press.

Home Office. (1982). *Unrecorded Offences of Burglary and Theft in a Dwelling in England and Wales: estimates from the General Household Survey.* Home Office Statistical Bulletin 11/82. London: Home Office.

Home Office. (1992). *Criminal Statistics, England and Wales, 1991.* Cm. 2134. London: HMSO.

Hope, T. (1987). 'Residential aspects of autocrime'. *Research Bulletin,* No. 23. London: Home Office Research and Planning Unit.

Hough, M. and Mayhew, P. (1985). *Taking Account of Crime: key findings from the 1984 British Crime Survey.* Home Office Research Study No. 86. London: HMSO.

Houghton, G. (1992). *Car Theft in England and Wales: the Home Office Car Theft Index*, Crime Prevention Unit Paper No. 33. London: Home Office.

Kinsey, K. and Anderson, S. (1992). *Crime and the Quality of Life: public perceptions and experiences of crime in Scotland.* Central Research Unit Paper. Edinburgh: Scottish Office.

Lea, J., Jones, T., Woodhouse T. and Young, J. (1988). *Preventing Crime: the Hilldrop Environmental Improvement Survey. First report.* Centre for Criminology. Middlesex: Middlesex Polytechnic.

Lewis, H. and Mo, J. (1986). 'Burglary insurance: findings from the British Crime Survey'. *Research Bulletin*, No. 22. London: Home Office Research and Planning Unit.

Light, R. Nee, C. and Ingham, H. (1993). *Car Theft: the offender's perspective.* Home Office Research Study No. 130. London: HMSO.

Litton, R.A. (1987). 'Crime and insurance'. *The Geneva Papers on Risk and Insurance.* Vol. 12, No. 44, July, 198-225.

Maguire, M. (1980). 'Burglary as opportunity'. *Research Bulletin*, No. 10. London: Home Office Research and Planning Unit.

Maguire, M. and Wilkinson, C. (1993). *Contact with Victims.* Home Office Research and Planning Unit Occasional Paper. London: Home Office.

Mayhew, P. (1985). 'The effects of crime: victims, the public and fear'. In, Research on Victimisation. *Collected Studies in Criminological Research.* Vol. XXIII. Strasbourg: Council of Europe.

Mayhew, P. (1990). 'Opportunity and vehicle crime'. In, Gottfredson, D.M. and Clarke, R. (Eds.), *Policy and Theory in Criminal Justice: contributions in honour of Leslie T. Wilkins.* Cambridge Study in Criminology. Aldershot: Gower.

Mayhew, P. and Aye Maung, N. (1992). *Surveying Crime: findings from the 1992 British Crime Survey.* Research Findings No. 2. London: Home Office Research and Statistics Department.

Mayhew, P. and Elliott, D. (1988). 'Trends in residential burglary in England and Wales: an update. *Research Bulletin*, No. 25. London: Home Office Research and Planning Unit.

Mayhew, P., Elliott, D. and Dowds, L. (1989). *The 1988 British Crime Survey.* Home Office Research Study No. 111. London: HMSO.

Mayhew, P. and Smith, L.J.F. (1985). 'Crime in England and Wales and Scotland: a British Crime Survey comparison'. *British Journal of Criminology*, 25, 2, 148-159.

McAllister, D., Leitch, S. and Payne, D. (1993). *Crime Prevention and Housebreaking in Scotland: findings from the 1989 and 1990 Labour Force Surveys.* Central Research Unit Paper. Edinburgh: Scottish Office.

Nee, C. and Taylor, M. (1988). 'Residential burglary in the Republic of Ireland: a situational perspective'. *Howard Journal of Criminal Justice*, 27, 105-116.

Newburn, T. and Merry, S. (1990). *Keeping in touch: police-victim communication in two areas.* Home Office Research Study No. 116. London: HMSO.

NOP Market Research Limited. (1985). *1984 British Crime Survey Technical Report.* Nop/9888. London: NOP Market Research Limited.

NOP/SCPR. (1989). *1988 British Crime Survey Technical Report.* London: NOP Market Research Limited/SCPR.

Office of Population Censuses and Surveys (OPCS). (1993). *The 1991 General Household Survey.* London: HMSO.

Painter, K. (1992). 'Different social worlds: the spatial, temporal and social dimensions of female victimization'. In, *Crime, Policing and Place, Evans, D.,* Fyfe, N. and Herbert, D.T (Eds.). London: Routledge.

Painter, K., Lea, J. Woodhouse, T. and Young, J. (1989). *Hammersmith and Fulham Crime and Policy Survey.* Centre for Criminology. Middlesex: Middlesex Polytechnic.

Payne, D. (1992). *Crime in Scotland: findings from the 1988 British Crime Survey.* Central Research Unit Paper. Edinburgh: Scottish Office.

Pease, K. (1988). *Judgements of Crime Seriousness: evidence from the 1984 British Crime Survey.* Home Office Research and Planning Unit Paper No. 44. London: Home Office.

Polvi, N., Looman, T. Humphries, C. and Pease, K. (1990). 'Repeat break-and-enter victimisation: time, course and crime prevention opportunity'. *Journal of Police Science and Administration,* 17, 8-11.

Reynolds, T., Viney, A., Aye Maung, N. and Phillips, M. (1993). *A Survey of Victim Support Volunteers.* London: Victim Support.

SCPR. (1993). *1992 British Crime Survey Technical Report.* London: Social and Community Planning Research.

Shaw, C. (1988). 'Latest estimates of ethnic minority populations'. *Population Trends,* No. 51. London: HMSO.

Skogan, W.G. (1984). 'Reporting crime to the police: the status of world research'. *Journal of Research in Crime and Delinquency,* 21, 113-137.

Skogan, W.G. (1986). 'Methodological issues in the study of victimisation'. In, E.A. Fattah (Ed.), *From Crime Policy to Victim Policy.* Basingstoke: Macmillan.

Skogan, W.G. (1990). 'The Polls—a Review. The National Crime Survey Redesign'. *Public Opinion Quarterly,* 54: 256-272.

Skogan, W.G. (Forthcoming). *Contacts between Police and Public: findings from the 1992 British Crime Survey.* Home Office Research Study. London: HMSO.

Skogan, W.G. and Antunes, G.E. (1979). 'Information, apprehension and deterrence: exploring the limits of police productivity.' *Journal of Research in Crime and Delinquency,* 21, 113-137.

Sparks, R.F. (1980). 'Criminal opportunities and crime rates'. In, Feinberg, S.E., and Reiss, A.J. (Eds.), *Indicators of Crime and Criminal Justice: quantitative studies.* Bureau of Justice Statistics, US Department of Justice. Washington, DC: Government Printing Office.

Sparks, R.F. (1981). 'Surveys of Victimisation—an optimistic assessment'. In, Tonry, M. and Morris, N. (Eds.), *Crime and Justice: an annual review of research.* Vol. 3. London: University of Chicago Press.

Sparks, R.F., Genn, H. and Dodd, D.J. (1977). *Surveying Victims.* London: John Wiley.

Tuck, M. and Southgate, P. (1981). *Ethnic minorities, Crime and Policing.* Home Office Research Study No. 70. London: HMSO.

US Department of Justice. (1976). *Criminal Victimization in the United States, 1976.* A National Crime Survey report. Washington DC: Government Printing Office.

van Dijk, J.J.M. (1982). 'The victim's willingness to report to the police: a function of prosecution policy'. In, Schneider, H.J. (Ed.), *The Victim in International Perspective.* Berlin and New York: Gruyter.

van Dijk, J.J.M. and Mayhew, P. (1993). *Criminal Victimisation in the Industrialised World: key findings of the 1989 and 1992 International Crime Survey.* The Hague: Directorate of Crime Prevention, Ministry of Justice.

Victim Support. (1992). *Annual Report: 1991/92.* London: Victim Support.

Waller, I. (1982). 'Crime victims: needs, services and reforms. Orphans of a social policy'. Paper presented at the IVth International Symposium on Victimology, Tokyo/Kyota, 1982.

Webb, B., Brown, B. and Bennett, T. (1992). *Preventing Car Crime in Car Parks.* Crime Prevention Unit Paper No. 34. London: Home Office.

Webb, B. and Laycock, G. (1992). *Tackling Car Crime: the nature and extent of the problem.* Crime Prevention Unit Paper No. 32. London: Home Office.

Publications

---

*   Out of print

4. *Firearms in crime. A Home Office Statistical Division report on indictable offences involving firearms in England and Wales. A. D. Weatherhead and B. M. Robinson. 1970. viii + 39pp. (11 340104 3).

5. *Financial penalties and probation. Martin Davies. 1970. vii + 39pp. (11 340105 1).

6. *Hostels for probationers. A study of the aims, working and variations in effectiveness of male probation hostels with special reference to the influence of the environment on delinquency. Ian Sinclair. 1971. ix + 200pp. (11 340106 X).

7. *Prediction methods in criminology—including a prediction study of young men on probation. Frances H. Simon. 1971. xi + 234pp. (11 340107 8).

8. *Study of the juvenile liaison scheme in West Ham 1961-65. Marilyn Taylor. 1971. vi + 46pp. (11 340108 6).

9. *Explorations in after-care. I—after-care units in London, Liverpool and Manchester. Martin Silberman (Royal London Prisoners' Aid Society) and Brenda Chapman. II—After-care hostels receiving a Home Office grant. Ian Sinclair and David Snow (HORU). III—St. Martin of Tours House, Aryeh Leissner (National Bureau for Co-operation in Child Care). 1971. xi + 140pp. (11 340109 4).

10. *A survey of adoption in Great Britain. Eleanor Grey in collaboration with Ronald M. Blunden. 1971. ix + 168pp. (11 340110 8).

11. *Thirteen-year-old approved school boys in 1962s. Elizabeth Field, W. H. Hammond and J. Tizard. 1971. ix + 46pp. (11 340111 6).

12. *Absconding from approved schools. R. V. G. Clarke and D. N. Martin. 1971. vi + 146pp. (11 340112 4).

13. *An experiment in personality assessment of young men remanded in custody. H. Sylvia Anthony. 1972. viii + 79pp. (11 340113 2).

14. *Girl offenders aged 17-20 years. I—Statistics relating to girl offenders aged 17-20 years from 1960 to 1970. II—Re-offending by girls released from borstal or detention centre training. III—The problems of girls released from borstal training during their period on after-care. Jean Davies and Nancy Goodman. 1972. v + 77pp. (11 340114 0).

15. *The controlled trial in institutional research—paradigm or pitfall or penal evaluators? R. V. G. Clarke and D. B. Cornish. 1972. v + 33pp. (11 340115 9).

16. *A survey of fine enforcement. Paul Softley. 1973. v + 65pp. (11 340116 7).

17. *An index of social environment—designed for use in social work menum research. Martin Davies. 1973. vi + 63pp. (11 340117 5).

18. *Social enquiry reports and the probation service. Martin Davies and Andrea Knopf. 1973. v + 49pp. (11 340118 3).

19. *Depression, psychopathic personality and attempted suicide in a borstal sample. H. Sylvia Anthony. 1973. viii + 44pp. (0 11 340119 1).

20. *The use of bail and custody by London magistrates' courts before and after the Criminal Justice Act 1967. Frances Simon and Mollie Weatheritt. 1974. vi + 78pp. (0 11 340120 5).

21. *Social work in the environment. A study of one aspect of probation practice. Martin Davies, with Margaret Rayfield. Alaster Calder and Tony Fowles. 1974. ix + 151pp. (0 11 340121 3).

22. *Social work in prison. An experiment in the use of extended contact with offenders. Margaret Shaw. 1974. viii + 154pp. (0 11 340122 1).

23. *Delinquency amongst opiate users. Joy Mott and Marilyn Taylor. 1974. vi + 31pp. (0 11 340663 0).

24. *IMPACT. Intensive matched probation and after-care treatment. Vol I—The design of the probation experiment and an interim evaluation. M. S. Folkard, A. J. Fowles, B. C. McWilliams, W. McWilliams, D. D. Smith, D. E. Smith and G. R. Walmsley. 1974. v + 54pp. (0 11 340664 9).

---

* Out of print

25. *The approved school experience. An account of boys' experiences of training under differing regimes of approved schools, with an attempt to evaluate the effectiveness of that training. Anne B. Dunlop. 1974. vii + 124pp. (0 11 340665 7).
26. *Absconding from open prisons. Charlotte Banks, Patricia Mayhew and R. J. Sapsford. 1975. viii + 89pp. (0 11 340666 5).
27. *Driving while disqualified. Sue Kriefman. 1975. vi + 136pp. (0 11 340667 3).
28. *Some male offenders' problems. I—Homeless offenders in Liverpool. W. McWilliams. II—Casework with short-term prisoners. Julie Holborn. 1975. x + 147pp. (0 11 340668 1).
29. *Community service orders. K. Pease, P. Durkin, I. Earnshaw, D. Payne and J. Thorpe. 1975. viii + 80pp. (0 11 340669 X).
30. *Field Wing Bail Hostel: the first nine months. Frances Simon and Sheena Wilson. 1975. viii + 55pp. (0 11 340670 3).
31. *Homicide in England and Wales 1967-1971. Evelyn Gibson. 1975. iv + 59pp. (0 11 340753 X).
32. *Residential treatment and its effects on delinquency. D. B. Cornish and R. V. G. Clarke. 1975. vi + 74pp. (0 11 340672 X).
33. *Further studies of female offenders. Part A: Borstal girls eight years after release. Nancy Goodman, Elizabeth Maloney and Jean Davies. Part B: The sentencing of women at the London Higher Courts. Nancy Goodman, Paul Durkin and Janet Halton. Part C: Girls appearing before a juvenile court. Jean Davies. 1976. vi + 114pp. (0 11 340673 8).
34. *Crime as opportunity. P. Mayhew, R. V. G. Clarke, A. Sturman and J. M. Hough. 1976. vii + 36pp. (0 11 340674 6).
35. *The effectiveness of sentencing: a review of the literature. S. R. Brody. 1976. v + 89pp. (0 11 340675 4).
36. *IMPACT. Intensive matched probation and after-care treatment. Vol. II—The results of the experiment. M. S. Folkard, D. E. Smith and D. D. 1976. xi + 40pp. (0 11 340676 2).
37. *Police cautioning in England and Wales. J. A. Ditchfield. 1976. v + 31pp. (0 11 340677 0).
38. *Parole in England and Wales. C. P. Nuttall, with E. E. Barnard, A. J. Fowles, A. Frost, W. H. Hammond, P. Mayhew, K. Pease, R. Tarling and M. J. Weatheritt. 1977. vi + 90pp. (0 11 340678 9).
39. *Community service assessed in 1976. K. Pease, S. Billingham and I. Earnshaw. 1977. vi + 29pp. (0 11 340679 7).
40. *Screen violence and film censorship: a review of research. Stephen Brody. 1977. vii + 179pp. (0 11 340680 0).
41. *Absconding from borstals. Gloria K. Laycock. 1977. v + 82pp. (0 11 340681 9).
42. *Gambling: a review of the literature and its implications for policy and research. D. B. Cornish. 1978. xii + 284pp. (0 11 340682 7).
43. *Compensation orders in magistrates' courts. Paul Softley. 1978. v + 41pp. (0 11 340683 5).
44. *Research in criminal justice. John Croft. 1978. iv + 16pp. (0 11 340684 3).
45. *Prison welfare: an account of an experiment at Liverpool. A. J. Fowles. 1978. v + 34pp. (0 11 340685 1).
46. *Fines in magistrates' courts. Paul Softley. 1978. v + 42pp. (0 11 340686 X).
47. *Tackling vandalism. R. V. Clarke (editor), F. J. Gladstone, A. Sturman and Sheena Wilson (contributors). 1978. vi + 91pp. (0 11 340687 8).
48. *Social inquiry reports: a survey. Jennifer Thorpe. 1979. vi + 55p. (0 11 340688 6).
49. *Crime in public view. P. Mayhew, R. V. G. Clarke, J. N. Burrows, J. M. Hough and S. W. C. Winchester. 1979. v + 36pp. (0 11 340689 4)
50. *Crime and the community. John Croft. 1979. v + 16pp. (0 11 340690 8).
51. *Life-sentence prisoners. David Smith (editor), Christopher Brown, Joan Worth, Roger Sapsford and Charlotte Banks (contributors). 1979. iv + 51pp. (0 11 340691 6).

---

* Out of print

52. *Hostels for offenders. Jane E. Andrews, with an appendix by Bill Sheppard. 1979. v + 30pp. (0 11 340692 4).

53. *Previous convictions, sentence and reconviction: a statistical study of a sample of 5,000 offenders convicted in January 1971. G. J. O. Phillpotts and L. B. Lancucki. 1979. v + 55pp. (0 11 340 693 2).

54. *Sexual offences, consent and sentencing. Roy Walmsley and Karen White. 1979. vi + 77pp. (0 11 340694 0).

55. *Crime prevention and the police. John Burrows, Paul Ekblom and Kevin Heal. 1979. v + 37pp. (0 11 340695 9).

56. *Sentencing practice in magistrates' courts. Roger Tarling, with the assistance of Mollie Weatheritt. 1979. vii + 54pp. (0 11 340696 7).

57. *Crime and comparative research. John Croft. 1979. iv + 16pp. (0 11 340697 5).

58. *Race, crime and arrests. Philip Stevens and Carole F. Willis. 1979. v + 69pp. (0 11 340698 3).

59. *Research and criminal policy. John Croft. 1980. iv + 14pp. (0 11 340699 1).

60. *Junior attendance centres. Anne B. Dunlop. 1980. v + 47pp. (0 11 340700 9).

61. *Police interrogation: an observational study in four police stations. Paul Softley, with the assistance of David Brown, Bob Forde, George Mair and David Moxon. 1980. vii + 67pp. (0 11 340701 7).

62. *Co-ordinating crime prevention efforts. F. J. Gladstone. 1980. v + 74pp. (0 11 340702 5).

63. *Crime prevention publicity: an assessment. D. Riley and P. Mayhew. 1980. v + 47pp. (0 11 340703 3).

64. *Taking offenders out of circulation. Stephen Brody and Roger Tarling. 1980. v + 46pp. (0 11 340704 1).

65. *Alcoholism and social policy: are we on the right lines? Mary Tuck. 1980. v + 30pp. (0 11 340705 X).

66. *Persistent petty offenders. Suzan Fairhead. 1981. vi + 78pp. (0 11 340706 8).

67. *Crime control and the police. Pauline Morris and Kevin Heal. 1981. v + 71pp. (0 11 340 707 6).

68. *Ethnic minorities in Britain: a study of trends in their position since 1961. Simon Field, George Mair, Tom Rees and Philip Stevens. 1981. v + 48pp. (0 11 340708 4).

69. *Managing criminological research. John Croft. 1981. iv + 17pp. (0 11 340709 2).

70. *Ethnic minorities, crime and policing: a survey of the experiences of West Indians and whites. Mary Tuck and Peter Southgate. 1981. iv + 54pp. (0 11 340765 3).

71. *Contested trials in magistrates' courts. Julie Vennard. 1982. v + 32pp. (0 11 340766 1).

72. *Public disorder: a review of research and a study in one inner city area. Simon Field and Peter Southgate. 1982. v + 77pp. (0 11 340767 X).

73. *Clearing up crime. John Burrows and Roger Tarling. 1982. vii + 31pp. (0 11 340768 8).

74. *Residential burglary: the limits of prevention. Stuart Winchester and Hilary Jackson. 1982. v + 47pp. (0 11 340769 6).

75. *Concerning crime. John Croft. 1982. iv + 16pp. (0 11 340 770 X).

76. *The British Crime Survey: first report. Mike Hough and Pat Mayhew. 1983. v + 62pp. (0 11 340786 6).

77. *Contacts between police and public: findings from the British Crime Survey. Peter Southgate and Paul Ekblom. 1984. v + 42pp. (0 11 340771 8).

78. *Fear of crime in England and Wales. Michael Maxfield. 1984. v + 57pp. (0 11 340772 6).

79. *Crime and police effectiveness. Ronald V. Clarke and Mike Hough 1984. iv + 33pp. (0 11 340773 3).

80. The attitudes of ethnic minorities. Simon Field. 1984. v + 49pp. (0 11 340774 2).

---

*   Out of print

81. Victims of crime: the dimensions of risk. Michael Gottfredson. 1984. v + 54pp. (0 11 340775 0).
82. The tape recording of police interviews with suspects: an interim report. Carole Willis. 1984. v + 45pp. (0 11 340776 9).
83. Parental supervision and juvenile delinquency. David Riley and Margaret Shaw. 1985. v + 90pp. (0 11 340799 8).
84. Adult prisons and prisoners in England and Wales 1970-1982: a review of the findings of social research. Joy Mott. 1985. vi + 73pp. (0 11 340801 3).
85. Taking account of crime: key findings from the 1984 British Crime Survey. Mike Hough and Pat Mayhew. 1985. vi + 115pp. (0 11 341810 2).
86. Implementing crime prevention measures. Tim Hope. 1985. vi + 82pp. (0 11 340812 9).
87. Resettling refugees: the lessons of research. Simon Field. 1985. vi + 66pp. (0 11 340815 3).
88. Investigating burglary: the measurement of police performance. John Burrows. 1986. vi + 36pp. (0 11 340824 2).
89. Personal violence. Roy Walmsley. 1986. vi + 87pp. (0 11 340827 7).
90. *Police-public encounters. Peter Southgate. 1986. vi + 150pp. (0 11 340834 X).
91. Grievance procedures in prisons. John Ditchfield and Claire Austin. 1986. vi + 87pp. (0 11 340839 0).
92. The effectiveness of the Forensic Science Service. Malcolm Ramsay. 1987. v + 100pp. (0 11 340842 0).
93. The police complaints procedure: a survey of complainant's views. David Brown. 1987. v + 98pp. (0 11 340853 6).
94. The validity of the reconviction prediction score. Denis Ward. 1987. vi + 46. (0 11 340882 X).
95. Economic aspects of the illicit drug market enforcement policies in the United Kingdom. Adam Wagstaff and Alan Maynard. 1988. vii + 156pp. (0 11 340883 8).
96. Schools, disruptive behaviour and deliquency: a review of literature. John Graham. 1988. v + 70pp. (0 11 340887 0).
97. The tape recording of police interviews with suspects: a second interim report. Carole Willis, John Macleod and Peter Naish. 1988. vii + 97pp. (0 11 340890 0).
98. Triable-either-way cases: Crown Court or magistrate's court. David Riley and Julie Vennard. 1988. v + 52pp. (0 11 340891 9).
99. Directing patrol work: a study of uniformed policing. John Burrows and Helen Lewis. 1988. v + 66pp. (0 11 340891 9).
100. Probation day centres. George Mair. 1988. v + 44pp. (0 11 340894 3).
101. Amusement machines: dependency and delinquency. John Graham. 1988. v + 48pp. (0 11 340895 1).
102. The use and enforcement of compensation orders in magistrates' courts. Tim Newburn. 1988. v + 49pp. (0 11 340 896 X).
103. Sentencing practice in the Crown Court. David Moxon. 1988. v + 90pp. (0 11 340902 8).
104. Detention at the police station under the Police and Criminal Evidence Act 1984. David Brown. 1988. v + 88pp. (0 11 340908 7).
105. Changes in rape offences and sentencing. Charles Lloyd and Roy Walmsley. 1989. vi + 53pp. (0 11 340910 9).
106. Concerns about rape. Lorna Smith. 1989. v + 48pp. (0 11 340911 7).
107. Domestic violence. Lorna Smith. 1989. v + 132pp. (0 11 340925 7).
108. Drinking and disorder: a study of non-metropolitan violence. Mary Tuck. 1989. v + 111pp. (0 11 340926 5).
109. Special security units. Roy Walmsley. 1989. v + 114pp. (0 11 340961 3).

---

*   Out of print

110. Pre-trial delay: the implications of time limits. Patricia Morgan and Julie Vennard. 1989. v + 66pp. (0 11 340964 8).
111. The 1988 British Crime Survey. Pat Mayhew, David Elliott and Lizanne Dowds. 1989. v + 133pp. (0 11 340965 6).
112. The settlement of claims at the Criminal Injuries Compensation Board. Tim Newburn. 1989. v + 40pp. (0 11 340967 2).
113. Race, community groups and service delivery. Hilary Jackson and Simon Field. 1989. v + 62pp. (0 11 340972 9).
114. Money payment supervision orders: probation policy and practice. George Mair and Charles Lloyd. 1989. v + 40pp. (0 11 340971 0).
115. Suicide and self-injury in prison: a literature review. Charles Lloyd. 1990. v + 69pp. (0 11 3409745 5).
116. Keeping in touch: police-victim communication in two areas. Tim Newburn and Susan Merry. 1990. v + 52pp. (0 11 340974 5).
117. The police and public in England and Wales: a British Crime Survey report. Wesley G. Skogan. 1990. vi + 74pp. (0 11 340995 8).
118. Control in prisons: a review of the literature. John Ditchfield. 1990. (0 11 340996 6).
119. Trends in crime and their interpretation: a study of recorded crime in post-war England and Wales. Simon Field. 1990. (0 11 340994 X).
120. Electronic monitoring: the trials and their results. George Mair and Claire Nee. 1990. v + 79pp. (0 11 340998 2).
121. Drink driving: the effects of enforcement. David Riley. 1991. viii + 78pp. (0 11 340999 0).
122. Managing difficult prisoners: the Parkhurst Special Unit. Roy Walmsley (Ed.) 1991. x + 139pp. (0 11 341008 5).
123. Investigating burglary: the effects of PACE. David Brown. 1991. xii + 106pp. (0 11 341011 5).
124. Traffic policing in changing times. Peter Southgate and Catriona Mirlees-Black. 1991. viii + 139pp. (0 11 341019 0).
125. Magistrates' court or Crown Court? mode of trial decisions and sentencing. Carol Hedderman and David Moxon. 1992. vii + 53pp. (0 11 341036 0).
126. Developments in the use of compensation orders in magistrates' courts since October 1988. David Moxon, John Martin Corkery and Carol Hedderman. 1992. x + 48pp. (0 11 341042 5).
127. A comparative study of firefighting arrangements in Britain, Denmark, the Netherlands and Sweden. John Graham, Simon Field, Roger Tarling and Heather Wilkinson. 1992. x + 57pp. (0 11 341043 3).
128. The National Prison Survey 1991: main findings. Roy Walmsley, Liz Howard and Sheila White. 1992. xiv + 82p. (0 11 341051 4).
129. Changing the Code: police detention under the revised PACE Codes of Practice. David Brown, Tom Ellis and Karen Larcombe. 1992. viii + 122pp. (0 11 341052 2).
130. Car theft: the offender's perspective. Roy Light, Claire Nee and Helen Ingham. 1993. x + 89pp. (0 11 341069 7).
131. Housing, community and crime: the impact of the Priority Estates Project. Janet Foster and Tim Hope. 1993. xi + 119pp. (0 11 341078 6).

ALSO

Designing out crime. R. V. G. Clarke and P. Mayhew (editors). 1980. viii+186pp. (0 11 340732 7).
(This book collects, with an introduction, studies that were originally published in HORS 34, 47, 49, 55, 62 and 63 and which are illustrative of the 'situational' approach to crime prevention.)

---

*   Out of print

Policing today. Kevin Heal, Roger Tarling and John Burrows (editors). v+181pp. (0 11 340800 5).
(This book brings together twelve separate studies on police matters produced during the last few years by the Unit. The collection records some relatively little known contributions to the debate on policing.)

Managing Criminal Justice: a collection of papers. David Moxon (ed.). 1985. vi+222pp. (0 11 340811 0).
(This book brings together a number of studies bearing on the management of the criminal justice system. It includes papers by social scientists and operational researchers working within the Research and Planning Unit, and academic researchers who have studied particular aspects of the criminal process.)

Situational Crime Prevention: from theory into practice. Kevin Heal and Gloria Laycock (editors). 1986. vii+166pp. (0 11 340826 9).
(Following the publication of *Designing Out Crime*, further research has been completed on the theoretical background to crime prevention. In drawing this work together this book sets down some of the theoretical concerns and discusses the emerging practical issues. It includes contributions by Unit staff as well as academics from this country and abroad.)

Communities and crime reduction. Tim Hope and Margaret Shaw (eds.). 1988. vii+311pp. (11 340892 7).
(The central theme of this book is the possibility of preventing crime by building upon the resources of local communities and of active citizens. The specially commissioned chapters, by distinguished international authors, review contemporary research and policy on community crime prevention.)

New directions in police training. Peter Southgage (ed.). 1988 xi+256pp. (11 340889 7).
(Training is central to the development of the police role, and particular thought and effort now go into making it more responsive to current needs—in order to produce police officers who are both effective and sensitive in their dealing with the public. This book illustrates some of the thinking and research behind these developments.)

The above HMSO publications can be purchased from Government Bookshops or through booksellers.

The following Home Office research publications are available on request from the Home Office Research and Planning Unit, 50 Queen Anne's Gate, London SW1H 9AT.

Research Unit Papers (RUP)

1. Uniformed police work and management technology. J. M. Hough. 1980.

2. Supplementary information on sexual offences and sentencing. Roy Walmsley and Karen White. 1980.

3. Board of visitor adjudications. David Smith, Claire Austin and John Ditchfield. 1981.

4. Day centres and probation. Suzan Fairhead, with the assistance of J. Wilkinson-Grey. 1981.

---

* Out of print

Research and Planning Unit Papers (RPUP)

5. Ethnic minorities and complaints against the police. Philip Stevens and Carole Willis. 1982.

6. *Crime and public housing. Mike Hough and Pat Mayhew (editors). 1982.

7. *Abstracts of race relations research. George Mair and Philip Stevens (editors). 1982.

8. Police probationer training in race relations. Peter Southgate. 1982.

9. *The police response to calls from the public. Paul Ekblom and Kevin Heal. 1982.

10. City centre crime: a situational approach to prevention. Malcolm Ramsay. 1982.

11. Burglary in schools: the prospects for prevention. Tim Hope. 1982.

12. *Fine enforcement. Paul Softley and David Moxon. 1982.

13. Vietnamese refugees. Peter Jones. 1982.

14. Community resources for victims of crime. Karen Williams. 1983.

15. The use, effectiveness and impact of police stop and search powers. Carole Willis. 1983.

16. Acquittal rates. Sid Butler. 1983.

17. Criminal justice comparisons: the case of Scotland and England and Wales. Lorna J. F. Smith. 1983.

18. Time taken to deal with juveniles under criminal proceedings. Catherine Frankenburg and Roger Tarling. 1983.

19. Civilian review of complains against the police: a survey of the United States literature. David C. Brown. 1983.

20. Police action on motoring offences. David Riley. 1983.

21. *Diverting drunks from the criminal justice system. Sue Kingsley and George Mair. 1983.

22. The staff resource implications of an independent prosecution system. Peter R. Jones. 1983.

23. Reducing the prison population: an exploratory study in Hampshire. David Smith, Bill Sheppard, George Mair, Karen Williams. 1984.

24. Criminal justice system model: magistrates' courts sub-model. Susan Rice. 1984.

25. Measures of police effectiveness and efficiency. Ian Sinclair and Clive Miller. 1984.

26. Punishment practice by prison Boards of Visitors. Susan Iles, Adrienne Connors, Chris May, Joy Mott. 1984.

27. *Reparation, conciliation and mediation: current projects and plans in England and Wales. Tony Marshall. 1984.

28. Magistrates' domestic courts: new perspectives. Tony Marshall (editor). 1984.

29. Racism awareness training for the police. Peter Southgate. 1984.

---

* Out of print

30. Community constables: a case study of a policing initiative. David Brown and Susan Iles. 1985.

31. Recruiting volunteers. Hilary Jackson. 1985.

32. Juvenile sentencing: is there a tariff? David Moxon, Peter Jones, Roger Tarling. 1985.

33. Bringing people together: mediation and reparation projects in Great Britain. Tony Marshall and Martin Walpole. 1985.

34. Remands in the absence of the accused. Chris May. 1985.

35. Modelling the criminal justice system. Patricia M. Morgan. 1985.

36. The criminal justice system model: the flow model. Hugh Pullinger. 1986.

37. Burglary: police actions and victim views. John Burrows. 1986.

38. Unlocking community resources: four experimental government small grants schemes. Hilary Jackson. 1986.

39. The cost of discriminating: a review of the literature. Shirley Dex. 1986.

40. Waiting for Crown Court trial: the remand population. Rachel Pearce. 1987.

41. Children's evidence the need for corroboration. Carol Hedderman. 1987.

42. A preliminary study of victim offender mediation and reparation schemes in England and Wales. Gwynn Davis, Jacky Boucherat, David Watson, Adrian Thatcher (Consultant). 1987.

43. Explaining fear of crime: evidence from the 1984 British Crime Survey. Michael Maxfield. 1987.

44. Judgements of crime seriousness: evidence from the 1984 British Crime Survey. Ken Pease. 1988.

45. Waiting time on the day in magistrates' courts: a review of case listings practises. David Moxon and Roger Tarling (editors). 1988.

46. Bail and probation work: the ILPS temporary bail action project. George Mair. 1988.

47. Police work and manpower allocation. Roger Tarling. 1988.

48. Computers in the courtroom. Carol Hedderman. 1988.

49. Data interchange between magistrates' courts and other agencies. Carol Hedderman. 1988.

50. Bail and probation work II: the use of London probation/bail hostels for bailees. Helen Lewis and George Mair. 1989.

51. The role and function of police community liaison officers. Susan V. Phillips and Raymond Cochrane. 1989.

52. Insuring against burglary losses. Helen Lewis. 1989.

53. Remand decisions in Brighton and Bournemouth. Patricia Morgan and Rachel Pearce. 1989.

54. Racially motivated incidents reported to the police. Jayne Seagrave. 1989.

55. Review of research on re-offending of mentally disordered offenders. David J. Murray. 1990.

---

* Out of print

56. Risk prediction and probation: papers from a Research and Planning Unit workshop. George Mair (editor). 1990.

57. Household fires: findings from the British Crime Survey 1988. Chris May. 1990.

58. Home Office funding of victim support schemes—money well spent? Justin Russell. 1990.

59. Unit fines: experiments in four courts. David Moxon, Mike Sutton and Carol Hedderman. 1990.

60. Deductions from benefit for fine default. David Moxon, Carol Hedderman and Mike Sutton. 1990.

61. Monitoring time limits on custodial remands. Paul F. Henderson. 1991.

62. Remands in custody for up to 28 days: the experiments. Paul F. Henderson and Patricia Morgan. 1991.

63. Parenthood training for young offenders: an evaluation of courses in Young Offender Institutions. Diane Caddle. 1991.

64. The multi-agency approach in practice: the North Plaistow racial harassment project. William Saulsbury and Benjamin Bowling. 1991.

65. Offending while on bail: a survey of recent studies. Patricia M. Morgan. 1992.

66. Juveniles sentenced for serious offences: a comparison of regimes in Young Offender Institutions and Local Authority Community Homes. John Ditchfield and Liza Catan. 1992.

67. The management and deployment of police armed response vehicles. Peter Southgate. 1992.

68. Using psychometric personality tests in the selection of firearms officers. Catriona Mirrlees-Black. 1992.

69. Bail information schemes: practice and effect. Charles Lloyd. 1992.

70. Crack and cocaine in England and Wales. Joy Mott (editor). 1992.

71. The National Probation Survey 1990. Chris May. 1993.

72. Public satisfaction with police services. Peter Southgate and Debbie Crisp. 1993.

73. Disqualification from driving: an effective penalty? Catriona Mirrlees-Black. 1993.

74. Detention under the prevention of Terrorism (Temporary Provisions) Act 1989: Access to legal advice and outside contact. David Brown. 1993.

75. Panel assessment schemes for mentally disordered offenders. Carol Hedderman. 1993.

76. Cash-limiting the probation service: a case study in resource allocation. Simon Field and Mike Hough. 1993.

Research Bulletin

The Research Bulletin is published twice a year and consists mainly of short articles relating to projects which are part of the Home Office Research and Planning Unit's research programme.

---

* Out of print

Printed in the United Kingdom for HMSO
Dd297174 C25 10/93